100%
CUSTOMER DELIGHT

Creating Operations Excellence That Delivers Promised Results Every Time

DAVID MCCLASKEY

DEDICATION

This book is dedicated to all those leaders and managers who are no longer willing to settle for ordinary and are willing to do what it takes to step up to extraordinary by ensuring their products and services meet 100% of their brand requirements, 100% of the time.

This book is based on proven practices for how role-model companies ensure their products and services meet 100% of their brand requirements every time. Many leaders have contributed to this book, but two leaders of Baldrige-winning role-model companies that I would like to particularly recognize for all the time they spent with me sharing their extraordinary systems are: Thom Crosby of Pal's Sudden Service and Horst Schulze, formerly of The Ritz-Carlton Hotel Company.

CONTENTS

PILLAR 3: PROCESS EXCELLENCE

PILLAR 4: PEOPLE EXCELLENCE

IMPLEMENTING THE PATH TO EXCELLENCE AND MAINTAINING EXTRAORDINARY OPERATIONS

EPILOGUE

ACKNOWLEDGMENTS

GLOSSARY OF KEY TERMS

BIBLIOGRAPHY, CHAPTER NOTES, AND RESOURCES

AUTHOR BIOGRAPHY

FOREWORD

*By Horst Schulze, Co-founder, Former President
& COO of The Ritz-Carlton Hotel Company*

Transforming Excellence from Dream to Reality

I'll never forget that evening with Roger Milliken, Chief Executive Officer (CEO) of Milliken and Company and an American industrialist and philanthropist. Ritz-Carlton had just been named the best hotel company in America, and while my team celebrated, I felt strangely hollow.

"Mr. Milliken," I confessed, "maybe we are the best in our industry. But if we are the best, we're the best of a lousy lot—because we are not good."

That moment changed everything.

Determined to improve, I turned to The Baldrige Criteria, a framework developed by the U.S. government to recognize organizations that achieve the highest levels of performance excellence. The framework promised a structured, measurable way to build world-class quality into an organization. But the deeper I went, the more frustrated I became. The language was abstract, the concepts academic. I sat through seminar after seminar, listening to experts who spoke in terms that made no practical sense to me. I knew we needed to get better, but I couldn't see how to translate theory into reality.

For 8 months, I struggled. Then I met David McClaskey.

In one conversation, he cut through all the complexity and made it beautifully simple: have a process, pilot it, implement it, measure it, improve it. Then start again.

It was like a light switch. For the first time, I could see not just what needed to change, but how to think about organizational excellence itself. Organizational excellence was no longer an abstract ideal or an aspiration. David turned something that had felt complex into something simple and easy to understand.

We began to think differently.

That shift in thinking transformed the Ritz-Carlton brand. Like many companies, we had been focused on cutting costs, believing that was the path to efficiency. But most cost-cutting efforts are shortsighted—the equivalent of buying cheaper soap to save a few cents. Real efficiency isn't about reducing—it's about eliminating waste. We learned to stop blaming employees for failures and instead to examine the processes that set them up for success or failure. We redesigned how we selected, trained, and supported our staff. We standardized excellence so that a guest walking into a Ritz-Carlton in Shanghai would experience the same level of service as a guest in Philadelphia.

The results were extraordinary. We became more sophisticated in how we did things. We saw a massive impact in metrics across the board. We saw results such as room complaints drop from 46 per 1,000 occupied rooms to just 1 per 10,000. We went from being Number 1 in the hotel industry to becoming a world class organization setting a leadership standard across all industries. We won The Baldrige Award not once, but twice, an accomplishment only achieved by a handful of companies since its inception.

The level of consistency and excellence we achieved became so powerful that today, investment firms specifically seek out Ritz-Carlton-trained leaders to run their companies. Over thirty executive leaders have come from our leadership ranks, not because we had some secret formula, but because we systematically built excellence into our culture, our processes, and our way of thinking.

None of this would have happened without David McClaskey. I was on the verge of abandoning the pursuit of organizational excellence entirely because I couldn't see a clear path forward. David didn't just give me a framework—he changed the way I thought about organizational excellence. That transformation in thinking changed Ritz-Carlton, and in turn, it changed an entire industry.

The book you hold in your hands contains the same clear, practical wisdom that helped me transform Ritz-Carlton into the finest hotel company in the world. This book will give people the means of running their organizations better. David has a rare ability to take complex ideas and simplify them without losing their power. He will show you how to move from hoping for excellence to systematically creating it.

Don't just read this book—study it. Apply it. Your organization stands at the same crossroads where I once stood. One path leads to systematic excellence and sustainable success. The other leads to stagnation and decline. The choice is yours.

The pursuit of excellence cannot wait. Your competitors certainly won't. The time to act is now.

Horst Schulze

Co-founder, Former President & COO of The Ritz-Carlton Hotel Company
Founder, Former Chairman & CEO of Capella Hotel Group

THE JOURNEY TO EXTRAORDINARY OPERATIONS

"Observing many companies in action, I am unable to point to a single instance in which stunning results were gotten without the active and personal leadership of the upper managers."

Joseph M. Juran, author, Guru of the Quality Movement

In today's hyper-competitive business landscape, the difference between success and failure often comes down to one critical factor: operational excellence. Yet, for many organizations, achieving and maintaining this level of performance remains an elusive goal. Why do some companies consistently outperform their peers, delighting customers and setting new industry standards, while others struggle to keep up? Jim Collins, author of Good to Great: Why Some Companies Make the Leap... and Others Don't, stated the following: "The good-to-great leaders … were seemingly ordinary people quietly producing extraordinary results." Related to operations excellence, would you like to know how they achieved extraordinary results while most leaders produced ordinary results?

This book shows a proven process to get your products and services right—*every* time.

This process not only delights customers but also takes the hassle out of it. A great way to make more money with less hassle.

By working with role-model companies, I have discovered what they do to get their products and services right *every* time. We at The McClaskey Excellence Institute have been teaching and assisting companies to implement this process for over 25 years.

This process not only delights customers by getting products and services right *every* time—it also engages your employees by setting them up for 100% success. The result? Increased revenue, profits, positive recommendations, and repeat business.

I vividly recall a moment working with Pal's Sudden Service when the true impact of this role-model level of operational excellence hit me like a bolt of lightning. As I stood in one of their restaurants, watching the seamless flow of operations and the genuine smiles on the faces of both employees and customers during the greeting and that everyone was focused, engaged, productive, and self-directed on their job, I realized that this was more than just a business strategy – it was a way of life. The energy, the passion, and the unwavering commitment to excellence were palpable, and I knew right then and there that I had found my challenge. My quest became to fully understand how Pal's, The Ritz-Carlton Hotel Company and other role-model companies that I worked with consistently obtained this level of operations excellence so I could share this process or Path to Excellence, as I came to call this proven process, with others so they could achieve a similar level of extraordinary operations for their companies.

The answer lies in pursuing what I call "extraordinary operations" - a state in which every product, service, and customer experience is delivered 100% to brand requirements, 100% of the time, under 100% of conditions. This isn't just a lofty ideal; it's a practical, achievable reality that can transform your organization from ordinary to extraordinary. And we can show you how to do it.

In the world of **extraordinary** operations, *every* business interaction leaves you feeling delighted, valued, and eager to return.

In the world of **ordinary** operations, you walk into a convenience store and receive no greeting or a greeting from someone just going through the motions.

Which world would you, as a customer, want to be in? Which world would you like your organization's customers to be in?

If your answer is the world of extraordinary operations, then welcome to the "McClaskey° Triple 100° Path to Excellence."

This book will give you an overview and familiarity with the McClaskey° Triple 100° Path to Excellence for achieving and maintaining extraordinary operations and its benefits. After leaders are familiar with the process, the path to implementation leads them to the McClaskey Excellence Institute's Achieving World-Class Results class, where we guide companies through the implementation of the Path to Excellence. Then consulting helps them achieve full and sustained implementation within the company. Whether you're a seasoned executive looking to take your company to the next level, a manager striving to improve your team's performance, or an entrepreneur building a business from the ground up, the principles and practices outlined in these pages will provide you with a clear roadmap to success.

Why I Wrote This Book

To make this world a better place. OK, that's a little broad. To help leaders of just about every company make their workplace a better and more productive place to work. Sharing the McClaskey° Triple 100° Path to Excellence is the first step in a process that will lead every company to extraordinary operations. It is what I know and how I can help. I care about companies being extraordinary rather than ordinary in their operations because when they are extraordinary, their customers, managers, employees, the company, and the community are better off. This includes many good, caring people who go to work every day. Here is how leaders, managers, customers, employees, companies, and communities will be better when companies have extraordinary operations.

Leaders and Managers: I have been consulting with leaders and managers for over 50 years. While people may make distinctions between leaders and managers, I believe that all leaders are also managers, and all managers are also leaders. In this book, I use the terms leader and manager interchangeably. It is so disappointing when I talk to leaders and managers who are discouraged because they have tried to improve their operations only to find they have gotten nowhere. In way too many cases, they were using approaches that are almost guaranteed to fail. We can give them a proven path so their hard work has a good chance of succeeding.

Customers: As a customer, it is irritating not to get precisely what you ordered or to have your experience diminished by mediocre, half-hearted service from someone who does not seem to care about you. This is so unnecessary and ruins many businesses. Extraordinary operations can make your company one that customers can count on because you always show them you care, and one of the ways you do that is to deliver your products and services 100% to your brand requirements, every time.

Employees: I always loved what I did for a living. But many people do not. We spend far too much time at work for it not to be a place we want to be. I like my work so much that people must tell me to stop. I wish you the same problem. One of the main reasons people do not like their work is not the work itself, but the things that happen at work that never should have happened in the first place. The top two complaints that I have heard from countless employees are being treated disrespectfully and not being set up for 100% success. Extraordinary operations will stop both problems from occurring. Your employees will enjoy their jobs, be more engaged, contribute more, and stay longer.

Your Company: When customers are delighted and employees are engaged, the company makes more revenue, profits, and repeat business, and you get more positive recommendations. This gives them a good chance to stay in business and thrive. With extraordinary operations, you get all these benefits with less hassle, a more engaged workforce, and less turnover.

Your Community: The community is better off when people are employed by companies with extraordinary operations. The people in their community have good, stable jobs, doing work they enjoy.

Our vision at The McClaskey Excellence Institute is not just for thousands of companies, but for over 100,000 companies with extraordinary operations. This book is part of the effort to help achieve that vision. The book will give you an understanding of the process. The McClaskey Excellence Institute's Achieving World-Class Results class will guide you through the initial implementation. McClaskey Excellence Institute-certified consultants can then help you achieve full implementation and make extraordinary operations an integral part of your culture. Many have found it helpful to have a partner who helps them succeed. I want you to know that when you need that partner, we at the McClaskey Excellence Institute are here to help you succeed.

As you journey through these pages, you'll learn:

- The mindset of the leaders of extraordinary organizations and how that differs from the mindset of leaders of ordinary organizations.
- The importance of aligning every task and decision with your mission and customer needs so everyone is working toward a common goal.
- How to determine if your processes are designed and written for 100% execution, and if not, what is missing.
- The key elements of setting up a team to deliver the desired products and services every time.

This book is not just about incremental improvements or quick fixes. It's the start of a process that will fundamentally transform how your organization operates, thinks, and performs. It's about setting a new standard of excellence that will differentiate you in the marketplace and drive sustainable success.

The question for you to consider is whether you are ready to leave ordinary operations behind and embrace extraordinary operations. The future of your business, your team, and your own legacy hangs in the balance. The benefits are so much greater than the costs, making this one of the best investments you could make in your business.

The choice is yours. Will you settle for the ordinary, or will you seize this moment and embark on a journey to extraordinary operations? Turn the page, and let's begin the journey to operational excellence together.

THINK EXCELLENCE

"Change starts with a change in your thinking."

Thom Crosby, CEO of Pal's Sudden Service

The journey to extraordinary operations begins not with action, but with thought.

Welcome to Pillar 1 of the McClaskey Triple 100° Path to Excellence: Think Excellence. This foundational pillar is where we challenge our preconceptions, redefine our standards or requirements, and set the stage for a transformative journey from ordinary to extraordinary.

Think Excellence is more than just a catchy phrase—it's a fundamental shift in mindset that separates world-class organizations from the rest. In this section, we'll delve deep into the thought processes that drive exceptional performance, exploring how leaders of extraordinary operations think differently from those content with mediocrity. To lead your organization to ongoing extraordinary performance, you need the mindset of an extraordinary leader. In Pillar 1, I will present case studies that demonstrate the fantastic benefits of extraordinary operations, provide an overview of the Path to Excellence, and explain what the extraordinary mindset is and why it is crucial to achieving extraordinary performance.

Throughout my years of working with thousands of service organization leaders, I've observed a startling trend: 90% settle for mediocrity. This section will not only expose the faulty thinking that leads to this complacency but will also present a compelling case for why leaders must break free from these mental constraints and strive for true excellence.

I will explore the critical element of Think Excellence:

- The 100% Mindset: Discover how shifting from "most" to "every" can revolutionize your operations. I will examine why accepting anything less than 100% performance sets a ceiling on your organization's potential and how embracing a 100% mindset can unlock unprecedented levels of quality and consistency.

By the end of this section, you'll understand why Think Excellence is the crucial first step on the path to transforming your organization. You'll be equipped with the mindset necessary to demand that every product and service meets 100% of the brand requirements, 100% of the time, under 100% of conditions.

Pillar 1 section of this book consists of three elements, each with its own chapter:

Element 1: EXTRAORDINARY OPERATIONS:
A GREAT INVESTMENT

Element 2: OVERVIEW AND ORIGIN OF THE
MCCLASKEY® TRIPLE 100® PATH TO EXCELLENCE

Element 3: THINK EXCELLENCE:
HOW EXTRAORDINARY LEADERS THINK
DIFFERENTLY

The Next Chapter

Prepare to challenge your assumptions, elevate your standards, and embark on a journey that will redefine what's possible for your organization. The path to extraordinary begins here, with a simple yet powerful shift in how we think about excellence. To start that mind shift, Chapter 1 will reveal the profound benefits that await organizations that obtain extraordinary operations. Going from ordinary to extraordinary operations may be one of the best and least risky investments you can make.

CHAPTER 1

EXTRAORDINARY OPERATIONS: A GREAT INVESTMENT

"A satisfied customer is the best business strategy of all."

Michael LeBoeuf,
author of "How to Win Customers and Keep Them for Life"

Delivering Expectations Every Time

What if I told you that a single fast-food restaurant brand outperforms global giants by 400% in repeat business, all while charging full price? Or a hotel that delights even its most discerning guests with its extraordinary care and comfort, which the guests find a great value, even when they are paying two to ten times the price of an average hotel room. Welcome to the world of extraordinary operations.

Imagine a world where *every* time you interact with a business, you know *exactly* what to expect and are never disappointed: a world where products and services are delivered flawlessly, consistently, and with genuine care; a world where you don't have to worry about unfulfilled promises, shoddy quality, people not caring, or lackluster service. This is the world of extraordinary operations, and it's a world where every organization that wants to have extraordinary operations can.

What you need to enter this world is a proven path to extraordinary operations. This book is here to give you that path. I will reveal the proven path these role-model organizations used to create extraordinary operations for their companies. Operations that will delight your customers every time. I have been helping companies learn and implement the Path to Excellence for 25 years.

Customer Experience - The Competitive Battleground

In a world where competition is fierce and customer expectations are high, extraordinary operations have become the cornerstone of business success. You want to be ready to win on this battleground.

The numbers don't lie:

- According to a Gartner study, 89% of companies now compete primarily based on customer experience.
- In the battle for customer loyalty, businesses that go the extra mile stand out from the crowd. By embracing extraordinary operations, companies can create the exceptional experiences that customers crave—and are willing to pay for. An American Express study found that 70% of Americans were willing to spend an average of 13% more with companies they believe provide excellent customer service.

The Pal's Sudden Service Story

To truly understand the power of extraordinary operations, let's examine a real-world success story that exemplifies these principles in action.

Pal's Sudden Service began as a humble startup in the fast-food industry, conceived by founder Pal Barger. What set Pal's apart from the competition was its unwavering dedication to extraordinary operations, driven by a passionate team, and guided by a visionary leader. Over the years, Pal's has continued to rise in prominence, leaving an indelible mark on the industry with its commitment to exceptional service and quality.

When Thom Crosby assumed the role of President and CEO, he furthered Pal's pursuit of excellence, fostering an environment where innovation thrived and employees flourished. Together, Barger and Crosby crafted a culture of excellence that became deeply embedded within the organization's DNA.

As time went on, Pal's continued to garner recognition and accolades for its role-model excellence in operations. Its notable achievements include being the first restaurant chain in the United States to receive the esteemed Malcolm Baldrige National Quality Award in 2001, an honor that validates the chain's unwavering dedication to quality and customer satisfaction. This award makes Pal's a national role-model from which others can learn.

Despite its success, Pal's Sudden Service remains steadfast in its pursuit of continual improvement and growth. The extraordinary results Pal's achieved serve as both a testament to its accomplishments and an inspiration for other organizations striving for operational excellence. As Pal's story continues to unfold, one thing that remains clear is that the commitment to extraordinary operations is the key to its phenomenal results, enduring success, and lasting legacy.

Witnessing the Pal's Sudden Service Magic

I recall my first visit to a Pal's Sudden Service drive-thru, having heard countless tales of its unparalleled food, accuracy, speed, and friendly service. As I pulled up, not to the speaker but to talk to a real person, a friendly person greeted me and took my order. I could see the smile on their face and hear the friendly tone of voice that clearly said, "We are glad you are here." Within minutes, I had my meal in hand, 100%

accurate, freshly prepared, and perfectly packaged. The experience left me in awe, a testament to the power of extraordinary operations.

While personal experiences are powerful, the true measure of extraordinary operations lies in the numbers. Let's look at the remarkable results Pal's achieves through their commitment to excellence.

Pal's Extraordinary Results

The dedication to extraordinary operations at Pal's Sudden Service has yielded remarkable results, including:

- Four times the repeat business of their best competitor
- Four times faster service than their best competitor
- One complaint per 3,500 orders, which is approximately 10 times better than their competitors
- 40 years of consecutive market share growth
- 40 years of consecutive same-store sales growth
- Some of the best profitability per square foot of just about any restaurant

These achievements serve as a beacon for other organizations striving for excellence, proving that the pursuit of extraordinary operations is not just a lofty ideal but a strategic necessity. You can see from this data that all three major stakeholders win at the same time when a company uses extraordinary operations. The customer receives the products and services promised every time, and shows how much they value that by coming back 4 times more often. The employee is respected and set up for 100% success, and stays twice as long with little to no economic incentive. The company has decades of same-store sales and market share growth. The company has some of the highest profitability per square foot of any restaurant brand in the country.

What's in Pal's Secret Sauce?

"You don't have to look in the bag. You know it's right."
- Frequently said by Pal's Customers.

What sets Pal's apart from its competitors? Let's break down the key elements that contribute to their extraordinary operations.

1. **Customer Satisfaction**: Pal's Sudden Service has made it their mission to achieve 100% customer satisfaction.

2. **Consistency to 100% in products, services, and customer experience**: A crucial aspect of Pal's success is its ability to maintain near-perfect consistency in its operations. Customers know they can rely on Pal's to deliver the same high-quality service and food every time they visit, fostering trust and loyalty.

3. **Remarkable Repeat Business Metrics**: The impact of Pal's dedication to excellence is evident in its astounding 400% higher repeat business compared to the global leaders in the industry.

4. **Frequency of Customer Visits**: While customers of the national quick-service restaurant (QSR) brands typically visit about three times per month, Pal's Sudden Service enjoys a much higher frequency, with customers returning four times more often, or approximately three times per week.

5. **Full-Price Strategy and Limited Choices**: What makes Pal's 400% higher repeat business even more impressive is the fact that they achieve this with fewer menu options and no discounting.

6. **Customer Loyalty**: The extraordinary operations at Pal's Sudden Service inspire such customer loyalty that many customers are willing to drive past one to five national brand locations to reach a Pal's restaurant.

7. **Comparison of Service Times**: Speed is a critical factor for quick-service restaurants, and Pal's excels in this area as well. On average, a car leaves Pal's drive-through every 18 seconds—a staggering 4 times faster than the average 72 seconds or more it takes at national competitors

8. **Order Accuracy and Customer Trust**: In addition to its impressive 4 times faster speed, Pal's Sudden Service maintains an exceptional level of accuracy that is 10 times more accurate, with only one complaint per 3,500 orders. Pal's being 1,000 percent more accurate than its competitors fosters a deep sense of trust among customers. Customers don't even feel the need to check their orders, confident that Pal's dedication to extraordinary operations ensures accuracy every time.

9. **Employee Turnover and Workforce Characteristics**: Pal's Sudden Service boasts a remarkably low employee turnover rate, maintaining approximately half the industry average for over a decade.

10. **Company Performance Against Competitors**: For 40 consecutive years, Pal's has experienced market share growth, same-store sales growth, and some of the highest profitability per square foot in the industry. Pal's extraordinary operations give it a sustainable competitor advantage.

11. **The Core of Pal's Operational Excellence**: At the heart of Pal's success lies an unwavering commitment to consistency and excellence through operations excellence.

Overall Benefits of Extraordinary Operations

When you have fully implemented the McClaskey "Triple 100" Path to Excellence, your:

- Customers will be delighted, sing your company's praises, be loyal, and come back more often because you deliver the products and services right, not most of the time, but 100% right every time.

- Employees will be productive and love to come to work because the company has created a work environment where they are set up for 100% success, so they can deliver the products and services right, not most of the time, but every time. A work environment that focuses everyone towards a worthy purpose to which each person not only contributes but can see the impact of their contribution. Your employees will be happy, love to come to work, and become loyal employees who stay. In the words of Simon Sinek, "your employees are in a work environment that will enable them to give you their best."

- The company will have high revenues, good profitability, and your competitors will find it is tough to compete against you because you deliver what you promised your customers every time, and thus have loyal customers who sing your praises to others.

Since all three stakeholders win when a company uses the McClaskey® Triple 100® Path to Excellence, I call this the Triple Win™. We want to achieve this triple win for all businesses. It is one of the best investments you can make.

Operating your company with extraordinary operations has significant benefits and very modest costs. This makes extraordinary operations one of the best and safest investments a service company can make.

If extraordinary operations is such a great investment, why is it that most service businesses choose to operate at an ordinary level? Having talked with thousands of service company executives about this, the main reasons are that the customers don't demand it, their competitors operate at the same ordinary level of operations that they operate, so there is little competitive pressure, leaders believe it cannot be done in the service business, and leaders believe that the benefits would not justify the costs. The first of the four reasons is mostly true: customers don't demand it, and almost all of your competitors are operating at the ordinary level, where getting it right most of the time is accepted as the best we can do. We will show that the last two reasons, that it cannot be done in the service industry and the benefits are not worth the costs, are untrue. This will give you some rare knowledge that only the best leaders know. With this information, many leaders' answers shift from settling for ordinary operations to leading their organizations to extraordinary operations, because it has been proven to be one of the best, least risky investments you can make in your business.

The Costs of Going from Ordinary to Extraordinary Operations

Yes, most companies incur one-time costs to set their employees up for 100% success, but the ongoing costs might be the same or even lower. I am not allowed to share Pal's cost of operations, but you will find their costs are within the normal ranges expected for Quick Service Restaurants (QSRs). That does not mean all costs are the same. Pal's probably spends slightly more on setting their employees up for 100% success and spends less money on all the costs related to things that never should have happened in the first place to include things like rework, complaints, excessive turnover, excess food costs due to both waste and incorrect portioning, low productivity, and employees not working together to serve the customer. Training costs are an example of Pal's spending more upfront on training while still having the same or lower annual training costs as their competitors. Pal's probably spends somewhat more per employee on training, training every employee to 100%, but since they have half the turnover —meaning employees stay twice as long —they only have to train half as many employees per year as their competitors. This makes Pal's annual training costs similar to those of its competitors, even though it spends more per employee on training. Think about all the benefits of having employees who are twice as experienced and who are trained to 100% instead of at a lesser level, as is the case in most other companies.

Throughout this book, I will return to role-model examples of extraordinary operations, such as Pal's Sudden Service and others. These case studies will be woven throughout multiple chapters, illustrating various concepts with examples you are familiar with and providing valuable insights. By revisiting these same success stories, you will see that they are model examples across all aspects of extraordinary operations. Since we have already introduced the company, you will gain a deeper understanding of how different principles of extraordinary operations can be applied in real-world contexts. It's time to turn our attention to your business.

The impact of extraordinary operations extends beyond a single organization. Let's examine how Pal's success inspired another company to pursue excellence. Don Fox, who was the CEO of Firehouse Subs when he took our Achieving World-Class Results class, told me that one of the great validations of the Path to Excellence being taught was that other companies are improving their performance by implementing it. He said it is nice to hear success stories, but you want to learn something you can apply to your company to make it better. K&N Management is one such example that illustrates this validation.

K&N Management: A Journey to Extraordinary Operations

In 2001, I had the pleasure of meeting Ken Schiller and Brian Nolan, the owners and driving forces behind K&N Management. Recognizing the potential of extraordinary operations, they sought out role-model restaurants to help them transform their business from ordinary to extraordinary. Their determination and vision would ultimately lead K&N Management to become the second restaurant company to win the coveted Malcolm Baldrige National Quality Award and thus be a nationally designated role-model.

The journey of K&N Management exemplifies the power of dedication, innovation, and a relentless pursuit of operational excellence. By studying K&N's path to success, we can uncover valuable insights and strategies that can be applied across industries, inspiring organizations worldwide to embrace extraordinary operations and achieve remarkable outcomes.

Ken and Brian initiated a long-term association with The McClaskey Excellence Institute, then known as the Pal's Business Excellence Institute, to learn the practices and principles used by Pal's and others to create extraordinary operations. Through this partnership, K&N Management learned that extraordinary operations are possible with the resources available to most organizations and the proven Path to Excellence that will elevate their operations from ordinary to extraordinary. They just needed to "raise the bar," as Ken Schiller would often say.

Under the guidance of David McClaskey and The McClaskey Excellence Institute, K&N Management diligently implemented various operational practices taught in the Institute's Achieving World-Class Results (AWCR) class, based on Pal's and others' proven role-model practices. By having all their managers attend The McClaskey Excellence Institute's "Achieving World-Class Results" Class, they learned firsthand what to do and were inspired to put it into practice. They discovered a step-by-step approach that taught what to do, why each is important, and how to do it.

Learning the Path to Excellence is the easier part. Implementation is where the heavy lifting comes in. I had the pleasure of working with them as their consultant and guide as they did the heavy lifting. The K&N Management managers and leaders customized and implemented these practices to work within K&N Management's culture. The managers and leaders implemented the four pillars of the McClaskey° Triple 100° Path to Excellence, enabling K&N to achieve extraordinary operations. With extraordinary operations, they consistently delivered their products and services to 100% of their brand requirements, to every customer, every time. Across all their restaurants and both their brands, K&N's dedicated efforts led to every store performing at extraordinary levels throughout the day. This commitment to excellence produced impressive results, demonstrating the power of adopting extraordinary operations to achieve long-lasting success. It also demonstrates the ability of McClaskey Excellence Institute's classes and consulting to enable companies to go from ordinary to extraordinary results. It was a pleasure to work with Ken, Brian, and all their directors, including Allyson Young, Craig Haley, and Marlis Oliver, as well as their managers, as they transformed K&N Management from ordinary to extraordinary operations. We then worked to make them Baldrige-winning national role-models.

K&N Management Results

In 2010, the year K&N Management became only the second restaurant to win The Baldrige Award. They had two brands when they won the Baldrige Award: Rudy's "Country Store" and Bar-B-Q and Mighty Fine Burgers, Fries & Shakes. Here are some of the results they posted:

- Rudy's increased average unit sales from just over $3 million in 2000 to slightly more than $7.5 million in 2010 (for food sales only).

- Mighty Fine increased annual unit sales from just over $2 million in 2007, when it started up, to more than $3.5 million in 2010, triple the unit sales of its best competitor.

- Overall customer satisfaction ratings are over 4.7 out of 5 for both brands, beating the best competitor.

- Over 95% of K&N Management team members reported they are proud to work for the company.

- In 2010, the Austin American-Statesman named the firm "the best place to work in Austin."

The Impact of Excellence

The remarkable journeys of both Pal's Sudden Service and K&N Management underscore the far-reaching effects of committing to and achieving extraordinary operations. By setting new industry standards and serving as role-models for excellence, these companies exemplify the sustainable competitive advantage that can be gained through obtaining and maintaining extraordinary operations.

The Transformative Power of Extraordinary Operations

Organizations with extraordinary operations often experience:

- **Enhanced customer loyalty and positive recommendations:** As demonstrated by Pal's Sudden Service, a steadfast commitment to delivering 100% on brand standards can lead to unparalleled customer trust and loyalty.

- **Sustained market share growth:** Like Pal's and K&N Management, companies that prioritize excellence see sustained growth, often outperforming competitors in challenging markets.

- **Significant increases in revenue and profitability:** The financial benefits of extraordinary operations, such as those seen in Pal's and K&N Management, show that operational excellence can drive profitability without additional ongoing costs.

- **Dramatically improved employee engagement and reduced employee turnover:** Both Pal's and K&N Management exemplify how setting employees up for 100% success fosters a supportive work environment, leading to higher employee retention and satisfaction.

These benefits highlight that extraordinary operations are not an additional cost but a strategic investment that pays dividends across all facets of the business. The key lies in adopting proven processes and strategies, as successfully employed by companies like Pal's and K&N.

Implementing these principles isn't without challenges. You may encounter resistance to change, resource constraints, or difficulties in maintaining consistency. However, as our case studies have shown, these challenges can be overcome. Overcoming these challenges can lead to extraordinary results that distinguish you in your industry.

Extraordinary operations aren't just about what you do—they're about who you become as an organization. The journey requires constant commitment, adaptation, and a willingness to challenge the status quo. But the rewards, in terms of performance, reputation, and competitive advantage, can be truly transformative.

Call to Action

- How does your organization currently approach operational excellence?
- What specific areas within your organization would benefit most from embracing extraordinary operations?
- How can you actively contribute to fostering a culture of excellence within your workplace?

Key Takeaways for Chapter 1: Extraordinary Operations: A Great Investment

1. Extraordinary operations is a great return on investment: Extraordinary operations, where you achieve the McClaskey® Triple 100® Level of Operations of delivering your products, services, and customer experience 100% to the brand requirement, 100% of the time, under 100% of the conditions, give you a competitive advantage with a great return on investment.

2. Extraordinary operations are not an additional cost but a strategic investment that pays high returns and provides dividends across all facets of the business. Three things that make extraordinary operations such a great investment are high returns, low risk, and, in most cases, low costs, with expenses consisting mainly of one-time investments.

3. Extraordinary operations leads to the Triple 100® Win™: Customers are delighted because you deliver what you promised every time; employees are engaged because you set them up for 100% success and there is lower turnover; and the organization gets a sustainable competitive advantage which maximizes its revenue, profitability, and positive customer comments.

The Next Chapter

Now that we see the significant benefits of extraordinary operations, let us look at the path to achieving them. The next chapter is an overview of the proven Path to Excellence that takes us from ordinary to extraordinary operations.

CHAPTER 2

OVERVIEW AND ORIGIN OF THE MCCLASKEY® TRIPLE 100® PATH TO EXCELLENCE

"Before you are a leader, success is all about growing yourself. When you become a leader, success is all about growing others."

Jack Welch, former Chairman and CEO of General Electric

The Path to Extraordinary Operations

The McClaskey® Triple 100® Path to Excellence is a proven path for companies to go from ordinary to extraordinary operations. The Path to Excellence consists of implementing the following four pillars:

1. Think Excellence
2. Focus Excellence
3. Process Excellence
4. People Excellence

Think Excellence
Your Target is Every Instead of Most

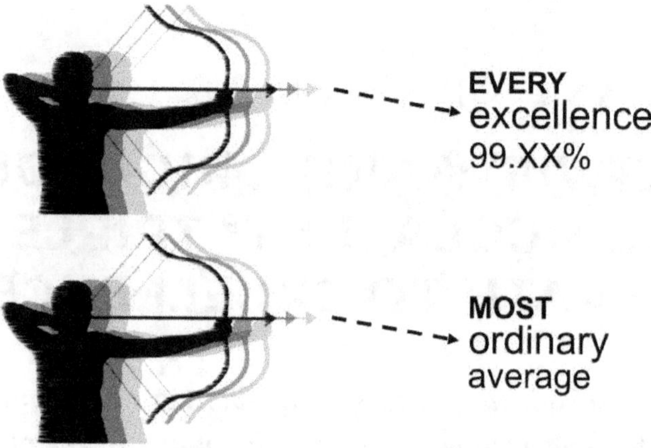

1. **Think Excellence:** is a mindset where the only acceptable standard is that products and services meet brand requirements every time.

At the core of this transformation is a shift in the leader's mindset or paradigm from accepting "most" to requiring "every." This mindset sets the tone for what is considered acceptable quality throughout the organization. It's about shifting from a mindset that accepts ordinary operations where getting it mostly right, most of the time, is accepted to a mindset that requires extraordinary operations where the only acceptable standard is that the products and services meet 100% of the brand requirements, 100% of the time, under 100% of conditions. This pillar challenges leaders and employees alike to refuse any compromise on quality or consistency, ensuring that delivering 100% becomes the standard in every aspect of the business.

This mindset distinction is key because an organization can never consistently deliver to a higher standard than the standard set by its leader. What the leader accepts is the true standard. When a leader sets "most" as their standard, it creates the lid on how well that organization can perform. John C. Maxwell, author of *The 21 Irrefutable Laws of Leadership*, stated this as the "law of the lid." In essence, leaders of ordinary businesses have authorized their employees to deliver the organization's products and services mostly to the brand requirements most of the time and therefore most become the lid. Another huge downside of accepting getting the products and services right most of the time is that, by default, ordinary businesses have also authorized their employees to deliver their products and services "wrong" some of the time. This is true because Most plus Some equals All. If leadership and managers accept that it is OK for the company to deliver its products and services 100% to its requirements most of the time, they are equally OK with products and services not being delivered to 100% of their requirements some of the time. In fact, they have authorized it by their acceptance of most.

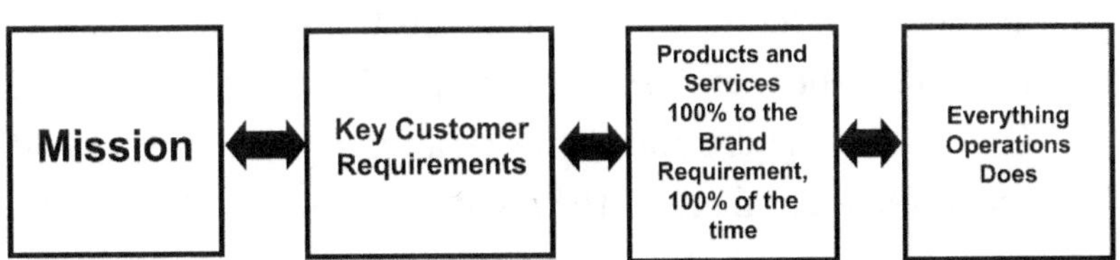

McClaskey® Triple 100® Path to Excellence
Focus Excellence

2. **Focus Excellence**: is aligning every aspect of your operations with your mission and key customer requirements or KCRs. The alignment builds the "why" into everything everyone in a company does, providing a common purpose for all to buy into.

By creating this laser focus for everything your company does, you build unshakeable customer trust and loyalty by consistently meeting their KCRs.

Every organization I know of that has extraordinary operations has every employee who works for them linked to and aligned with their mission. The mission is the organization's purpose. It is essential to align people to a common mission or purpose if you want them to work together productively. When groups of people are not aligned to a common mission, a certain percentage of their actions work against each other because of this lack of alignment.

Leaders of extraordinary organizations know how important it is to align everyone around a common mission so that all their efforts work toward accomplishing it. This alignment of every task an employee performs with the mission statement gives the "why" behind the task's importance and how it contributes to the mission. It provides purpose for the work. Employees knowing how each process or task they work on contributes toward the mission is critical for employee engagement. This alignment of each task employees perform with the mission is achieved by showing how each task links to one or more KCRs.

The KCRs are what you promised the customer. The KCRs are the key factors on which the customer will judge if your products and services are acceptable. These are the key factors that determine if the customer gives you a positive recommendation and if they will give you repeat business.

Operations fulfill their part of meeting the KCRs when they deliver your products and services that 100% meet your brand's requirements every time.

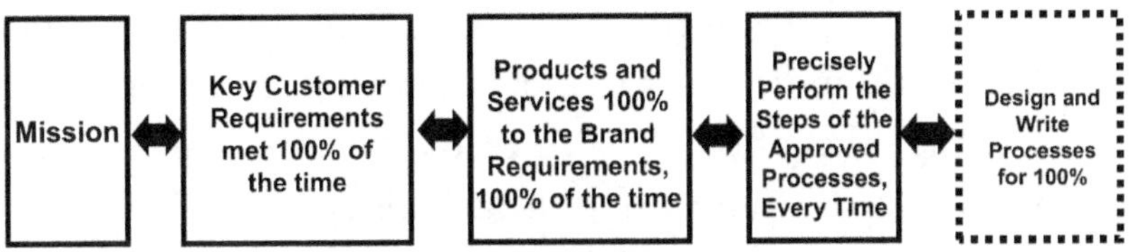

3. **Process Excellence**: is to design and document processes that will deliver the desired process outputs every time in the most efficient manner.

The desired process outputs are those that 100% meet your brand standards or requirements, 100% of the time, under 100% of the conditions. I am going to define standards as your brand requirements, since they are requirements, not suggestions. I will use the words' standards 'and 'requirements' interchangeably. Here, we delve into designing and documenting processes for 100% success. Processes are designed and documented for 100% when each step of the approved process is precisely performed, the process output is 100% to the brand requirements, every time, and in the most efficient manner. This standard ensures your operations are effective and efficient. This systematic approach leaves nothing to chance, creating a foundation for consistent excellence.

Most service processes in most companies are designed to only deliver the product and service, mostly to the requirements for that product or service. This is because, for ordinary companies, the accepted standard is to deliver the products and services mostly right most of the time.

In extraordinary companies, whose standard is to deliver the products and services 100% to their requirements every time, the processes that deliver these products and services must be designed for 100%. Most of the thousands of service processes that I have seen are designed to get the product or service mostly right, but could easily be designed to get the product 100% right. Taking the process from mostly right to 100% right requires about 15% more effort in the design portion. Companies had to design the process 85% correctly to deliver the product and service correctly most of the time. This extra 15% is put into the design process only when it is the company's standard to deliver the products and services 100% to the brand requirements. To get the value from processes designed for 100%, there needs to be a written company policy that the approved process will be used everywhere applicable. This is referred to as standardizing the process.

The last element of process excellence is systematically and sustainably improving the process as needed. As your organization learns better ways to make the product or service, the process needs to be adjusted to incorporate those improved methods. If processes are not updated so they remain the best-known way to deliver that product or service, employees will tend to stop using outdated processes that don't reflect the best way to produce the process output.

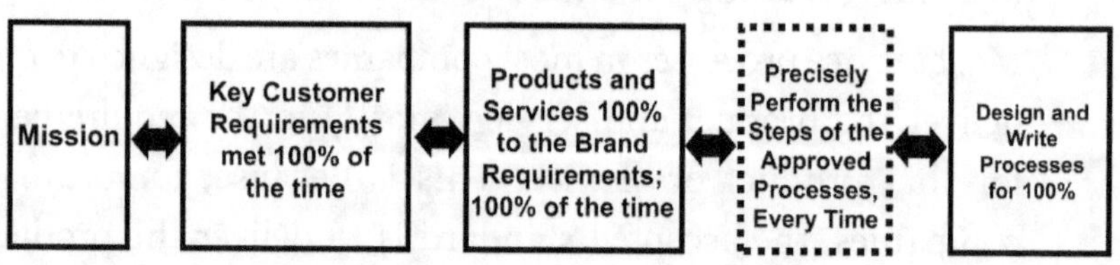

- **People Excellence:** focuses on setting employees up for 100% success, fostering a culture of pride, engagement, and accountability.

People Excellence is about employee behaviors on the job. At a very high level, the only two behaviors needed to produce an organization's products and services 100% to the brand requirements are for the employees to follow the conditions of employment at all times and to precisely perform the steps of the approved processes connected to their jobs every time, even if there is no supervision in the area. When these two behaviors occur every time, an organization gets 100% in People Excellence. The conditions of employment are the behaviors the company requires as a condition of working for your organization. It should be noted that we are talking about your employees' behaviors, which are always their choice. Extraordinary organizations that consistently deliver their products and services 100% to the brand requirements use nine elements to set up an environment where employees will choose their behaviors in such a way that they will fully comply with the conditions of employment every time and precisely perform each step of the approved process, every time, even when no supervision is in the area. These nine elements will be taught as part of the People Excellence pillar.

These four pillars form the McClaskey° Triple 100° Path to Excellence - a proven methodology that has helped organizations across industries achieve and maintain extraordinary operations and remarkable results. This is a proven path because it is based on what companies actually do to obtain extraordinary operations.

Throughout this book, we will explore each of these pillars in-depth, providing the knowledge, tools, and strategies to implement in your organization. I will describe the what, why, and how behind successfully implementing each of the four pillars.

You'll discover how companies like Pal's Sudden Service, The Ritz-Carlton, K&N Management, and others have applied these pillars to become leaders in their fields. Throughout this book, we'll explore the four pillars of excellence to help you adapt them to your company's unique context and culture.

The Three Principles of Extraordinary Operations

There are three principles of extraordinary operations incorporated into every pillar and the overall McClaskey® Triple 100° Path to Excellence. The principles are the key concepts that make the Path for Excellence work. Each of the four pillars accomplishes the objective of the pillar in a way that is consistent with all three principles. These three principles are:

1. **Set everyone up for 100% success.**
2. **Eliminate gray areas.**
3. **Improve operations so it is a win/win for customers, and employees, and the company, all at the same time.**

Set everyone up for 100% success: This means that, for whatever you are asking someone to do, they have the training, work environment, tools, and motivation, so you are so sure it will happen that you would make the McClaskey® $1,000 Bet. The bet is, would you bet 1,000 U.S. Dollars of your own money that the next time the process is performed, it will be done 100% right? I have asked thousands of managers and employees whether they would make that bet on their organization, and almost no one would. They know that the people who work for them are not set up for 100% success and are not following the process steps 100% of the time. They are set up to do it mostly right.

Eliminate gray areas: I am defining "gray" as anything that can be reasonably interpreted in more than one way. This can be something you wrote or said. You cannot manage gray, so you need to remove it.

Improve operations so it is a win/win: Improve operations so it is a win/win for customers, employees, and the company, all at the same time.

That means you are not making tradeoffs. Everything done during the McClaskey® Triple 100® Path to Excellence is done in such a way that the customer, employee, and the company all benefit. For example, training to 100% is one of the elements within the People Excellence pillar. Training an employee to do their job 100% right instead of the very common 75% right, When you train to 100%, (a) the customer wins - they are delighted because they get the products and services 100% to the brand requirements every time; (b) the employee wins - they are set up to do their jobs 100% right which gives them control over the work and ensures they can make it right every time; and (c) the company wins, because when the customers are delighted and the employees are engaged and productive, the company gets increased revenue, profits, repeat business, and positive recommendations.

The Universal Applicability of Extraordinary Operations

The beauty of the McClaskey® Triple 100® Path to Excellence lies in its universal applicability – it can be adapted and implemented in any context, empowering organizations of all types to unlock their full potential and achieve sustainable success. The principles and practices of extraordinary operations are not limited to any particular industry or company size. Whether you're a small startup looking to disrupt your market, a mid-sized organization seeking to optimize your processes and then grow, or a global corporation aiming to maintain your competitive edge, the Path to Excellence is open to you as a proven path to go from ordinary to extraordinary operations.

The Power of Extraordinary Operations

The true power of extraordinary operations lies in their transformative nature. It's not about perfecting a single aspect of your business but about creating a system where 100% excellence is the default, not the exception, for all aspects of your operations.

The key revelation is this: extraordinary operations are not about doing extraordinary things, but about doing ordinary things at an extraordinary level. It's about infusing every action, every process, and every interaction with an unwavering commitment to excellence, rather than settling for 'mostly right'. '

This shift in mindset—from seeing excellence as a goal to viewing it as the only acceptable standard—is what separates truly extraordinary companies from the rest. It is what allows a regional chain like Pal's to outperform global giants.

Implementing these pillars isn't without challenges. You may encounter resistance to change, resource constraints, or difficulties in maintaining consistency. However, as our case studies have shown and will continue to show, these challenges and obstacles can be overcome, and doing so can lead to extraordinary results that distinguish you in your industry.

Consider How the Four Pillars Could Transform Your Own Organization:

As you consider the journey toward extraordinary operations, reflect on these pivotal questions, grounded in the Four Pillars of Excellence:

- **Unwavering Commitment to 100% Excellence (Think Excellence):** What if everyone in your company had as their standard and was fully committed to doing their part in delivering 100% of brand requirements in every interaction?

- **Alignment to the Mission and Purpose (Focus Excellence):** Imagine the clarity, focus, and sense of purpose your organization could achieve if everyone had a crystal-clear understanding of how everything they do contributes to the company's mission and the Key Customer Requirements.

- **All Processes Show the Steps to 100% meeting the requirements (Process Excellence):** How would your operations improve if all your processes were clearly written and, if followed, led to the product and service meeting 100% of your brand requirements?

- **Employees Set Up for 100% Correct Execution (People Excellence):** How much better would your service be if every employee were trained to the level of your best performer, consistently delivering top-notch results?

The Source of the Process

It is important to know where this path came from. Even though I have been consulting with hundreds of companies for over 50 years, and I have trained over 15,000 leaders in operations excellence-related topics, I did not invent the Path to Excellence I will share and have taught leaders to use over the last 25 years. My background enabled me to understand and see the pattern or path used by multiple role-model companies to achieve extraordinary operations. As I worked with and understood how these role-model companies delivered their products and services 100% of the time with the same resources as companies with ordinary operations, I saw a pattern. A common path that they used became clear. It is this proven Path to Excellence developed by these role-model companies that I have named the McClaskey® Triple 100® Path to Excellence.

I learned from many role-model companies and leaders. I am indebted to everyone who contributed to my knowledge and enabled me to share my understanding with others. I want to mention, by name, a few of the many leaders and companies that were very instrumental in my learning the key elements that are the basis of the Path to Excellence. They, along with others within their companies, designed and implemented their own path. Each of their paths contained the common elements taught in the Path to Excellence that led to extraordinary operations. Leaders like: Thom Crosby and Pal Barger of Pal's Sudden Service; Horst Schulze, of The Ritz-Carlton Hotel Company; Ken Schiller and

Brian Nolan of K&N Management; Rulon Stacey and Priscilla Nuwash of Poudre Valley Health System; Joe Alexander, of Monfort College of Business at Northern Colorado University; Don Evans and Roger Quayle of OMI, and Earnie Davenport, Eastman Chemical Company.

This is a special list. Not only did I think these companies were role-models, but the U.S. government designated them as role-models as well. I got to know these companies and their leaders, as well as their businesses in depth, because I was their Baldrige Consultant when they applied and won the Malcolm Baldrige National Quality Award. This award is a country-level award, awarded by the U.S. government and awarded in the name of the U.S. President. The Baldrige Award is given to only a few companies each year, which serve as role models for their excellence in operations and sustained high performance. Role-models are those from whom others can learn and improve.

Remember, extraordinary operations aren't just about what you do; they're about who you become as an organization. The journey requires constant commitment, adaptation, and a willingness to challenge the status quo. But the rewards—in terms of performance, reputation, and competitive advantage—can be truly transformative.

Call to Action

1. What percentage of your products and services are currently delivered 100% to their brand requirements?

2. What percentage of your customers only experience all of your products and services 100% to your brand requirements during their last transaction with your company?

3. How does not delivering your products and services 100% to your brand requirements impact your customers and their repeat business rate?

Key Takeaways for Chapter 2: Overview and Origin of the McClaskey® Triple 100® Path to Excellence

1. The McClaskey® Triple 100® Path to Excellence is a proven path for companies to transform ordinary operations into extraordinary ones.

2. The Path to Excellence consists of implementing the following four pillars: Think Excellence, Focus Excellence, Process Excellence, and People Excellence.

3. Underlying the Path to Excellence are three principles that are used to make each of the four pillars have an excellent impact: Set everyone up for 100% success; Eliminate gray areas; Improve operations so it is a win/win for customers, employees, and the company, all at the same time.

4. There are obstacles and challenges to implementing the Path for Excellence, but these can be overcome.

5. The McClaskey® Triple 100® Path to Excellence is a proven path derived from the in-depth, first-hand study of role-model companies that have achieved and maintained extraordinary operations.

6. You don't have to implement the Path to Excellence yourself. There are others, like McClaskey Excellence Institute, who can help you.

The Next Chapter

In the next chapter, I will discuss Think Excellence: How Extraordinary Leaders Think Differently. The Path to Excellence starts with changing your mindset, or your paradigms. These are the assumptions you believe that shape how you process information. In the next chapter, we'll explore how leaders of organizations with extraordinary operations think differently from leaders of organizations with ordinary operations. You'll discover how this mindset shift can dramatically impact your organization's performance, customer satisfaction, and employee engagement.

The choice is yours: Will you settle for the ordinary, or will you dare to be extraordinary?

CHAPTER 3

THINK EXCELLENCE: HOW EXTRAORDINARY LEADERS THINK DIFFERENTLY

"An organization can't please every human being every time.
But it never hurts to try."

Horst Schulze, former President & COO of
The Ritz-Carlton Hotel Company; author of "Excellence Wins"

The McClaskey® $1,000 Bet

Would you take this bet?

You're waiting in the drive-through at your favorite national fast-food restaurant with a friend. Your mouth is watering in anticipation of those perfectly crisp, golden french fries when your friend looks at you and smirks.

She says, "I bet you $1,000 the fries won't be hot."

How confident are you that the fries will be hot? Do you take the bet that the fries will be hot?

If you're like most people, your thoughts immediately go to your experiences with cold fries, greasy fries, oversalted fries, and any number of other subpar experiences with your fries.

Nope, not taking that bet.

But, what if . . . ?

What if you could confidently bet the fries will be perfectly hot, crispy, and golden every single time? As you know, there is a fast-food chain where you can confidently make that bet. Every customer, every time, gets the food and service exactly right. A restaurant where operational excellence isn't just a lofty goal, but a way of life. And they do it with the same resources most other restaurants have. That place exists. It's Pal's Sudden Service, a shining example of what I call "extraordinary operations."

Together, we will explore businesses that consistently deliver their products and services right, every single time. More importantly, we'll show you how to transform your own company into one that unfailingly delivers your products and services right, every time, delighting your customers. I will delve deeper into Pal's Sudden Service and the McClaskey® $1,000 Bet shortly, but first, let's address the challenges this book aims to solve.

A Tale of Two Fast-food Chains!

Picture this: Two restaurants stand side-by-side in the heart of a bustling city. One, a stark monument to mediocrity – let's call it Company A. The other, a gleaming beacon of unwavering excellence, known as Company B. What lies between these two contrasting worlds? An invisible line, marking the boundary between the realms of the ordinary and the extraordinary.

In the grand narrative of business, these chains embody two distinct paths, and two opposing mindsets. One is mired in the stagnant swamp of mediocracy. The other dares to reach for the stars, propelled by the unstoppable force of the Excellence Mindset.

Prepare to be astonished as we journey into the heart of these divergent worlds, unraveling the threads that weave together the fabric of their success—or lack thereof. Discover the power of the Excellence Mindset, the engine that drives innovation and catapults organizations to new heights.

The extraordinary advantage awaits those who dare to venture beyond the boundary and embrace this transformative way of thinking. Will you join them?

The Power of the Excellence Mindset

As we step across the divide into the realm of Company B, prepare to witness a world where mediocrity has no foothold. While Company A settles for the commonplace, Company B thrives on delivering excellence in every detail, every moment, and every experience.

At Company A, you might find a perfectly average fast-food restaurant. They operate with ordinary operations that mostly deliver on their promises most of the time. Their food is mostly what it should be, their service is somewhat friendly, and their bathrooms are more or less clean. By all accounts, they're "no worse than anyone else" in their business. And because they deliver most of the time, they do have some cars in their drive-through line.

But Company B? Ah, Company B is where the magic happens! They operate with extraordinary operations. Here, every single french fry is a symphony of flavor and texture—hot, crispy, and perfectly salted. Every burger is a masterpiece of juicy perfection, nestled in a fresh, fluffy bun. Every order, no matter how complex, is accurate and prompt, a testament to their unwavering commitment to delighting customers.

The warmth and genuine hospitality of Company B's service leave you feeling not just satisfied but truly valued and appreciated. And their bathrooms? They're not just clean; they're immaculate, sparkling sanctuaries that redefine the very notion of customer care. And because they deliver every time, they have a steady stream of fast-moving cars in their drive-through line.

The stark contrast between these two establishments lays bare the chasm separating the realm of ordinary operations from that of extraordinary operations. The difference is palpable and all-encompassing, and it is this relentless pursuit of excellence that sets Company B on the path to remarkable success, leaving Company A in the shadows of mediocrity. The stage is set for a tale of business triumph, born of the unyielding determination to be not just good, but truly extraordinary in their mindset.

The Perils of "Most" and the Path to "Every"

When leaders are asked if every customer in their service business is greeted according to their brand's requirements, the resounding response is "most." This word, "most," represents not only the level of actual performance but also the level of acceptance by the leaders. Leaders have come to accept that their service businesses will perform at a level where most customers receive most of the brand requirements for their products and services most of the time. This is the very definition and effect of settling for ordinary operations.

This acceptance of "most" as the norm dulls the alarm bells that should be ringing when things go wrong. Errors become a normal part of business, with service providers unsurprised when customers point out mistakes or promises that were made but not fulfilled. Everyone would like things to be right every time. Still, leaders have resigned themselves to the idea that perfection is unattainable, and so "most" becomes the accepted standard for how well the company's products and services meet the brand requirements.

The ordinary way of thinking dictates that you can't get it right every time, so it's acceptable to get it right most of the time. However, this mindset only perpetuates mediocrity and hinders an organization's potential for greatness. When leaders accept "most" as their standard, they have capped the level to which an organization can perform.

John Maxwell's first law of his *21 Irrefutable Laws of Leadership* is the Law of the Lid. An organization will not exceed the level that leaders accept. The lid on your company's performance is set by the level that the leaders accept. If leaders accept "most," then that is the best level at which the business will perform. The journey to extraordinary operations begins by shifting our mindset from settling for "most" to only accepting "every". You will not have extraordinary operations if you accept most.

The Power of "Every": Lessons from Industry Leaders

The dedication to "every" rather than settling for "good enough" is exemplified by the following case studies:

The Ritz-Carlton Hotel Company. As the Ritz-Carlton Baldrige consultant both times they won the Baldrige Award, I had to learn about all their excellent systems in depth, how they worked, and how they are all integrated together to provide exceptional service that delights every guest, every time. Horst's standard was every. It would never be okay with him to have any customer complaints or to fail to delight every customer. He never accepted most.

One of many policies and processes he put in place to help make this level of service to guests as close to reality as possible was empowering employees to spend up to $2,000 per guest without managerial approval. This was a direct result of Horst's leadership mindset of 'every.' When leaders set a standard of 'every,' many creative practices emerge to achieve this with their existing workforce.

Another great example is Ritz-Carlton's Lateral Service policy. Whenever any Ritz-Carlton employee sees a customer who needs help right now, they stop what they are doing, help the guest, and then return to what they were doing. They don't need a manager's approval for this activity. Every employee is authorized and empowered to do it. These are two of many practices that enable the Ritz-Carlton hotels to provide an exceptional level of hospitality while keeping labor costs reasonable. His dedication is to enable all Ritz-Carlton employees to provide every guest an experience that "enlivens the senses, instills well-being, and fulfills even the unexpressed wishes and needs of our guests." This commitment to "every" guest, every time, has established the brand as an icon of extraordinary service and the first, and currently, the only hotel company to win the Baldrige Award twice.

Toyota. The company's "kaizen" improvement philosophy exemplifies a relentless pursuit of perfection by identifying and eliminating all waste and defects in its production processes. It does not matter how small the waste or imperfections are. Toyota's commitment to improving every process every time has solidified its position as one of the world's most admired manufacturers.

Zappos. The brand's unique offer for new hires to quit after training and receive payment reflects its dedication to maintaining a team fully committed to providing "WOW" service every time. By refusing to compromise, Zappos has cultivated a culture of unwavering excellence.

Apple. One of Steve Jobs' biggest fears was that Apple would accept hiring B-level employees rather than just A-level employees. He wanted to create exciting product releases with every product release and knew that would not happen with B-level employees.

Football Coach. Vince Lombardi captured the mindset of leaders whose companies have extraordinary operations: "Perfection is not attainable, but if we chase perfection, we can catch excellence." With this mindset, he created an American football dynasty, starting with a below-average team before he became the coach. He is such a standout that the Super Bowl championship trophy, the highest award in American football, is named after him.

These industry leaders have embraced the mindset that striving for "every" is not only valuable but necessary for achieving extraordinary operations, employee engagement, and sustained business success. By following their lead, you too can unlock your organization's true potential and transform "most" into "every."

The Hidden Perils of Accepting "Most"

"Most" is generally considered a favorable word, reflecting a reasonable effort and a job well done. However, in business operations, this commonplace acceptance of "most" has an insidious underside. When leadership accepts most as its standard, leadership also implicitly authorizes a standard of getting things wrong "some" of the time. All companies that have most as their standard, which includes most service companies, could, and maybe should, post the following sign on their website or door to their business:

> Dear Customer,
>
> If you choose to do business with our company, we have authorized our employees to meet what we promised you most of the time. We have also authorized our employees not to deliver all that we promised some of the time.
>
> The Management

This concealed standard of "some", buried within the acceptance of "most," means that organizations are designed, managed, and rewarded with the expectation of sometimes falling short of their brand specifications.

By accepting "most" as the operational standard, leaders inadvertently cause their organizations to operate below their full potential. This insidious "some" undermines the pursuit of excellence and fosters a culture of complacency. Leaders easily rationalize accepting some by believing sayings like "to err is human." Therefore, if we have humans working for us, then we must have errors. It just goes with the territory.

But what if the main reason for most errors was that management has accepted that errors will happen, treating them as an unavoidable cost of doing business? Nothing we can do about it. To break free from mediocrity and achieve extraordinary operations, leaders must recognize and reject this hidden pitfall and embrace the transformative power of aiming for "every" instead.

Alcoa's Journey to Zero - Transforming a Company Through the Power of "Every"

In 1987, Alcoa, the world's leading aluminum manufacturer, found itself in crisis. Workplace accidents were rampant, employee morale was low, and profits were stagnant. The company desperately needed a change.

Enter Paul O'Neill, an unconventional choice for CEO with no industry experience. Despite skepticism, O'Neill made a bold declaration: Alcoa would become the safest company in America with a goal of zero workplace injuries.

O'Neill revolutionized Alcoa's culture from the ground up, making safety the top priority above profits and productivity. His goal and mindset of zero workplace injuries was what changed first. Then many actions followed. It is important to note that the first step was a change in the leader's mindset. He stopped accepting that injuries and fatalities were inevitable. Actions consistent with his new mindset started to happen. He empowered workers, fostered transparency, and maintained a relentless focus on safety. O'Neill's vision took hold.

Accidents declined, morale soared, and productivity skyrocketed. The results were remarkable as Alcoa reduced its workplace injury rate by 95% during O'Neill's tenure, while profits and market value reached record highs.

Alcoa's story exemplifies the power of the "every" mindset. O'Neill's refusal to accept anything less than zero injuries challenged mediocrity, fostering a culture of excellence and accountability. Alcoa's transformation serves as an inspiration to leaders across industries.

Leadership Expectations in the Airline and Automobile Industries

The safety records of commercial airlines and automobiles reveal a powerful lesson about the impact of leadership expectations on quality outcomes. Despite the intricate nature of flying a commercial jet compared to driving a car, air travel remains significantly safer. Consider these striking statistics:

- According to the National Safety Council, the U.S death rate per 100 million passenger miles for passenger vehicles is significantly higher than for airlines, with passenger vehicles being over 1,200 times more dangerous than airlines. https://injuryfacts.nsc.org/home-and-community/safety-topics/deaths-by-transportation-mode/
- In 2022 in the U.S., passengers in cars and trucks were injured at a rate of 42 per 100 million miles traveled. For U.S. air travel, it was 0.007 per 100 million miles. That makes injuries from car and truck travel 6000 times more common than those from U.S. air travel. https://usafacts.org/articles/is-flying-safer-than-driving/
- The National Safety Council reports a 1 in 101 lifetime odds of dying in a motor vehicle crash, compared to 1 in 9,821 for air and space transport. The average American will get in 3 or 4 accidents throughout their lifetime.

Does it not seem strange that the commercial airplane, a mode of transportation that is many times more complex than a car, is many times safer than the simpler mode of transportation? These disparities can be attributed to the fundamental difference in the number of fatalities that leaders in each industry are willing to accept.

In commercial aviation, CEOs and regulators maintain a zero-tolerance approach to accidents, recognizing that even a single crash is unacceptable. With a target of zero fatalities, commercial airline companies have implemented comprehensive systems and protocols to mitigate risks, including rigorous training, strict maintenance schedules, redundant safety features, and real-time monitoring. The entire industry is unified around the unwavering goal of zero accidents and, thus, zero fatalities. In contrast, society has come to accept a higher level of risk on our roads.

While efforts are made to improve driving safety, there is no equivalent to aviation's relentless pursuit of zero accidents. Political leaders seldom prioritize eliminating traffic fatalities, and automakers often balance safety with other factors, such as cost and performance. Individual drivers are willing to accept the risk because that is all they have ever known. The level of traffic accidents could be many times lower, even with the existing roads and cars, if our standard were zero fatalities. We could implement many changes to reduce traffic fatalities at little to no cost. Instead, we settle for a "most" standard for traffic fatalities, where it is ok to have "some" fatalities. This standard of most is one of the major causes that we kill tens of thousands of people each year in traffic accidents, just in the United States.

A personal example of setting a zero-traffic accident policy is one I set for myself and my family when my daughter was born. At that time, the leading cause of deaths of children under 30 was car accidents. I wanted to reduce the probability of my daughter dying in a car accident. I set the following zero accident policy: You cannot hit anything with the car, and you can never allow anything to hit the car. If the car is in an accident, you will have to pay if you want it fixed. So far, 21 years later, zero accidents and, of course, no fatalities. Some examples of cost-effective actions every family or individual could take to reduce the probability they will be in an accident: set a zero accident standard; take defensive driving classes, these are often offered free of charge; have a zero distraction policy when you drive, don't get distracted by cell phones, or anything else when you are driving; keep a safe minimum distance between your car and the car in front of you; have good tread on your tires; have good windshield wipers, etc.

These case studies demonstrate that the quality an organization achieves is heavily influenced by the standards its leaders accept and act on. When leaders tolerate some level of failure, they inadvertently promote a culture of mediocrity. Conversely, when they set 100% goals and refuse to accept anything less, they empower their organizations to reach new heights. The level of errors leaders accept sets the lid on how close to 100% any organization can achieve. When you go from settling for most to having a standard that only accepts right every time, you raise the lid. Your organization generally cannot, over a long period of time, exceed the standard that the leaders accept.

Business leaders must recognize the power of their standards and what they accept in shaping quality outcomes. Embracing a zero-defect mentality is the first element that sets their teams up to do their very best, Leaders only accepting a standard of 100% right for anything that can impact the quality of the products and services is an essential starting point to enabling a business to escape the trap of "good enough" and unleash the full potential of their organizations to deliver truly exceptional results that are as close to 100% right as possible.

Crossing the Chasm from Ordinary to Extraordinary

The divide between ordinary and extraordinary operations lies in the mindset of an organization's leaders. Leaders who achieve extraordinary levels of operations embrace what we call the McClaskey® Triple 100® Level of Operations. This principle demands that for every customer interaction, products and services meet 100% of brand requirements, 100% of the time, under 100% of conditions. It's a standard that leaves no room for compromise or excuses.

To illustrate this principle, let's examine the transformation of Pal's Sudden Service, a quick-service restaurant founded in 1956. For decades, Pal's operated as a well-run business whose operations were better than most restaurants but still considered in the ordinary range of operations. However, in the mid-1980s, founder Pal Barger had an epiphany that would revolutionize his approach to operations.

Pal shared with me the pivotal moment that sparked this change. He began to critically examine the quality standards he had accepted for years. His reasoning was simple yet profound: if a customer pays full price and receives products and services that are 100% to Pal's requirements, it's a fair transaction. However, if the customer pays full price but receives anything less than 100%, they're being cheated. This realization led to a powerful declaration: Pal would set as his brand's standard that every order would be right.

But what did "right" mean in this context? For Pal, it meant nothing less than 100% adherence to all its brand requirements, 100% of the time, under 100% of conditions. This wasn't just a lofty goal—it became the new operational standard for the entire organization.

This commitment set Pal's on a transformative journey. Led by President and CEO Thom Crosby, the company embarked on a decade-long mission to elevate every aspect of its operations. They meticulously developed processes and systems designed to achieve this unprecedented level of quality, all while working within normal resource constraints.

The results were nothing short of extraordinary. By 1997, Pal's was operating at an exceptional level across almost all key performance metrics. The true testament to their achievement lies in what happened next. Nearly three decades later, this extraordinary level of performance hasn't just been maintained—it's been enhanced and ingrained into the very fabric of the organization's culture. Every store and every transaction Pal's delivers the products and services 100% to the brand requirements. This standard has been maintained even as

Pal's has grown its store count. Extraordinary operations significantly help you successfully and profitably scale your operations.

Today, Pal's stands as a beacon of operational excellence, benchmarked by many in the industry. Their journey from good to extraordinary demonstrates the power of unwavering commitment to excellence.

This principle to 100% extends beyond just quality control of products and services. The standard permeates every aspect of the organization, from hiring practices to employee training, from process design to customer interaction, from the mindset that guides managers to the mindset that guides every Pal's employee's actions. It creates a holistic culture that leaves no room for mediocrity or complacency.

The key takeaway is that the first step to extraordinary operations is for leaders to commit to the 100% standard, and nothing less is acceptable. When leaders commit to nothing less than 100% excellence, they set in motion a cascade of improvements that elevate the entire organization. It's not about perfection—it's about the relentless pursuit of excellence in every interaction, every process, every time.

Breaking Barriers in Belief

Despite the clear success of companies like Pal's, many organizations struggle to achieve this level of operational excellence. The most common objection? "It's impossible to achieve 100% all the time." Others argue that striving for such a high standard is too costly, too stressful for management and employees, or simply unnecessary in their industry.

These objections, while understandable, miss the fundamental point. The goal isn't literal perfection—it's about setting the bar at 100% and then doing everything in your power to reach it. Setting the bar at 100% gets you closer to 100% operational excellence than setting the bar at most. It's about creating a culture where "good enough" is never good enough.

Moreover, the costs of not striving for 100% are often underestimated. Consider the long-term impact of customer dissatisfaction, employee turnover due to frustration with subpar systems, or the cumulative effect of small inefficiencies multiplied across thousands of transactions.

The reality is that organizations whose leaders accept most as their standard fail to achieve extraordinary operations, not because it's impossible, but because their leaders can't or won't commit to a 100% standard and then act to make the standard a reality. They settle for "most" or "good enough," thereby setting a ceiling on their company's potential for excellence.

This underscores a fundamental truth: an organization will never exceed the expectations of its leaders. The journey to extraordinary operations begins with a shift in mindset at the top—a commitment to 100% excellence that permeates every level of the organization. This commitment, by itself, does not cause the organization to improve its quality. The commitment to 100% sets in motion a chain of events that would not have happened without the leader's commitment to 100%. The actions leaders who are committed to 100% take to achieve operations excellence will be described in this book.

As mentioned in the previous chapter, the first step in the Path to Excellence is for the leaders to commit to the standard of extraordinary operations, which states that the only acceptable level is to deliver the products 100% to the brand requirements, 100% of the time, under 100% of the conditions.

What Uncompromising Commitment to Excellence Looks Like

Horst Schulze, when he was President and Chief Operating Officer (COO) of The Ritz-Carlton Hotel Company, exemplifies the power of an uncompromising commitment to excellence. Under his leadership,

The Ritz-Carlton became a byword for luxury and exceptional service, setting a new benchmark for the hospitality industry.

Schulze's philosophy was encapsulated in the company's credo, "We are Ladies and Gentlemen serving Ladies and Gentlemen." This was not merely a catchy phrase but a deeply ingrained belief that shaped every aspect of the hotel's operations. For Schulze, guest satisfaction could not be compromised - every interaction and detail had to be 100% to The Ritz-Carlton standards, 100% of the time. His standard was 100% guest satisfaction and zero guest complaints. Nothing else is acceptable.

To achieve this goal, Schulze implemented a comprehensive training program for all employees, from housekeepers to executives. The training went beyond technical skills and included fostering a deep sense of pride and purpose in each team member. Employees were trained to anticipate guests' needs, immediately respond to any guest need they saw, pay attention to details, and go the extra mile to create unforgettable experiences. In its operations, the company set the target of "defect-free" experiences for guests.

The impact of Schulze's vision and leadership was profound. I had the pleasure of learning directly from Horst Schulze when I was the Baldrige Consultant for the Ritz-Carlton Hotel Company, both times they won the Baldrige Award. The Ritz-Carlton was the first hotel company to win the Malcolm Baldrige National Quality Award. To add to that, 7 years later, they won it again, which continued to make them national role-models. They consistently topped customer satisfaction rankings. It built a loyal customer base and a reputation for unparalleled service that endures to this day. An essential driver of this level of ongoing performance was the uncompromising standards of their leader.

Some of the results the Ritz-Carlton reported when they won the Baldrige Award were:

- 99 percent of guests said they were satisfied with their overall experience

- Pre-tax return on investment and earnings (before income taxes, depreciation, and amortization) nearly doubled over 4 years

- Revenue Per Available Room (the industry's measure of market share) continues to grow, exceeding the industry average by more than 300 percent

Schulze's story demonstrates the potential of the 100% mindset to revolutionize industries. By refusing to accept anything less than 100% compliance with brand standards, he challenged his team to redefine hospitality norms. Schulze showed that extraordinary performance is not only about having the resources and talent, but also about setting a standard of 100% excellence at every level, from the President to each employee.

Achieving this level of performance requires challenging conventional wisdom, empowering employees, and making 100% excellence a non-negotiable standard. As The Ritz-Carlton's story reveals, the rewards for those who embrace this uncompromising standard are immeasurable. By striving for 100% every time, leaders can build organizations that achieve extraordinary results and make a lasting impact on their customers' lives.

Schulze's book, *Excellence Wins*, contains many more examples of processes Schulze and his leaders put in place to obtain national role-model levels of excellence within The Ritz-Carlton Hotel Company.

Where Excellence Begins

Transformation begins with a shift in mindset. Our mental framework shapes how we process information, make decisions, and act. The same data, filtered through different mindsets, can lead to vastly different outcomes. This realization—that significant change starts with altering the paradigms or mindsets of a company's leaders—is why "Think Excellence" is the first of four pillars in the McClaskey° Triple 100° Path to Excellence.

The specific mindset shift we're advocating is moving from "most," which defines ordinary operations, to "every," which defines extraordinary operations. It's a transition from accepting that it's okay for most of your company's products and services to meet brand requirements most of the time to embracing the 100% mindset. This extraordinary perspective demands that every product and service meet 100% of the brand requirements, 100% of the time, under 100% of conditions, thus satisfying all KCRs for every customer, every time.

Leaders who aspire to elevate their organizations from ordinary to extraordinary operations must first scrutinize their own expectations, beliefs, and standards they accept. By recognizing that an organization's quality level directly reflects the standards accepted by its leaders, leaders can identify areas where their current mindset may be limiting their company's potential. This self-examination and resetting standards to 100% is the crucial first step towards operational excellence.

Adopting a 100% mindset isn't about unrealistic perfectionism; it's about setting an unwavering standard that propels continuous improvement and exceptional performance. When leaders embrace this mindset, they redefine what's possible within their organization. Instead of settling for "good enough" or "better than most," they set their sights on true 100% excellence. This shift in thinking cascades throughout the organization, influencing every decision, process, and interaction.

The 100% mindset creates a clear, unambiguous target. This clear standard eliminates the gray areas where mediocrity can hide and forces everyone to confront and address shortcomings head-on. When 99% isn't acceptable, the standard drives innovation, problem-solving, and a constant push for improvement. Moreover, this mindset fosters a culture of accountability. When the standard is crystal clear, there's no room for excuses or rationalizations. Every team member understands what's expected and is empowered to meet those expectations.

Most importantly, while the 100% mindset aims high, it's not about achieving instant perfection - it's about the journey towards it. It's about creating systems, processes, and a culture that consistently strives for the highest possible standards. This ongoing pursuit of excellence becomes self-reinforcing, continually raising the bar and pushing the organization to new heights of performance.

The impact of this mindset is profound. This mindset permeates every aspect of the organization, from hiring practices and employee training to process design and customer interaction. This mindset is a holistic approach that leaves no room for mediocrity or complacency. By adopting this mindset, leaders don't just improve their operations - they fundamentally transform the DNA of their organization, creating a legacy of excellence that stands the test of time.

Let's look at another real-world example of how one organization broke free from setting for ordinary to setting extraordinary as its standard. Fransmart, a franchise development company that is one of the industry's leading partners for entrepreneurs looking to build wealth through franchising, faced a common challenge in their industry - the acceptance of "industry standard" performance as the benchmark for success. But they chose a different path.

Fransmart implemented a system that holds every aspect of franchise support to the highest standards. They developed a proprietary training program that goes beyond basic franchise operations, focusing on instilling a mindset of excellence in every Fransmart brand's franchisee. This approach ensures that franchisees understand and commit to delivering 100% to brand requirements in all conditions.

The results were transformative. Fransmart's brands' franchises began consistently outperforming industry averages. More importantly, they created a culture where excellence was not just encouraged but expected. They broke the chain of mediocrity by refusing to accept it as inevitable.

For leaders, this shift may necessitate a reevaluation of their approach to problem-solving, decision-making, and employee empowerment. This questioning often involves asking challenging questions and confronting uncomfortable truths about their organization's performance. However, this process of self-examination can uncover hidden potential and identify unprecedented opportunities for growth.

The extent to which a leader accepts products and services that fall short of brand requirements is crucial because, invariably, the average company's performance will not exceed the leader's accepted standard. This underscores the critical role of leadership in setting the bar for excellence.

Moreover, the journey towards extraordinary performance is not a solitary endeavor. By instilling this mindset throughout the organization, leaders can harness the collective power of their entire workforce to drive change. This mindset involves cultivating an environment where employees at every level feel empowered to take ownership of quality and actively contribute to the organization's success.

In essence, achieving extraordinary performance requires both personal and organizational transformation. The process begins with leaders thinking differently and evolves into a shared commitment to excellence across the entire company. The 100% mindset challenges leaders to aim higher, work smarter, and never stop improving. It's this commitment to excellence that separates truly extraordinary organizations from the rest.

Remember, when we accept anything less than 100%, we inadvertently set a lower standard for our entire company. By embracing this 100% mindset, leaders can unleash their company's full potential and propel their organizations to new heights of success and customer satisfaction. The key takeaway is this: extraordinary operations begin with leaders setting the standard at 100%. When leaders commit to nothing less than 100% excellence, this decision sets in motion a cascade of improvements that elevate the entire organization.

Implementation Steps: Translating the 100% Mindset into Action

The Ritz-Carlton Hotel Company's journey towards operational excellence offers valuable insights into how organizations can put the 100% mindset into practice. Here are some key steps they took and how other organizations can apply these principles:

1. Set a clear, measurable 100% goal: The Ritz-Carlton aimed for "defect-free" guest experiences, seeking to eliminate all problems. This unambiguous goal set by Horst Schulze guided their decisions and actions. Organizations should establish clear, quantifiable targets that reflect their commitment to 100% excellence.

2. Implement measurement systems: To monitor progress towards their 100% goal, The Ritz-Carlton developed a robust measurement system. This system helped them identify areas for improvement and celebrate achievements. Organizations should implement similar systems to track their progress and maintain accountability.

3. Empower employees: The Ritz-Carlton enabled every employee to address immediate guest needs through Lateral Service. All employees were authorized to (a) pause their tasks when they noticed a guest had a need, (b) assist the guest, and (c) then resume their work. Companies should empower their employees to take ownership of quality and make decisions that benefit customers.

4. Provide extensive training: To ensure employees had the skills to deliver on their 100% promise, The Ritz-Carlton invested heavily in training. Organizations should prioritize employee development and provide comprehensive training programs to equip their employees for 100% success.

5. Integrate the 100% goal into strategy and culture: The pursuit of 100% customer satisfaction and operational excellence was a core part of The Ritz-Carlton's strategy and culture. Organizations should make the 100% mindset a fundamental part of their operations, designing every process for 100% execution and reinforcing this commitment through every interaction, from hiring to daily operations to executive decision-making.

Organizations that aspire to achieve The Ritz-Carlton's success can adopt these practices and adapt them to their unique context. By making the 100% mindset the leadership standard and a guiding principle that impacts every aspect of their operations, organizations can propel themselves towards 100% performance and long-term success.

Throughout this chapter, we've explored the transformative power of the 100% mindset. From Pal's Sudden Service's commitment to getting every order right, to Alcoa's relentless pursuit of zero workplace injuries, to The Ritz-Carlton's dedication to flawless guest experiences, we've seen how this mindset can revolutionize organizations across diverse industries. These examples illustrate that the journey from ordinary to extraordinary operations begins with a fundamental shift in leadership thinking. By rejecting the acceptance of "most" and embracing the pursuit of "every," leaders set a new standard that permeates every aspect of their organization. This mindset shift is not just about setting lofty goals; it's about creating a culture where 100% is the only acceptable outcome, where every team member is enabled and empowered to deliver on the organization's promises 100% of the time, and where continuous improvement is woven into the fabric of daily operations.

Call to Action: The Decision to Be Extraordinary is Yours

The journey to extraordinary operations begins with a single decision: for your company and its managers to make as its standard to settle for nothing less than 100% of your products, services, and customer experience to meet 100% of our brand requirements, 100% of the time, under 100% of the conditions.

It's a high bar, but it's the bar that separates the ordinary from the truly extraordinary. It starts with you, the leader, setting that expectation for yourself and refusing to accept anything less than 100% of your products and services that are delivered 100% to your brand requirements. Setting the standard is a necessary first step to making the 100% standard a reality for your company. Are you ready to make that commitment?

Key Takeaways for Chapter 3: Think Excellence: How Extraordinary Leaders Think Differently

1. It starts with mindset: Transformation from ordinary to extraordinary begins with a shift in the leaders' mindset. Our mental framework shapes how we process information, which influences the decisions we make, which in turn shape the actions we take. The same data, filtered through different mindsets, can lead to vastly different actions and outcomes.

2. Shift your mindset from most to every: Shift from the "most" mindset of ordinary leaders to the "every" or "100%" mindset of extraordinary leaders. This extraordinary perspective has as the only acceptable standard that every product and service meet 100% of the brand requirements, 100% of the time, under 100% of conditions. When this happens, all the

operations-related KCRs for every customer are met every time. This is the McClaskey® Triple 100® Level of Operations. Ordinary leaders accept that it is okay for their organization's products and services to mostly meet the brand requirements, most of the time. This acceptance of "most" designs in errors, mistakes, and dissatisfaction as an authorized management policy. This shift in mindset—from seeing 100% as a goal to view it as the only acceptable standard—is what separates truly extraordinary companies from the rest.

3. Your organizational performance will never be higher than the level the leaders accept: Over the long term, your organization can never perform better than the standards the leadership accepts. As a leader, your beliefs and expectations are the lid on your organization's potential. Thus, when leaders accept that it is ok to deliver some products and services at less than 100%, they make that a self-fulfilling prophecy.

The Next Pillar

With leaders having shifted their mindset from most to every, let us move on to the second pillar of the McClaskey® Triple 100® Path to Excellence: Focus Excellence. In this pillar, the goal is to align everyone in the company with the company's mission and KCRs.

PILLAR 2

FOCUS EXCELLENCE

"If you could get all the people in an organization rowing in the same direction, you could dominate any industry, in any market, against any competition, at any time."

Patrick Lencioni, author of The Five Dysfunctions of a Team

Focus Everything You Do as the Best Way to Accomplish Your Mission

With the foundation of the 100% mindset established, we now turn our attention to a critical question: How do we channel this commitment to excellence into focused, purposeful action? Welcome to Pillar 2 of the McClaskey® Triple 100® Path to Excellence: Focus Excellence.

Focus Excellence is about harnessing the power of alignment. It's the art of ensuring that every individual, every task, and every decision in your organization is laser-focused on achieving a common goal: your mission. In this section, we'll explore how to transform your mission from mere words on a wall into a living, breathing force that drives your organization forward.

Many organizations struggle with alignment, resulting in wasted effort, conflicting priorities, and unrealized potential. Through Focus Excellence, we'll show you a proven, straightforward process that any organization can implement to achieve true alignment. More importantly, we'll demonstrate how to leverage this alignment to create tangible value, driving decisions and behaviors that propel your organization towards extraordinary performance.

In this pillar, we'll delve into six key elements of Focus Excellence. The six elements are:

Element 1: Clarifying the Mission: Learn how to craft a clear, compelling mission statement that serves as a true north for your organization.

Element 2: Identifying Key Customer Requirements (KCRs): Discover techniques for pinpointing what truly matters to your customers and how to make these requirements the cornerstone of your operations.

Element 3: Aligning Every Task to the Mission through KCRs: Explore strategies for ensuring that every action in your organization contributes directly to fulfilling your mission and meeting customer requirements.

Element 4: Using Mission and KCRs to Make Decisions: Learn a powerful framework for decision-making that ensures every choice moves your organization closer to its goals.

Element 5: The Manager's Role in Embedding Mission and KCRs into Organizational Culture: Understand how leaders at all levels can reinforce alignment and make the mission a lived reality throughout the organization.

Element 6: The Unit Operations Manager's Role: Dive into the specific responsibilities of unit operations managers in maintaining focus and driving excellence in day-to-day activities.

By mastering Focus Excellence, you'll create an organization where every employee understands not just what they do but why they do it. You'll eliminate inefficiencies caused by misalignment and harness the full power of your team's efforts toward a common purpose.

Prepare to clarify your organization's purpose, align your team's efforts, and create a focused force capable of achieving extraordinary results. The Path to Excellence continues here, where vision meets action and purpose drives performance.

CHAPTER 4

MISSION: THE PURPOSE OF EVERYTHING AN ORGANIZATION DOES

"As a leader, your job is to energize people around the mission and vision you've articulated."

Jack Welch

Excellence Occurs When Everyone is Aligned to a Common Purpose

In the words of Peter Drucker, management consultant, educator, and author, whose writings contributed to the philosophical and practical foundations of modern management theory, "The most important thing in communication is to hear what isn't being said." This insightful quote highlights a critical truth about mission statements: their power lies not just in the words themselves, but in the behaviors and decisions they inspire. A well-crafted mission statement can transform an organization, but only if it is understood, embraced, and acted upon by every individual.

In the previous chapter, we explored the concept of the 100% mindset—the unwavering commitment to delivering products and services that meet customer requirements 100% of the time. This mindset is the foundation of extraordinary operations, only achieved when everyone in the organization is aligned and working towards a common purpose. That's where a clear, compelling mission statement comes in.

A mission statement is more than just a collection of words or a catchy slogan. It is a declaration of an organization's purpose, a light that guides every employee toward the same objective and illuminates the path to success. When crafted effectively, a mission statement provides a framework for decision-making, a filter through which every action and initiative can be evaluated. It answers the fundamental question, "Why does our organization exist?" and is the basis for everything an organization does. It is your organization's purpose.

Dairy Queen CEO Troy Bader said Warren Buffett taught him that zeal for the mission is more important than anything else; being "the smartest person in the world" won't outperform "somebody who has that passion." (Fortune magazine)

The mission serves as the basis for determining which actions an organization should take. In business, there are no absolute rights or wrongs. Only when you ask which decision best supports the organization's mission can you determine whether one decision is better than an alternative. For example, if an organization's mission is to provide Italian pizza in a way that delights customers and creates loyalty, and you are trying to determine if a more formal or a more casual type of customer greeting would be best, it is the one that best represents an Italian experience in a way that delights the customer and creates loyalty.

Another example is an employee determining if the pizza she is making should be put into the oven to be baked. She inspects the pizza to decide whether or not it fully meets the brand's requirements. She knows the pizza brand requirements were based on what is best to achieve the organization's mission. If the pizza meets all the brand requirements, she knows it's right and puts it in the oven. If it does not meet all the brand's requirements, she fixes it until it does, then puts the pizza in the oven.

In each example, the mission provides the purpose and the "why" and enables every action taken within the company to align with the organization's mission by making decisions that best support the mission. This process enables everyone related to the organization to align their collective actions to best support the mission. However, many organizations fall into the trap of creating mission statements that are vague, abstract, too long, or disconnected from the realities of their business. Leaders may have well-established mission statements, but if individuals within the organization don't understand how the mission applies to their specific roles and responsibilities and how it helps them make job-related decisions, the mission becomes a document with little to no impact or value. When an organization's mission statement fails to provide a clear, shared understanding of purpose and alignment, confusion leads to conflicting interpretations, misaligned priorities, and ultimately subpar performance.

To truly harness the power of a mission statement, organizations must go beyond mere words and ensure that every individual understands how the mission applies to them. Everyone in the organization must use the mission statement as a basis for aligning behaviors, guiding decisions, and understanding the "why" or larger purpose behind everything each employee does. Only then can leaders create a culture of excellence when everyone works towards a shared purpose.

The Alignment Challenge: Turning Mission into Action

Imagine two organizations in the same industry, each with a mission statement. Company A's mission statement is proudly displayed on the walls of their office, but when you ask employees what it means to them, you get a variety of answers. Some focus on financial performance, others on innovation, and still others on customer satisfaction. There's no clear consensus on how the mission statement translates into day-to-day behaviors and decisions.

In contrast, Company B has a different approach. They've created a clear, compelling mission statement and invested time and resources to ensure that every employee knows, memorizes, understands, and uses it—and how it applies to their job. As a result, Company B's employees are aligned and empowered. These employees know exactly what's expected of them and understand how their work contributes to the organization's success. When faced with a decision, they don't have to guess or rely on their interpretation of the mission statement. With a clear understanding of the organization's mission, they can make a choice that best aligns with the organization's purpose.

Over time, the difference between these two companies becomes clear. Company A struggles with inconsistency, conflicting priorities, and a lack of focus. It is hard for the hundreds of decisions made at all levels to be the best possible decisions to achieve the mission, since a clear understanding and consistent use of the mission statement has not been established. They may have pockets of excellence, but they fail to achieve sustained extraordinary operations. Company B, on the other hand, thrives. They can adapt to changing market conditions, innovate rapidly, and consistently deliver products and services that meet or exceed customer expectations. Their mission statement isn't just a plaque on the wall; it's a living, breathing part of their culture that guides every action and decision.

The Data Speaks: Measuring the Impact of Mission-Driven Cultures

The impact of a clear, well-understood mission statement on organizational performance is well-documented. According to Deloitte, mission-driven companies have 30% higher levels of innovation and 40% higher levels of retention. Other research also indicates that communicating mission and values effectively leads to a significant boost in employee engagement.

Facilitating Strategic Planning: A Personal Insight

In my experience leading hundreds of strategic planning sessions, I have seen that when a company's leaders have a clear understanding of the organization's mission and a shared view of its current state and future opportunities, they can swiftly agree on strategies that will best drive the organization forward. This result exemplifies the importance of aligning a group around a common mission.

Core Principles of Effective Mission Statements

A mission statement is as powerful as its implementation. To harness the full potential of an organization's mission, it's crucial to understand and apply several key principles. These principles transform a mission statement from mere words into a dynamic force that shapes culture, gives purpose to all activities, guides decisions, and drives extraordinary performance operations. By adhering to these core tenets, you can ensure your mission statement becomes a catalyst for alignment, purpose, and success throughout your organization. Let's explore these essential principles that elevate a mission statement from a static declaration to an active driver of organizational excellence:

1. An effective mission statement clearly, concisely, and compellingly states the organization's purpose. The mission statement must serve as a basis for alignment, purpose, actions, and decision-making.

2. The primary customer for the mission statement is the organization's employees, including its management.

3. Mission statements create most of their value when they are used to create alignment, purpose, and as a basis for actions and decision-making. Just having a mission statement but not using it creates little value.

4. For mission statements to be usable and provide value, they need to meet these criteria: concisely (is a short phrase) states the purpose of the organization; can be memorized by all; can be used to make decisions

5. For the mission to be useful, it needs to be known, memorized, and understood by all employees. This will not happen unless the statement is short and concise.

6. Every employee in the organization must understand how the mission statement applies to their specific role and responsibilities. This statement provides a sense of purpose, or the "why," behind every task by showing how what they are specifically doing contributes to accomplishing the organization's mission.

7. Every employee in the organization must use the mission statement to guide the many decisions they make to carry out their job responsibilities.

8. Mission statements do not have to be unique. Many organizations can have the same mission. For example, part of The Ritz-Carlton's mission, which they call their Credo, is "a place where genuine care and comfort of our guests is our highest mission." Tens of thousands of businesses could say the same thing, and that is okay.

9. The mission statement does not have to explain what your organization does for the customer. A separate, customer-oriented statement can be developed if the business feels the need for its marketing and sales efforts. The primary customers for the organization's mission statement discussed in this chapter are the employees, so they can all work toward a common purpose.

10. The mission statement should be a living, breathing, active part of the organization's culture, not just a plaque on the wall.

Addressing Skepticism Related to the True Value of Mission Statements

Some may argue that mission statements are nothing more than empty platitudes, disconnected from the realities of running a business. They may point to examples of organizations with well-crafted mission statements that fail to deliver extraordinary operations. While these challenges are valid, they miss the more significant point. A mission statement alone does not guarantee success, but a well-crafted, widely understood mission statement is a critical foundation for achieving extraordinary operations. When used effectively, a mission statement provides a framework for aligning behaviors, giving everything a company does purpose, guiding decisions, and defining the KCRs that drive success.

The real challenge lies not in crafting the perfect mission statement but in ensuring that every individual in the organization understands and uses it as a basis for action. This requires leadership that provides ongoing education, and role-model actions that consistently align with the best way to accomplish the mission. It means using the mission statement as a lens through which every decision is evaluated, every action is taken, and every customer interaction is approached.

Without this level of clarity and alignment, even the most well-crafted mission statement will fail to deliver its full potential. However, sustained extraordinary operations become possible when an organization commits to using its mission statement to drive behaviors, provide purpose, and make decisions. It becomes challenging to maintain extraordinary operations without everyone buying into and being guided by a common mission. When everyone is not brought into and guided by a common mission, too much of the organization's energy and resources are misdirected.

Bridging Purpose and Performance

The true power of a mission statement lies in its ability to serve as a basis for enabling employees at every level of the organization to understand how their work contributes to the bigger picture and to make decisions that align with the organization's mission.

However, achieving this level of clarity and alignment is no easy feat. This clarity requires a commitment from leadership to both craft a compelling mission statement and ensure that every employee in the organization understands, embraces, and uses it. This commitment means investing time and resources into communication, education, aligning actions with the best way to accomplish the mission, and reinforcement. When organizations get this action right, the results can be transformative. Employees are more engaged and empowered, customers are more satisfied and loyal, and the organization is better positioned to adapt to changing market conditions and achieve sustained extraordinary operations. The mission statement becomes not just a statement of purpose but a powerful tool to get everyone to work together for a common purpose and to drive behaviors and decisions that lead to success.

Implementation Steps for Mission Statement

1. Create a Clear and Compelling Mission Statement

Objective:

Create a mission statement or ensure that the existing organizational mission statement articulates the organization's purpose and reason for existence clearly, concisely, and in a compelling manner to serve as a basis for alignment, purpose, actions, and decision-making.

Action:

Either create a mission statement or review the current mission statement to ensure it is clear, concise (15-20 words or fewer are desirable), and compelling, ensuring that the mission statement can serve as a basis for alignment, purpose, actions, and decision-making. The primary audience for the mission statement is the organization's employees, including management.

Guidance on Developing a Mission Statement:

- In the McClaskey Excellence Institute Consulting Practice, we have found three basic formats that help companies draft an effective mission statement. Decide which format would best serve as a basis for employee alignment, purpose, actions, and decision-making.

Preferred Formats:

- **Customer Delight Format:**
  - State the purpose to delight customers in a way that causes repeat business.
  - Example: Pal's mission statement: "Delight Customers in a Way that Creates Loyalty."
  - Example: Creative Masonry: "Make sure every customer is 100% satisfied."
- **Overall Impact Format:**
  - State the overall impact you want to occur for your customers as a result of being a customer of your organization.
  - Example: Google's mission statement: "To organize the world's information and make it universally accessible and useful."
- **Product/Service Focus Format:**
  - State "to provide" and then state your organization's overall product and/or service (usually at a high level,

so only one covers it), then, at a very high level, say who your primary customer is.

- Example: Costco's mission statement: "To continually provide our members with quality goods and services at the lowest possible prices."

2. Communicate the Mission Throughout the Organization

Objective:

Ensure every employee knows, understands, and has memorized the mission and how it applies to their roles and responsibilities.

Action:

Create an ongoing communication plan that includes orientation, onboarding, company-wide meetings, team discussions, and visual reminders throughout the workplace. Use the mission statement during daily conversations, coaching, training, and team and company meetings to keep it top of mind. Chapter 8 will provide details on how to do this.

3. Enable and Empower Employees to Use

Objective:

Give employees the training, resources, and responsibility to make decisions that best support their job responsibilities and the mission.

Action:

Within the employee's job responsibilities and consistent with applicable processes and procedures, train and empower employees to make decisions that align with the mission. Chapter 7 will provide details on how to do this.

4. Create Accountability for Use for all Employees

Objective:

Develop and use accountability and coaching processes that hold employees accountable for knowing, memorizing, understanding, and using the mission to make their job-related decisions.

Action:

Managers at all levels need to hold themselves and their direct reports accountable for knowing, memorizing, understanding, and applying the mission when making job-related decisions. Review your accountability and coaching processes quarterly to ensure the mission statement serves as a basis for alignment, purpose, actions, and daily decision-making.

5. Communicate Success

Objective:

Reinforce the importance of the mission by sharing performance data and success stories.

Action:

Share metrics and success stories to motivate and align the team. Highlight how achieving the mission is critical to the organization's overall success. Share stories where decisions that were influenced by the mission led to a successful outcome.

6. Lead by Example

Objective:

Ensure leadership at all levels embodies the mission and demonstrates commitment to the KCRs.

Action:

Require leaders to model behaviors and decision-making skills aligned with the mission and KCRs, fostering a culture of accountability and excellence.

7. Revisit Your Mission Statement and Implementation Process

Annually:

As part of your strategic planning process, revisit your mission statement to determine whether any wording changes are needed. Use the mission statement during strategic planning as the key criteria for selection strategies.

By applying these principles and implementation steps, organizations can develop and implement an effective mission statement, turning these words into a powerful driver of operational excellence and customer satisfaction.

A Clear Path Forward

By completing the mission implementation steps, your organization has a clear, concise, compelling mission statement that articulates its purpose. It answers the question of why your organization exists. You have taken the time to communicate with every employee in your organization, so they know, have memorized, understand, and use the mission statement. You have an ongoing communication process that keeps the mission top of mind through daily use during conversations, written communication, training, coaching, and team and organizational meetings.

Harnessing the full power of your mission statement only occurs when every employee at all levels of the organization:

- Understand how everything they do contributes to accomplishing the mission (the purpose of their work); and

- Uses the mission statement as a basis for making the many decisions every employee makes each day to carry out their job responsibilities. Decisions mean choices, and when we have choices, we want to make the choice that best supports the mission.

Here is a dilemma we will now solve. Mission statements, by their very nature of having to describe the purpose of the entire organization, are vague and, by themselves, lead to multiple interpretations. Mission statements can also be so general that it is exceedingly difficult for every employee in the company to use the mission as a basis for making their specific job-related decisions. If we try to solve the problem by adding details to the mission statement, it becomes so complex as to be useless.

Mission statements, by themselves, provide only minimal value. But the goal is to make the mission statement not just a statement of purpose, but a compass that guides every decision and provides a purpose for everything done within the organization. The mission guides every step of the journey toward extraordinary operations.

We will solve this dilemma, and thus unleash the power of the mission statement, in the next chapter. We will add a separate but related component, the KCRs. This addition will both remove the vagueness (or gray) from how the mission statement is interpreted and enable every employee to use it to guide the many decisions made at all levels of the company. We will use the mission statement as a framework for defining your organization's KCRs.

Call to Action

1. Develop or revise your organization's mission statement so it fully meets the criteria for usable mission statements: is a short phrase that concisely states the purpose of the organization; can be memorized by all; can be used to make decisions.

2. Get the mission statement approved so it is the official mission statement of the organization

Key Takeaways for Chapter 4: Mission: The Purpose of Everything an Organization Does

1. The mission statement is your organization's purpose. These words answer the question, "Why does our organization exist?" and it is the basis for everything an organization does. It is a guiding light that gets every employee to work toward a common objective.

2. An effective mission statement clearly, concisely, and in a compelling manner states the organization's purpose. To provide value, the mission statement must serve as a basis for alignment, purpose, actions, and decision-making for every person in the organization.

3. For mission statements to be usable and provide value, they need to meet these criteria: concisely (is a short phrase) states the purpose of the organization; can be memorized by all; can be used to make decisions

4. A group of people can only effectively work together if they work for a common purpose. That common purpose is the organization's mission.

5. The true power of a mission statement lies in its ability to form the basis that enables all employees at every level of the organization to understand how their work contributes to the purpose of the company and to provide a guide for them to

make job-related decisions that best align with the company's mission.

6. The mission statement provides a framework for decision-making, a filter through which every action and initiative can be evaluated.

The Next Chapter

In the upcoming chapter, we'll explore how to translate your mission statement into specific, measurable requirements that drive behaviors and decisions at every level of the organization. Get ready to turn your mission from words to action and unlock your organization's full potential.

CHAPTER 5

IDENTIFY KEY CUSTOMER REQUIREMENTS

"Getting the right product or service into the customer's hands is the highest form of marketing."

Seth Godin, author, entrepreneur

Identify and Focus on What Matters Most to Customers

At the heart of any thriving organization lies a deep understanding of customer needs. This unwavering commitment to customer-centricity is the cornerstone of Focus Excellence, a critical component of the McClaskey° Triple 100° Path to Excellence. By identifying and focusing on what matters most to customers, businesses can create exceptional value and secure a competitive advantage.

In an era where customer expectations continue to evolve, companies must stay agile and attuned to meeting their customers' needs. By identifying and homing in on the essential or key requirements of their customers, organizations can tailor their offerings and operations to drive satisfaction, loyalty, and ultimately, extraordinary operations.

The importance of this focus cannot be overstated. Deeply understanding and prioritizing customer needs is key to achieving extraordinary performance.

As Founder and former Amazon CEO Jeff Bezos aptly puts it, "The most important single thing is to focus obsessively on the customer. Our goal is to be Earth's most customer-centric company." The most successful companies make identifying and meeting KCRs a core part of their culture and processes, embedding this philosophy into every aspect of their operations.

Remember how we identified Zappos as a company that prioritizes excellence? Zappos fosters a culture that prioritizes customer satisfaction, encouraging call center employees to take as much time as needed to address customer concerns. This approach ensures that each customer interaction is thorough and tailored to that individual's needs.

As we delve into Chapter 5, we'll explore strategies and techniques for identifying KCRs. I will examine how to identify these crucial needs and prioritize them effectively.

The journey to Focus Excellence began with identifying your mission and writing it to meet the mission criteria we discussed in Chapter 4. The next element of the Focus Excellence journey is to identify the key needs and expectations of the customers. I will refer to the key customer needs or expectations as key customer requirements (KCRs). This chapter will enable you to add the second element of Focus Excellence: identifying your company's KCRs.

Defining What Matters Most to Your Customers: their KCRs

Picture yourself holding a satisfaction survey for a business you recently visited. They ask you to rate your overall satisfaction on a scale of 1 to 5, with 5 being very satisfied and 1 being very dissatisfied. What factors come to mind as you consider your response?

These factors likely represent your KCRs for that business - the aspects that matter most when choosing that particular product or service. What are the most essential aspects of a customer's experience that, if not fully met, would cause you not to be delighted with the experience? This expectation may differ for different types of businesses or products. However, customers have roughly the same set of requirements for a given product or service.

For instance, over the years, we have asked thousands of McClaskey Excellence Institute class participants: "What are your essential or key requirements when being a customer of a quick-service restaurant?" Almost everyone, regardless of their age, the country they live in, etc., lists these six KCRs: 1) the quality of the food, 2) friendly service, 3) speed of service, 4) accuracy of order, 5) cleanliness of the facility, and 6) overall value (based on the overall experience versus the price). Since KCRs are so fundamental, they are easy for company leaders to identify. I know this because during our classes or consulting sessions, we have helped thousands of companies identify their KCRs in just a few minutes.

Each KCR significantly influences how customers judge their overall satisfaction. Missing even one KCR has a significant impact on the overall customer experience. How well a business meets all their KCRs for a given customer affects how delighted they are with the overall experience, how often they return as repeat customers, and whether they provide positive or negative recommendations about the business. Ultimately, these KCRs serve as the essential buying criteria for customers.

Businesses can create a competitive advantage and elevate their performance by having everyone in their organization understand and focus on meeting their KCRs. Identifying the KCRs is the second element within the Focus Excellence component of the McClaskey® Triple 100® Path to Excellence. This focus helps to provide alignment with the customer and the mission essential to creating a work environment that can transform ordinary operations into extraordinary operations.

Customer service expert Kate Zabriskie's insight, "The customer's perception is your reality," emphasizes the importance of understanding and addressing customer needs to shape a positive perception and drive success. A Gartner study highlights this point, revealing that 89% of companies now compete primarily based on customer experience.

As businesses strive to create exceptional experiences, they must identify and focus on the KCRs, heeding Twitter co-founder Jack Dorsey's advice: "Make every detail perfect and limit the number of details to perfect." A prime example is Chick-fil-A, where a case study found that their obsession with speed, accuracy, and friendly service was a key driver of their industry-leading customer satisfaction ratings.

By having everything focused on these critical KCRs, organizations can cultivate a loyal customer base, drive repeat business, and solidify their position as industry leaders. As the late Steve Jobs said, "We have to treat our customers like guests when they buy our products," emphasizing the need to understand and meet customer expectations. Satisfaction surveys offer valuable insights into how well companies are doing just that.

These surveys allow businesses to assess their performance across various touchpoints, with common factors including product/service quality, value for money, staff responsiveness, ease of experience, and overall satisfaction. By analyzing survey data, patterns emerge, revealing the KCRs that most significantly impact satisfaction and loyalty. Customer surveys, when designed around KCRs, can provide trend data on how well your customers perceive you are meeting or exceeding their KCRs.

To achieve excellence in operations, companies take this a step further, probing deeper into the "why" behind the ratings and mining qualitative feedback for gold. This deeper understanding allows an organization to identify and refine their KCRs and understand what the company is or is not doing to fully satisfy customers' KCRs. This analysis enables the ability to adapt to evolving customer needs, refine your product and service requirements, stay ahead of the competition, and maintain your position as industry leaders.

Building Competitive Advantage Through Customer Insights

The benefits of identifying and focusing on KCRs and delivering exceptional customer experiences are well-documented. Here are some compelling statistics that showcase the high returns of customer-centricity:

1. A study by Deloitte found that customer-centric companies are 60% more profitable than companies not focused on the customer.

2. Research by Forbes found that 86% of customers are willing to pay more for a better customer experience.

3. A Walker study discovered that the customer experience will overtake price and product as the key brand differentiator.

4. Data from Bain & Company showed that businesses that lead in customer experience grow revenues 4-8% above their market, while those that lag fall behind by 2-3%.

5. A Gartner survey found that organizations that effectively execute customer experience strategies are three times more likely to exceed their business goals.

These findings highlight the significant impact of prioritizing, focusing on, and consistently meeting the KCRs on an organization's bottom line. By fostering a customer-centric approach and continuously adapting to evolving customer needs, businesses can secure a competitive edge, boost profitability, and set themselves up for long-term success.

Identifying and Using Key Customer Requirements to Create Organizational Focus

To effectively focus on what truly matters for your organization, it's essential to identify and understand the KCRs. After establishing your mission statement, the next step to achieve Focus Excellence involves defining what your customers value most about their interactions with your organization. These are generally customer expectations or needs that the customer believes are due to them because they are doing business with you.

Step 1: List a Draft of Your Organization's Key Customer Requirements

A. Study your approved company mission statement that fully meets the mission criteria from the previous chapter.

B. The KCRs are the critical few (key) requirements the customer has, all of which must be fully met for the customer to be delighted with the customer experience with your organization. We have found that most companies have between 4 to 8 KCRs.

C. Most established businesses have a deep understanding of their customers, which can be leveraged to list KCRs. We have found that, for companies that have been in existence for at least 3 months, the leadership team usually knows, with a reasonable degree of accuracy, what their customers' key requirements are. It is just a matter of making a list.

D. Your draft list should only identify the vital few key customer requirements. Typically, organizations find that there are four to eight KCRs.

E. Write a brief description for each KCR that helps the reader understand what the KCR means. This description should be concise, usually less than a sentence.

Step 2: Do Some Limited Confirmation of the Draft of the Key Customer Requirements

A. **Talk with your customers:** It is beneficial to engage directly with customers to validate and refine your draft list of KCRs. I have found that these conversations mostly confirm or lead to moderate changes to the draft list the leadership team developed.

B. **Review your data from customers:** Briefly review the key outputs from customer surveys, interviews, focus groups, and online reviews to collect qualitative and quantitative insights from customers. Identify patterns in the feedback and highlight recurring themes that may reveal KCRs.

C. **Customer feedback:** Regular analysis of customer reviews, complaints, and feedback helps pinpoint what customers appreciate or criticize about their experiences. The most commonly mentioned comments often highlight the most significant aspects of customer satisfaction or dissatisfaction.

D. **Talk with your employees:** Show the draft KCRs list to your employees and see if they spot anything missing or communication issues where they interpret the words very differently from what you meant the words to mean.

E. **Research:** Do some internet and other searches on what similar companies have for their KCRs. To identify emerging KCRs, talk to experts in the field and researchers.

F. **Test:** If all the KCRs are met, are most customers delighted with the experience with your company? If not, determine whether a KCR is missing or needs to be modified. If yes, meeting all the KCRs is how you delight your customers.

G. **Test:** if any one of the KCRs is not met, are most customers less than delighted. If no, determine if the list of KCRs needs to be modified.

Step 3: Approve the Business Key Customer Requirements

A. Have the KCR list reviewed and approved by whoever in the company needs to approve such a list to make it official company policy. As we have mentioned, most companies have between 4 to 8 KCRs. You usually do not want a list longer than 8, if possible.

Step 4: Communicate the Key Customer Requirements

Ensure every employee in the company knows, has memorized, and understands the organization's mission and KCRs. Chapter 8 has specifics on how to do this.

A. This step will require multiple communication methods. It usually takes 2-6 weeks of deliberate and concerted effort to accomplish this. Communication needs to be worked on continuously, not just a one-shot-and-done. Managers can get very creative here, figuring out and using fun, effective ways to help everyone know, memorize, and understand the KCRs.

B. A lot of companies found that communicating the KCRs and the approved mission statement at the same time was very helpful. That way, they can explain the linkage between the two. This would illustrate that achieving the KCRs is key to fulfilling the company's mission and delighting customers.

C. There are three major milestones you want to achieve in your communication with every employee. Every employee needs to know, be able to recite from memory, and understand and explain the mission and KCRs. An employee understands the mission and KCRs when they can briefly explain them to others and how they all fit together to delight the customer.

D. Management at all levels must regularly use the actual words in the mission and KCRs as they talk to each other and all employees. It is critical to use the mission and KCRs when providing positive and corrective coaching and feedback.

E. As appropriate, communicate the mission and KCRs to other key stakeholders like customers, partners, suppliers, and investors. Everyone involved in helping to meet the mission and KCRs should know what they are.

Step 5: Use the Key Customer Requirements

A. The reason you want people to know, memorize, and understand the mission and KCRs is so they can use them. The mission and KCRs only create value if they impact the behaviors of your employees and other stakeholders who have an impact on the mission and KCRs.

B. Meeting all the KCRs is how you delight the customer and fulfill your mission.

C. Use the mission and KCRs to provide a worthy purpose for every task you ask employees to do. Every task should be linked to one or more KCRs. How to do this will be described in Chapter 6.

D. Use the mission and KCRs to influence the dozens of decisions that employees make every day as they go about accomplishing their jobs. Details about how to do this will be covered in Chapter 7.

Step 6: Measure the Key Customer Requirements (KCRs)

Measures of KCRs are usually a combination of customer-based indicators and feedback and internal company measures.

E. Develop customer-based measures for each of the KCRs. The customer-based measures are usually subjective indicators and can include customer observations, customer comments online and in person, customer surveys, which products and services customers order or use, the rate of repeat business, or other customer-based indicators. You want to ensure that when the KCRs are all met, the customer is delighted. If all KCRs are met but customers are not delighted, identify the cause and determine whether the KCRs or their definitions need to be modified.

F. Develop internally based measures that indicate whether or not the customer's KCRs are met. Examples of these types of measures include customer complaints; errors that impact the customer; service times; and audits. These measures are usually internal, objective measures.

Step 7: Maintain the Daily Use of the Mission and Key Customer Requirements

A. Regularly review daily, weekly, and monthly the measures of the KCRs for: (a) opportunities for improvement; (b) feedback to employees and units within the business; (c) opportunities to provide coaching and rewards; and (d) reviews and evaluations.

Step 8: Continue to Test your KCRs against Customer Delight:

A. Customer expectations are a moving target. They generally don't change rapidly, but they can change. You need to keep testing to ensure your current KCRs and how you define them are what delights your customer. When all the KCRs are met, is the customer delighted with the experience with your company? If not, determine what is missing, what changed, and whether the KCRs or their definitions need to be modified.

Key Linkage Between Mission and KCRs: Meeting All Key Customer Requirements Results in Delighted Customers, which accomplishes your mission:

Terms like "delight" and "satisfaction" in your mission statement are subjective and vague. I will use the term "gray" to refer to any word or phrase that can reasonably be interpreted in more than one way. You design the gray out of your mission statement (Delight, satisfy, etc.); by defining that the way you "delight or satisfy" your customers is to meet all their KCRs. Satisfying your KCRs is also how you achieve your mission. KCRs are usually very measurable in clear black and white terms. Therefore, the KCRs help translate the "delight" or "satisfaction" statement in your mission into clear, actionable behaviors and objectives. As already stated, for a quick-service restaurant, key requirements might include quality, friendliness, speed, accuracy, cleanliness, and overall value. All of which can be precisely measured. You delight your customers by fully meeting all of their KCRs.

Meeting the Key Customer Requirements is What You Do to Achieve Your Mission and Delight Customers

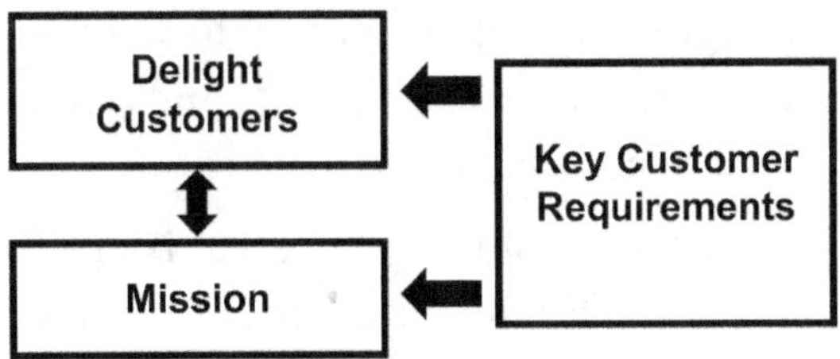

The simplest and most effective strategy for delighting customers is to fully meet all of their key requirements, every time. Failure to meet even one can significantly diminish the customer experience.

To truly delight your customers, it's not enough to meet most of their key requirements; you must strive to meet all their KCRs. Let me illustrate the concept that you need to meet all of your KCRs to delight customers, and that if even one KCR is not met, the customer will not be delighted.

Consider a quick-service restaurant scenario:

- If the food quality is high but the staff is unfriendly, customers are likely not delighted.

- If both food quality and friendliness are good, but service is slow, the experience still falls short and does not delight the customer.

- Even if food quality, friendliness, and speed meet expectations, an incorrect order can undermine the overall experience.

I have now defined what your organization does to delight the customers: fully meet all their KCRs, every time.

- Delighted Customers = All KCRs are Fully Met
- Mission Achieved Requires all KCRs to be Fully Met

I have now defined the term "delight" from your mission statement as fully meeting all the KCRs. With this definition, we have turned the term "delight" in your mission statement from a vague, very gray term into a measurable, clearly defined term that is black and white and cannot be reasonably interpreted in multiple ways.

This clarity focuses all of your organization's operations on fully meeting all the KCRs, every customer, every time. This clarity gives you the path that has the highest probability of consistently delighting every customer, every time.

When you consistently meet all the KCRs, every customer, every time, your organization creates delighted customers (your mission), which leads to repeat business, loyalty, and positive recommendations, which in turn drive revenue, profitability, and growth.

Call to Action

1. Develop your organization's KCRs. The KCRs are the critical few (key) requirements the customer has, all of which must be fully met for the customer to be delighted with the customer experience with your organization. We have found that most companies have between 4 to 8 KCRs.

2. Have your KCRs officially approved by the organization.

Key Takeaways for Chapter 5: Identify Key Customer Requirements

1. The simplest and most effective strategy for delighting customers is to fully meet all of their key customer requirements (KCRs), every time. KCRs are key; failure to meet even one can significantly diminish the customer experience.

2. The KCRs are the critical few, usually four to eight, customer needs or expectations, all of which must be fully met for the customer to be delighted with their experience.

3. The essential mission of any business is to delight its customers in a way that creates loyalty and repeat business. The KCRs translate the vague or gray word "delight" into clear, understandable, measurable KCRs.

4. Organizations delight their customers and, therefore, achieve their mission by fully meeting all their KCRs, every time.

5. The activities of a business need to be the best way to accomplish the KCRs.

The Next Chapter

Now that you have identified your company's KCRs, in the next chapter, let's explore how to align every task you ask your employees to do to your mission by how they impact one or more of the KCRs.

CHAPTER 6

ALIGN EVERY TASK TO THE MISSION THROUGH KEY CUSTOMER REQUIREMENTS

"You've got to think about big things while you're doing small things, so that all the small things go in the right direction."

Alvin Toffler, author of "Future Shock"

Create Purpose by Aligning Every Task to the Mission

In this chapter, we'll explore how aligning every task with your mission through the lens of KCRs can unleash your organization's full potential by focusing everything on the customer and providing a worthy purpose for everything employees do. Imagine the potential for success and growth if every task your team performed directly contributed to your organization's mission. Envision the employee engagement you will achieve if every employee understands how each task they perform contributes to satisfying one or more KCRs. This understanding provides a worthy purpose for everything employees do. Envision a workplace where each action, big or small, is a purposeful stepping stone toward fulfilling your organization's mission and the person performing that task knows it.

Understanding Alignment

With a clearly defined mission statement and a deep understanding of KCRs, the next step is to align every task within your organization to fulfill these essential elements. Alignment ensures that all aspects of your operations work harmoniously to achieve your mission and meet KCRs.

By connecting each employee's responsibilities and tasks to the organizational mission and KCRs, you can foster a sense of purpose and engagement while also driving effectiveness and efficiency. This alignment helps employees understand the importance of their roles and empowers them to make decisions and take actions that directly contribute to your organization's success.

Moreover, alignment can enhance your organization's agility and adaptability in a rapidly changing business landscape. With a clear focus on mission and KCRs, your organization can consistently meet KCRs, respond quickly to emerging trends, capitalize on new opportunities, and navigate challenges effectively.

McClaskey® Triple 100® Alignment to Mission:
Link and Align Every Job/Task to the Mission through the Key Customer Requirements

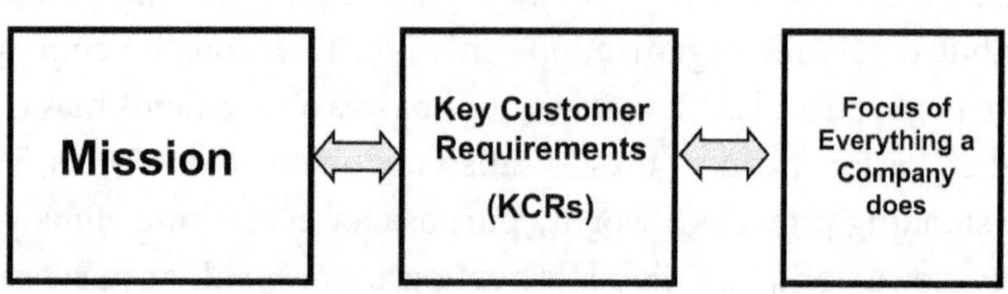

In summary, aligning every task with your mission and KCRs is a powerful way to drive employee engagement, empower employees to make work-based decisions, improve operational effectiveness and efficiency, and consistently create exceptional customer experiences. By embracing this approach, your organization can thrive in today's competitive marketplace, obtain a sustainable competitive advantage, and achieve long-term success.

The Power of Alignment: MidwayUSA

Meet MidwayUSA, a small business that experienced a remarkable transformation upon adopting the Baldrige Criteria for performance excellence. With a clear focus that included aligning their efforts with their mission and KCRs, MidwayUSA saw impressive improvements across the board.

After implementing Baldrige, MidwayUSA's sales have grown an average of 17% annually over the past 12 years, while net income has grown an average of 39% annually over the same period. Moreover, customer satisfaction reached an all-time high of 93%. President Larry Potterfield praised the Baldrige Criteria as the driving force that enabled the company to elevate its performance, providing a framework for sustainability and continuous improvement. One of the key elements of the Baldrige Criteria is that everything is assessed against how it impacts the organization's mission and meeting their KCRs. As a result of MidwayUSA's use of this and other aspects of the Baldrige criteria, as of this time, they have won the Baldrige Award 3 times. This shows they are a sustained role-model over a long period of time.

MidwayUSA's commitment to aligning its mission with daily operations was one of the key changes it made to achieve its breakthrough results. This simple yet effective process is essential to enabling your organization to unlock its full potential, drive growth, and achieve exceptional customer satisfaction. MidwayUSA's story is an inspiring example of how alignment can propel a business from great to truly exceptional.

Role-model Examples

Pal's Sudden Service and The Ritz-Carlton Hotel role-model companies in creating a culture where every employee is aligned with the mission and KCRs. In these companies, every employee knows, has memorized, and understands the mission and KCRs; knows how everything they do contributes to one or more of the KCRs; and makes all their many job-related decisions in a way that best contributes to the mission and KCRs.

Evidence Supporting Alignment

Numerous studies demonstrated the significant impact of alignment and line-of-sight on an organization's performance. According to a 2020 Harvard Business Review article, organizations with a strong alignment and line-of-sight between individual tasks and the overall mission have outperformed their competitors by a considerable margin. These organizations have shown higher revenue growth, increased market share, and enhanced employee satisfaction and retention rates.

In another study published in the Journal of Business Strategy in 2019, researchers found that organizations with well-defined alignment were more agile and responsive to changes in their environment. This adaptability improved innovation, better decision-making, and greater overall performance.

Key Principles for Effective Alignment

First, establishing and agreeing upon the organization's mission and validating KCRs (KCRs) is crucial. Without the agreed upon mission and KCRs, there is no agreed upon purpose or concise understanding of the customer's key expectations to focus on.

Once the mission and KCRs are in place, it is essential to align everyone's tasks and job responsibilities with these guiding principles.

Every task, no matter how seemingly small or insignificant, can and should be linked to one or more KCRs. By doing so, it becomes evident to both the individual and the organization how each individual's contribution impacts the organization's ability to fulfill its mission. This use provides each individual with a clear, relevant sense of purpose, which is critical to high, sustained employee engagement.

To create a culture of alignment and value creation, leaders must ensure that every employee understands the significance and purpose of their work in contributing to the KCRs and the organization's mission. This can be facilitated through management discussions and visual displays that clearly show the connections between tasks, KCRs, and the mission, and that are regularly discussed.

One of the best practices McClaskey Excellence Institute teaches in its classes and uses with its consulting clients is to write into the standard operating procedures (SOPs) and incorporate into the training for every task or process which KCRs that task or process contributes to. This step provides the "why" or purpose for the task or process. With this included, training is more effective since it includes the "why" as well as the what and how to do every task. This provides the purpose and alignment necessary for employees to feel engaged because they know all elements of their work make a meaningful contribution to the mission by contributing to the KCRs. When organizations drive alignment across all levels and tasks, it improves collaboration among individuals and teams, creates value, and increases employee engagement, job satisfaction, and retention.

It is important to highlight why we need the KCRs to connect tasks, processes, and jobs to the mission. It is because the mission, by its very nature as the purpose of the entire organization, contains vague or grey words like 'delight,' 'satisfy,' and 'wow.' Those grey words make it difficult for customers to connect with companies. We have put in place a connector that defines explicitly what the company needs to do to delight, satisfy, or wow customers. It means you need to meet all the KCRs.

Key customer requirements are much more specific, immediate, and measurable and all employees can relate to them. For a convenience store whose mission is to "delight every customer every time," connecting all employee job-related activities to delight would be difficult. That same convenience store has as its KCRs availability, timeliness, quality, friendliness, cleanliness, and value. Employees of convenience stores can relate to the KCRs because that is exactly what they require when they are customers of a convenience store. When they walk into a convenience store, they want to be greeted and feel welcomed. They want the items they came to buy to be of good quality and to be available, to be waited on in a timely manner, to be in a clean store, and to feel like they got a good value. They know how they feel when any of their KCRs are not met. Therefore, they can empathize with customers because they understand how customers feel when their KCRs are met or not. This makes words in the mission, like 'delight,' 'wow,' and 'satisfy,' something all employees can relate to.

Key customer requirements are much more objective and measurable than delight. All employee tasks can be directly linked to one or more of the KCRs. Meeting all six KCRs delights the customer and they come back. When all their tasks or jobs are linked to one or more KCRs, they can see and understand how that task contributes to the mission of delighting the customer. This alignment provides a sense of purpose, connecting the work to how it helps delight the customer.

Overcoming Challenges in Alignment

Integrating alignment into daily operations can present several challenges for organizations. Some of these challenges include:

Time: Alignment can be time-consuming, and leaders and managers may struggle to balance their regular duties with the additional responsibilities associated with alignment efforts. Managers may feel they do not have the time to adequately communicate, role-model, train, and coach so that employees know, are aligned with, and make decisions based on the mission and KCRs. Managers may feel particularly time-pressured when they are short-staffed and have to perform the tasks their employees would typically handle. Providing adequate resources and support can help managers handle these competing demands. Correct staffing levels, employees that are trained to do their jobs 100% right, 100% of the time, proper time management of the managers, and delegation and prioritization of tasks related to focus excellence are areas that can help ensure managers will have time to communicate, role-model, and reinforce the use of the mission and KCRs to align all employees and make decisions.

Lack of communication: Effective communication is crucial to successful alignment. Employees may become disengaged if they do not understand the organization's mission or how their tasks contribute to its success by impacting KCRs. Regular, transparent communication using many channels at all levels of the organization can help mitigate this issue. Examples of regular communications include meetings, newsletters, posters on bulletin boards, clever reminders, and acknowledgments/honors when people do it well.

Inconsistent leadership: Leaders must consistently model the behaviors they wish to see in their teams. Inconsistencies in leadership can lead to confusion and a lack of trust, making it difficult for employees to fully embrace alignment. Leaders must role-model so that all their decisions are guided by what is best for the organization's mission and KCRs. During corrective and positive coaching, leaders should explicitly state which KCRs are either adversely or positively affected by the behavior being coached.

Aligning Support Functions to Key Customer Requirements: Where aligning tasks that directly contribute to KCRs is relatively straightforward, the process of aligning support tasks and responsibilities with the mission and KCRs can be complex, particularly in large organizations. Many support functions do not directly impact the KCRs but do so indirectly by affecting employees or processes that, in turn, impact the KCRs. To connect with support processes, it is sometimes helpful to visualize the impact if the support function is not carried out or done incorrectly.

For example, suppose a support group forecasts, and the estimates are off. In that case, the people and materials might not be available in the required amounts, thereby affecting KCRs on timeliness and cost. If the recruiting process is not working correctly, the right people with the right skills will not be hired, which impacts the KCRs of quality, timeliness, and cost.

Despite these challenges, the benefits of integrating alignment into daily operations far outweigh the difficulties. By addressing these issues proactively and providing ongoing support, organizations can successfully align their teams, achieve their mission, and meet their KCRs with increased efficiency and effectiveness.

Transformational Insights and Revelations

Aligning every task and role responsibility to the mission is a transformative process that helps ensure all work is value-adding, drives the organization towards its mission, and consistently meets its KCRs. This alignment fosters a clear understanding of how each individual's work contributes to the greater purpose, giving their daily tasks meaning and importance and driving employee engagement, productivity, and retention.

Research consistently demonstrates the significance of meaningful work in fostering employee satisfaction, engagement, and overall well-being. Extraordinary organizations recognize this essential connection and intentionally integrate purpose into every job and task.

When employees understand the "why" behind their work, they become empowered to exert their maximum discretionary effort toward achieving the organization's mission and consistently meeting the KCRs.

This connection instills a sense of pride and joy in their contributions as they recognize the value of their work in the broader context.

Leaders often desire to engage their employees, yet many organizations struggle to create an environment that fosters genuine connection and commitment. By implementing a simple process that links tasks to the mission through KCRs, organizations can create meaningful work experiences, resulting in the "Triple Win." This powerful outcome benefits the customer, employee, and organization alike, as engaged employees become invested in their work and are driven to make a positive difference.

In essence, alignment is a catalyst, transforming standard tasks into impactful actions that drive organizational success. Organizations can unlock their full potential and achieve extraordinary results by fostering an environment where every team member understands the importance of their role and can experience the joy of meaningful work.

Personal Experience of linking KCRs and Mission to My Job at Pal's

To illustrate the effectiveness of this method, I will share a personal example from my time working at Pal's Sudden Service. I worked with Pal's as a co-founder and president of Pal's Business Excellence Institute (renamed The McClaskey Excellence Institute in 2020). At the Institute, we teach thousands of leaders from all over the world proven practices of operations excellence. Early in my journey to thoroughly understand Pal's role-model practices, I not only spent hundreds of hours talking with Pal's leaders and managers and observing their operations, but also worked as an employee in Pal's restaurants for 6 weeks. Experiencing role-model practices of operations excellence firsthand from a crew or team member perspective was an important part of my learning journey. This enabled me to incorporate the perspective of all levels of an organization, from the CEO to the team member, as I teach the Path to Excellence to leaders of just about every type of company. As a crew member, I experienced the hiring, orientation, training, and coaching processes, and everything Pal's did to set me and every other employee up for 100% success, 100% of the time. As a result of my training, I was certified as a french fry Maker. I operated the french fry process 100% right, 100% of the time, producing french fries that 100% met Pal's requirements for 6 weeks. This adds an extra level of depth to the material I am sharing in this book and in our McClaskey Excellence Institute classes, as it is validated by first-hand experience that it works. In short, my goal was to discover and share how to create and sustain a culture that enables ordinary people to routinely do extraordinary things.

I gained first-hand knowledge of how Pal's aligns every employee task with the organization's mission and KCRs. As a result, I knew exactly how my task of making french fries impacted the KCRs. I knew that the work I did, like everyone else's at Pal's, was essential if we were to meet all the KCRs for each and every customer. Together, doing each of our tasks 100% right, precisely performing the approved processes, we met Pal's mission to delight every customer in a way that creates loyalty. I made dozens of decisions per hour at my job, and each was the best choice to meet the KCRs and achieve the mission. It was a great job, and I loved working there. I hated having to leave after 6 weeks. That is how much engagement the alignment we are talking about can create among employees.

Pal's Sudden Service focuses on six KCRs: quality of food, friendly service, speed of service, accuracy of order, cleanliness of the facility, and overall value. Here's how the role of a french fry maker impacts these KCRs:

- **Quality of food:** The french fry Maker directly influences the taste of the fries, which significantly affects the customers' perception of food quality.

- **Speed of service:** Ensuring the fries are ready on time contributes to the overall service speed, which is crucial for a drive-through operation like Pal's.

- **Accuracy of order:** Delivering the correct size bag, weight, and amount of seasoning of fries is essential for achieving order accuracy.

- **Cleanliness of the facility:** Maintaining a clean fry station is vital and reflects on the overall cleanliness of the facility.

- **Value:** The combination of food quality, speed, and accuracy contributes to the perceived customer value.

At Pal's, the french fry Maker's role doesn't directly affect friendly service, since they have no direct contact with customers in the drive-through. They can indirectly affect friendliness by supporting employees who directly interact with customers. They play a vital role in meeting the other KCRs, ultimately contributing to the organization's mission. This example illustrates that all jobs affect at least one KCR, but few affect all of them.

This example from Pal's Sudden Service demonstrates how the McClaskey® Triple 100® Alignment to Mission method connects individual roles to KCRs and the mission. By clarifying these connections, organizations can foster a more engaged and motivated workforce, driving performance and customer satisfaction.

Real-World Application: Eastman Chemical Company

To further illustrate the importance of aligning tasks with KCRs, let's examine another real-world example from my 34-year career at the Baldrige-winning Eastman Chemical Company. Eastman Chemical manufactures chemicals used in various products, and its success hinges on meeting its customers' precise needs.

Eastman's customers had several key requirements:

- **Product Quality:** 100% conformity to product specifications, no contamination, and no damage to shipping containers.

- **Proper Amount:** Ensuring the correct quantity in each container and each order.

- **Proper Labels:** Accurate and undamaged labels on each container.

- **Delivered on Time:** Shipments arriving on the agreed-upon date or date range.

- **Proper Documentation:** Accurate billing and accompanying paperwork.

- **Delivered to the Right Location:** Ensuring products are sent to the correct address.

- **Responsive to Questions:** Quickly answer customer inquiries and resolve issues.

Let's focus on the role of a warehouse worker at Eastman, responsible for selecting 55-gallon drums from the warehouse, stacking them on pallets, loading them onto trucks, and completing the necessary paperwork. Here's how this role directly impacts the KCRs:

- **Product Quality:** The warehouse worker ensures that shipping containers are not damaged, maintaining the quality and integrity of the product during handling and transportation.

- **Proper Amount:** The warehouse worker ensures that customers receive the exact quantity they ordered by selecting the right containers as specified on the shipping order.

- **Proper Labels:** The warehouse worker inspects labels to ensure they are accurate and undamaged, preventing any confusion or errors in product identification.

- **Delivered on Time:** Timely picking and loading of orders contribute to meeting delivery schedules, ensuring that shipments arrive when expected.

- **Proper Documentation:** Providing accurate information for the invoice clerk ensures correct billing and accompanying documentation, which is crucial for customer records and payment.

- **Delivered to the Right Location:** Although this task concerns the logistics team, the warehouse worker indirectly supports this requirement by ensuring the correct items are prepared for dispatch.

- **Responsive to Questions:** While not typically involved in customer interactions, the warehouse worker supports overall responsiveness by ensuring orders are accurate and issues are minimized.

This example from Eastman Chemical Company highlights how every role, including those not directly customer-facing, plays a vital part in meeting KCRs. By understanding and aligning their tasks with these requirements, employees can contribute meaningfully to the organization's mission and enhance overall customer satisfaction. Understanding how their work creates value contributes to employees' sense of purpose, self-esteem, and importance, leading to higher levels of engagement, productivity, and retention.

Cross-Industry Impact of Aligning Practices with Key Customer Requirements

Aligning tasks with KCRs extends across various industries. Whether it's a quick-service restaurant or a company, the principle remains the same: every task contributes toward meeting one or more KCRs, and meeting KCRS drives the achievement of the organization's mission.

Implementation Steps: McClaskey® Triple 100® Alignment: Connect every task to the KCRs and Mission

To connect how each task impacts one or more KCRs, thus impacting the mission, follow these steps:

Develop and Approve Your Mission and Key Customer Requirements: For detailed guidance on developing your mission and identifying KCRs, refer to Chapters 4 and 5.

Integrate Key Customer Requirements into SOPs and Training: For each task, identify which KCRs it contributes to and incorporate this information into your Standard Operating Procedures (SOPs) related to that task. Make each task's contribution to KCRs, and thus how the task supports the mission, a fundamental part of training programs.

Ongoing Coaching and Management: Explain and repeatedly ask employees how their tasks contribute to the organization's mission and KCRs. During positive and corrective coaching, highlight how the behavior being addressed affects KCRs, reinforcing the importance of doing their jobs correctly.

By implementing these steps, you can create clear alignment between every task and the mission, fostering a culture in which every employee understands the value of their work in meeting the organization's KCRs and thus contributes to achieving the mission.

Harnessing the Power of Alignment for Transformational Change

As we've seen through the examples of Pal's and Eastman Chemical Company, the power of aligning tasks and practices with an organization's mission and KCRs cannot be overstated. The success stories shared underscore the potential for transformational change when leaders prioritize these vital elements.

Implementing this alignment is relatively straightforward and meets with little to no resistance. Employees appreciate it when the organization ensures that all work contributes to fulfilling the KCRs and helps them understand how their work creates value for the customer and the company. It creates a sense of purpose and pride, leading to employees being more engaged and productive, and staying longer.

Realigning Your Team for Success

In light of these insights, I encourage leaders across industries to critically examine their team's tasks and responsibilities. Ask yourself: How do each of our day-to-day actions and tasks contribute to our organization's mission and KCRs? Can each of the employees working for me say how each task they work on impacts one or more KCRs? If not, it's time to realign and refocus your efforts so that every employee can tell which key customer requirement is impacted by each task they perform. This alignment leads to a sense of purpose, worth, and pride.

By applying the practices discussed, you'll empower your team to drive performance, enhance customer satisfaction, and cultivate a culture that engages employees in their jobs and provides excellence to your customers. Remember, change starts at the top. As a leader, you have the unique opportunity to inspire and guide your organization toward a brighter, more successful future that is good for the customer, the employee, and the organization.

Unlocking Potential Through True Alignment

As we've seen throughout this exploration of organizational alignment, it's clear that the power to drive performance and customer satisfaction lies within our grasp. By connecting individual tasks to the organization's mission through the KCRs, we can unlock a world of potential and achieve extraordinary results. Remember, true alignment means turning every task into a contribution to KCRs and the mission. This gives purpose to everything that is done within the organization. Embrace this mindset, and watch your organization soar to new heights of success.

Building a Foundation for Excellence

With our understanding of aligning tasks and practices to the organizational mission and KCRs, we've laid a solid foundation for driving performance, creating a purpose that drives employee engagement, and achieving excellence. Aligning every task with the mission and KCRs is the first element of using the mission and KCRs to create value and drive extraordinary operations.

Call to Action

1. Start the process of aligning all processes or tasks to one or more KCR by selecting 2-5 processes to start. Document in the written procedure which KCRs each process support. Convey this to everyone who performs that process as part of the process training.

2. Train everyone who is performing those 2 to 5 processes you selected so they know which KCRs that process supports.

3. Ask these employees to tell you, from memory, which KCRs the process they are working on supports. Start with the processes you selected.

Key Takeaways for Chapter 6: Align Every Task to the Mission through Key Customer Requirements

1. Aligning each employee's responsibilities and tasks with the organization's mission through the KCRs provides the "why" or worthy purpose behind their work, which drives employee

engagement, empowers employees to make work-based decisions, improves operational effectiveness and efficiency, and consistently creates exceptional customer experiences.

2. Providing purpose and alignment is necessary for employees to feel engaged because they know all elements of their work make a meaningful contribution to the mission by contributing to the KCRs.

3. You accomplish the organization's mission by meeting all the KCRs for every customer, every time.

4. For each task, identify which KCRs the task contributes toward accomplishing.

The Next Chapter

The primary way the mission and KCRs drive extraordinary operations is by serving as a basis for decision-making. Every employee who works for your company makes dozens of decisions per day. In the next chapter, I will show you how to develop a culture where every decision made by every employee, every day, is based on the choice that best supports the KCRs and most contributes to the mission.

Turn the page and see how to bring this culture to your company.

CHAPTER 7

HOW TO USE YOUR MISSION AND KCRS TO MAKE DECISIONS

"Making good decisions is a crucial skill at every level."

Peter Drucker, management consultant, educator, and author

The Power of Mission-Driven Decision Making

Have you ever wondered how companies like Amazon, Apple, or Disney consistently make decisions that perfectly align with their brand and customer expectations? The secret lies in their unwavering commitment and alignment with their mission and KCRs.

Consider the story of Howard Schultz, who returned as Starbucks' CEO in 2008, when the company was struggling. His first major decision was to close all 7,100 U.S. stores for about 3 hours to retrain baristas to make the perfect espresso. This decision, which cost the company an estimated $6 million, was guided by Starbucks' mission to "inspire and nurture the human spirit – one person, one cup and one neighborhood at a time" and its KCR of providing high-quality coffee experiences.

The Foundation of Aligned Decision-Making

A clear mission statement and well-defined KCRs serve as an organization's North Stars, guiding every decision from strategic planning to day-to-day operations. This approach isn't new. Companies like Johnson & Johnson have been using their credo to guide decisions since 1943. However, in today's fast-paced business environment, making quick, aligned decisions is more crucial than ever.

A mission-driven organization creates a culture where every employee understands and is empowered to make decisions that align with that purpose. To visualize this process, imagine a decision-making flowchart where every choice passes through filters for mission alignment and KCR fulfillment, so the decision made is the one that best fulfills the KCR and contributes most to the mission. This mental model can help employees at all levels understand how to apply these principles in their daily work.

Mission in Action: The Unilever Example

Let's dive deeper into how mission-driven decision-making transformed Unilever under Paul Polman's leadership. In 2009, Polman became CEO and introduced the Unilever Sustainable Living Plan, aligning the company's mission with sustainable and socially responsible practices.

One pivotal decision came in 2016 when Unilever acquired Dollar Shave Club for $1 billion. On the surface, this might have seemed like just another acquisition. However, among other reasons for the acquisition, it was consistent with and supported Unilever's mission to "make sustainable living commonplace" and its KCR of providing affordable, quality products.

Dollar Shave Club's subscription model aligned perfectly with Unilever's sustainability goals by reducing packaging waste and transportation emissions. Moreover, the company addressed the KCR of affordability in the premium personal care market. This decision not only boosted Unilever's market share but also reinforced their commitment to their mission and KCRs.

Research Supporting Mission-Driven Decision-Making

Research supports the effectiveness of mission-driven decision-making:

- A study by Deloitte found that purpose-driven companies witnessed higher market share gains and grew three times faster on average than their competitors.

- A study published in the Strategic Management Journal found that firms with high-quality mission statements outperformed those without by 30% in terms of financial performance.

- A study by the Harvard Business Review found that companies with clearly articulated and widely understood mission statements had 30% higher levels of innovation and 40% higher levels of employee retention.

These statistics paint a compelling picture, but the real power of mission-driven decision-making lies in its ability to create a unified direction for an entire organization. When every employee, from the CEO to the front-line staff, uses the same criteria to make decisions, it creates powerful alignment that customers can feel and that competitors find hard to replicate. I have found that having a sustained, high-performing organization requires everyone to be brought in and guided by a common mission.

Mission-Driven Decision-Making in Leading Companies

The examples illustrate how leading companies leverage their missions and KCRs to guide decision-making at all levels of their organizations.

This approach creates a powerful alignment that resonates with customers and sets these companies apart from their competitors.

Amazon: Customer Obsession and Decision Velocity

Amazon's mission of customer obsession serves as the company's north star for all decisions. They've developed a sophisticated approach to decision-making that balances thoroughness with speed:

1. For consequential, irreversible decisions, Amazon takes a slow, methodical approach. These decisions are carefully evaluated against their potential impact on customer experience and long-term mission alignment.
2. For reversible decisions, Amazon empowers teams to move quickly. This approach enables rapid innovation and learning while keeping customer needs at the forefront.

Amazon's use of customer-centric metrics and data to evaluate decisions ensures that even quick choices are grounded in their mission of customer obsession. Their willingness to experiment and learn from failures demonstrates a commitment to continuous improvement in customer service.

Johnson & Johnson: The Power of a Long-standing Credo

Johnson & Johnson's (J&J) use of their Credo since 1943 showcases the enduring power of a well-crafted mission statement. By prioritizing the needs of patients, employees, communities, and shareholders in that order, J&J established a clear decision-making hierarchy.

This mission-driven approach was put to the test during the 1982 Tylenol crisis. Despite the significant short-term financial impact, J&J's decision to recall all Tylenol products was directly aligned with their Credo's emphasis on customer safety. This decision not only protected consumers but also solidified J&J's reputation as a trustworthy company, demonstrating the long-term benefits of mission-aligned decision-making.

Apple: User Experience and Brand Values

Apple's mission of providing the best user experience drives every product decision. This commitment extends beyond just product features to encompass all aspects of the customer journey.

A powerful example of Apple's mission-driven decision-making was its refusal to create an iPhone "backdoor" for the FBI. While potentially controversial, this decision was firmly rooted in Apple's commitment to user privacy, a key component of its overall mission to enhance the user experience.

Apple's focus on innovation and premium quality in their decision-making process reinforces their brand values and maintains their position as a leader in user experience.

Core Principles of Mission-Aligned Decision-Making

Across these examples, we see several common threads. To harness this power, consider these core principles:

1. **Alignment**: Every decision at every level should be the choice that best supports your mission and KCRs.
2. **Consistency**: Everyone should apply this approach to every decision across all levels of the organization.
3. **Communication**: Ensure everyone in the organization knows, has memorized, and understands the mission and KCRs for top-of-mind awareness and use.
4. **Best Known Ways**: Document the most effective methods to accomplish the mission and meet the KCRs in your standard operating procedures (SOPs).

5. **Measurement**: Regularly assess decisions against mission-related metrics, KCR fulfillment, and customer satisfaction.

By adopting these principles, companies can create a robust decision-making framework that drives consistent, mission-aligned choices at every level of the organization. This approach not only drives better business outcomes but also fosters a strong, unified culture that resonates with both employees and customers.

Steps to Implement Mission-Driven Decision-Making

To implement mission-driven decision-making in your organization, consider these steps:

- **Define and communicate**: Clearly articulate your mission and KCRs in concise, memorable terms. Use Chapter 4 on the mission statement and Chapter 5 on KCRs to develop a mission statement and KCRs that can drive focus and excellence. Then, systematically communicate the mission and KCRs to everyone in the organization.

- **Memorization**: Ensure all employees can recite the mission and KCRs from memory. This is important because you will not use it to make daily decisions if it is not at the top of your mind.

- **Connect the dots**: Regularly demonstrate how daily activities contribute to the mission and KCRs.

- **Create a framework**: Develop a decision-making model that prioritizes mission and KCR alignment.

- **Train employees**: Provide comprehensive training in using the mission and KCRs in decision-making.

- **Track and evaluate**: Implement a system to monitor decisions based on mission and KCR alignment. The key question to ask all employees is: "Tell me about decisions you made today, or in the last hour, which were influenced by the mission and KCRs?"

- **Review and adjust**: Periodically reassess your mission and KCRs during strategic planning sessions.

Interactive Exercise: Mission-KCR-Decision Alignment

To bring these steps to life in your organization, try this interactive exercise:

At the executive level, you could ask the following:

- Write down your organization's mission and KCRs.
- List five significant decisions made in the last quarter.
- For each decision, rate how well it aligns with your mission and KCRs on a scale of 1-10.
- Reflect on how you could improve this alignment in future decisions. At the individual employee level, you can ask: What decisions did you make in the last hour, day, or week that were influenced by the mission or KCRs? What were the last five job-related decisions you made? Did the mission or KCRs influence your decisions? If so, how?

Depending on the responses you heard, provide positive or corrective coaching. For executives, it should be part of coaching and considered in their performance evaluation.

This exercise can be a powerful tool for assessing your current decision-making processes and identifying areas for improvement.

Future Trends in Mission-Driven Decision-Making

As we look to the future, emerging trends are shaping mission-driven decision-making. AI-assisted decision alignment tools, real-time

KCR tracking dashboards, and even gamification of mission-aligned behaviors are on the horizon. While these technologies offer exciting possibilities, the core principle remains the same: aligning every decision with what is best to accomplish your mission and KCRs.

Call to Action

Start using your mission and KCRs as decision-making tools today. At all levels within the organization, from team members to the CEO, reflect on your decisions from the last week. How many were influenced by your mission or KCRs? List some examples. If you find it challenging to connect your decisions to these guiding principles, it's time to reevaluate either your decision-making process or the clarity of your mission and KCRs.

Once you've done this reflection, choose one upcoming decision and consciously apply your mission and KCRs to the process. Document and share the outcome with your team to inspire mission-driven decision-making throughout your organization.

Role-model and regularly share examples of decisions made because they were the best choice to achieve the mission and KCRs.

Systematically ask employees who work for you about how they made the decisions they made. Provide positive coaching if it was the best choice for the mission and KCRs and corrective coaching and mentoring if it was not.

Together, your mission and KCRs will guide you to success in the complex terrain of business. By consistently using your mission and KCRs to guide all decisions, you'll not only make better decisions but also create a more aligned, engaged, and successful organization.

Key Takeaways for Chapter 7: How to Use Your Mission and KCRs to Make Decisions

1. The Power of Mission-Driven Decisions:

   A. It improves the quality of decisions by enabling all decisions and actions to best contribute to accomplishing the KCRs and the mission.

   B. It promotes employee engagement by connecting the decisions each employee makes to the KCRs and the mission.

2. Use a systematic process to enable everyone who works for you to use your organization's mission and KCRs to drive decisions.

The Next Chapter

Now that we've explored how to use your mission and KCRs to guide decision-making, let's turn to the critical task of effectively communicating and reinforcing the daily use throughout your organization. In the next chapter, we'll discuss strategies for ensuring your mission and KCRs become an integral part of your company's culture and daily operations.

CHAPTER 8

THE MANAGER'S ROLE IN EMBEDDING MISSION AND KCRS INTO ORGANIZATIONAL CULTURE

"Your first and foremost job as a leader is to take charge of your own energy and then help to orchestrate the energy of those around you."

Peter Drucker

Building a Purpose-Driven Culture

Imagine walking into a store where every employee, from the newest hire to the seasoned manager, can articulate not just what they do, but why they do it. Where decisions, big and small, are made with unwavering alignment to the company's mission and key customer requirements (KCRs). This isn't a utopian dream—it's the reality of organizations where managers have mastered the art of making their mission and KCRs an active part of their culture. And you're about to learn exactly how they do it.

Setting the Stage: The Power of Mission-Driven Leadership

A well-crafted mission statement and clearly defined KCRs are starting points in today's hypercompetitive business landscape. The real differentiator lies in how these principles are woven into the fabric and used to drive decisions and daily operations. Companies like The Ritz-Carlton Hotel Company and Airbnb have shown that when managers successfully embed the mission and KCRs into every aspect of their team's work, it leads to remarkable success, customer loyalty, and a workforce united in purpose.

Excellence in Action: Real-World Examples

The Ritz-Carlton's Unwavering Commitment to Extraordinary Service

In the realm of luxury hospitality, one name stands out as a symbol of unparalleled service and dedication to guest satisfaction: The Ritz-Carlton Hotel Company. Its iconic lion-and-crown logo has become synonymous with excellence, setting the global standard for the industry. At the heart of this success lies the Credo Card, a powerful tool carried by every employee, from housekeepers to the hotel general manager.

The Credo Card encapsulates the company's philosophy, emphasizing that "the genuine care and comfort of our guests is our highest mission." This laminated card outlines key behaviors known as "the basics," including Lateral Service—a concept that empowers employees to break away from their regular work to address a guest's immediate needs. By prioritizing customer satisfaction, the Ritz-Carlton ensures extraordinary experiences that fulfill their mission.

A Personal Encounter with the Ritz-Carlton Culture, Horst Schulze, and the Magic of the Credo Card

During a visit to the Ritz-Carlton Buckhead in Atlanta, I experienced the true power of the Credo Card firsthand. One of the 20 Ritz-Carlton Basics, part of the Credo Card, was: "Escort Guest rather than pointing out directions to another area of the Hotel." When I got lost in the hotel's corridors, a staff member in charge of a large group preparing for a major event noticed I was wandering, paused his work, and personally escorted me to my meeting room, which was over 10 minutes away. Can you imagine how disruptive this was to his task, involving more than 20 people? He didn't hesitate. He gave a few quick instructions to his assistant, and then he accompanied me to my meeting. Along the way, we had great conversations about working for the Ritz-Carlton and what it meant to him. His steadfast dedication to service showcased the Ritz-Carlton's employees' commitment to guest satisfaction by following the Basics outlined in the Credo Card and always prioritizing the guest.

Another great example I experienced was part of the Credo itself: "fulfills even the unexpressed wishes and needs of our guests." I was at the Ritz-Carlton Buckhead with a lawyer whom the Ritz-Carlton had contracted to provide some legal services. We were working together, with me sharing information as a nationally recognized expert in performance excellence. We met at breakfast, and he expressed total amazement at what had happened to him that morning at the Ritz-Carlton. He always starts his day with the Wall Street Journal. He had checked in the day before but hadn't mentioned the paper to anyone, yet it was there at his hotel room door this morning. He checked the paper left outside other guests' rooms and was the only one who received the Wall Street Journal. After some thought, he figured out how they did it. He threw out the previous day's Wall Street Journal in the trash in his room the day before. The housekeeper must have noticed and arranged for a Wall Street Journal to be left outside his door the next morning. Talk about fulfilling the "unexpressed needs."

Later, in one of the many conversations I had with Horst Schulze, when he was President and COO of The Ritz-Carlton Hotel Company, he emphasized the importance of seeing employees as service "professionals," similar to an English butler. By instilling the values outlined in the Credo Card, Ritz-Carlton empowers its team to create memorable experiences that consistently surpass guest expectations.

This strong commitment to service excellence, embodied by the Credo Card, makes the Ritz-Carlton stand out as an industry leader. From my conversations with Horst Schulze and my personal experience working with The Ritz-Carlton, which has won the Baldrige National Quality Award twice, it is clear that the organization's success depends on a deeply rooted culture of service, built from the top down and nurtured at every level of the company.

The Credo Card: A Manager's Tool for Achieving Operational Excellence

In examining the Ritz-Carlton's commitment to extraordinary service, the Credo Card functions as an essential tool for managers striving for operations excellence. This laminated card, carried by every employee, summarizes the company's philosophy and highlights key behaviors known as "the basics." By adhering to these principles, Ritz-Carlton staff members consistently deliver unparalleled service that has become a hallmark of the brand.

The unit operations managers are responsible for ensuring that employees deliver products and services 100% to the brand standards outlined in the Credo Card and the procedures. They make sure employees are trained to 100%, Coach to 100% by observing and providing both positive and corrective feedback, and establish the work environment for 100% execution. They promote and ensure 100% execution to brand standards. For managers, the Credo Card functions as a blueprint for creating a culture of excellence. By encouraging behaviors described on the card, such as "Lateral Service," and by focusing on customer satisfaction, managers empower their teams to deliver outstanding service that supports the company's mission. The Credo Card also ensures that every employee, regardless of role, understands their responsibility to uphold the high standards of the Ritz-Carlton, fostering a unified approach to operations excellence.

Furthermore, the Credo Card serves as a reminder of the Ritz-Carlton's commitment to "the genuine care and comfort of our guests." By embedding this philosophy into their staff, managers can foster an environment where employees feel personally connected to the company's mission, motivating them to go above and beyond in delivering exceptional service.

The Ritz-Carlton's Credo Card demonstrates the importance of aligning a company's values with its daily operations. For managers, this tool offers a clear framework for achieving operations excellence and ensuring their teams consistently provide an exceptional experience for every guest.

Case Study: Airbnb's Mission in Action

Consider Airbnb's journey. Their mission, "to create a world where anyone can belong anywhere," isn't just a catchy phrase—it's a living, breathing entity that guides every decision. When Airbnb introduced its Experiences Platform, allowing hosts to offer unique local activities, it wasn't just expanding services. It was a deliberate move to deepen travelers' sense of belonging, directly aligning with their mission and meeting the KCR of providing unique, memorable experiences.

Evidence of Success: The Data Behind Purpose-Driven Organizations

The impact of mission-driven operations is not just anecdotal:

- A 2019 Deloitte study found that purpose-driven companies grew three times faster than their competitors, with higher workforce and customer satisfaction.

- The 2018 Cone/Porter Novelli Purpose Study revealed that 79% of Americans are more loyal to purpose-driven brands, and 73% are willing to defend them.

- A 2017 study in the Strategic Management Journal showed that firms with high-quality mission statements outperformed others in financial performance by 30%.

Key Strategies for Embedding Mission and KCRs in Everyday Operations

Here are some examples of how managers make the mission and KCRs an active part of their culture:

- **Daily Integration:** Use mission and KCR language in all communications, including coaching and feedback.

- **Make the mission and KCRs visible:** Make mission and KCR visibility a priority by posting them in key areas.

- **Make the mission and KCRs known and memorized:** Through various activities, games, and quizzes, encourage employees to memorize and apply the mission and KCRs in their daily decisions.

- **Coaching:** Use mission and KCR language in both positive and corrective coaching and feedback

- **Mission-Centric Meetings:** Dedicate time in team meetings to discuss the mission, KCRs, and their practical applications.

- **Purpose-Driven Task Alignment:** Explicitly link every task to relevant KCRs and the overall mission.

- **Mission-First Training:** Build in the "why" or purpose by beginning all task and process training by explaining the task's connection to KCRs and the mission.

- **Recognition and Accountability:** Reward and coach employees based on their understanding and application of the mission and KCRs.

Debunking the Myths: Does Mission-Driven Culture Stifle Innovation?

Some argue that such an intense focus on mission and KCRs could stifle innovation or flexibility. However, companies like Spotify prove otherwise. Their mission to "unlock the potential of human creativity" drives their innovative features and user-centric approach, demonstrating that a well-crafted mission can enhance agility and innovation.

Revelation: The True Power of a Mission-Driven Culture

The true power of these approaches lies in their consistency and pervasiveness. When managers commit to these practices, they create an environment where the mission and KCRs naturally guide decision-making at all levels. It's not about occasional reminders—it's about creating a cultural DNA where every action is instinctively aligned with the organization's purpose and customer focus.

Implementation Guide: Turning Theory into Action

- **Evaluate the Current State:** Assess how well your team understands and applies the mission and KCRs.

- **Select Strategies:** Choose three to seven systematic approaches that fit your team's needs that will create a culture of everyone knowing and using the mission and KCRs to make decisions.

- **Create an Action Plan:** Develop a 30-day plan to introduce these strategies.

- **Monitor Progress:** Continuously assess and refine your approach based on results.

- **Expand and Scale:** Once the foundation is solid, introduce more strategies to further embed the mission and KCRs.

The Manager as a Mission Catalyst

As a manager, you're not just a keeper of the mission—you're its living embodiment. Your daily actions can transform words on a wall into the heartbeat of your organization. Will you accept the challenge to breathe life into your mission and KCRs?

Call to Action: Your Role as a Cultural Architect

The unit operations manager needs to plan and conduct an ongoing set of daily and weekly activities and actions that will embed the organization's Mission and Key Customer Requirements in the everyday operations culture, so every employee who works for them:

1. Knows and has memorized the mission and KCRs.
2. Know what KCR every task they do contributes to, and thus know the purpose of their work.
3. Uses the KCRs and mission to guide them in every decision they make.

Unit operations managers need to identify the top three strategies they'll use to ensure the mission and KCRs are known, memorized, and used by every employee who works for them to make decisions. Commit to implementing these strategies consistently over the next 30 days. Some examples of methods that unit operations managers have successfully used to get the mission and KCRs known, memorized, and used include having examples of use by employees at every team meeting, having contests to see who can say the mission and KCR from memory, and using the words in the mission and KCRs as they coach.

Key Takeaways for Chapter 8: The Manager's Role in Embedding Mission and KCRs into Organizational Culture

The unit operations manager is responsible for getting every employee who works for them to:

4. Know and have memorized the mission and KCRs.
5. Know what KCR every task they do contributes to, and thus know the purpose of their work.
6. Uses the KCRs and mission to guide them in every decision they make.

The Next Chapter

You have now effectively communicated and reinforced the mission and KCRs' daily use throughout your organization. In the next chapter, I will define the unit operations manager's role in clear and unambiguous terms.

CHAPTER 9

THE UNIT OPERATIONS MANAGER'S ROLE

"Management by objective works - if you know the objectives. Ninety percent of the time you don't."

Peter Drucker

The Symphony of Operations

At the heart of every thriving business lies a well-oiled machine, a symphony of processes and people working harmoniously to deliver unparalleled products and services. This is the realm of the unit operations manager, the conductor who orchestrates beautiful music by getting the right music in front of each musician and then getting them to all play their part in harmony. What separates the ordinary from the extraordinary? How can a company transcend the boundaries of mediocrity and ascend to the pinnacles of success? One key part of the answer lies in clearly defining the unit operations manager's role and embracing a philosophy that demands nothing less than getting operations 100% right every time.

Redefining the Role of Operations and the Unit Operations Manager

Unit operations managers are often seen as the unsung heroes of the business world, toiling behind the scenes to bring the products and services to your customers. However, the traditional view of operations management as a mere facilitator of day-to-day activities fails to capture its true purpose. The significance of operations and operations management cannot be overstated. Operations is the company function that produces and delivers the company's products, services, and customer experience. Operations is the function that provides the products and services customers pay for and that fulfill the customer's KCRs.

Within a company's overall operations function, the customer interfaces with the operations unit to obtain the company's products and services. Depending on the company, the units might be called by many names, including a store, restaurant, or department; the unit operations manager is the person who heads each operations unit. The unit operations manager is known by many titles, including General Manager, Store Manager, Department Head, and Unit Manager, among others.

The unit operations managers are in charge of their unit and show up daily. All assistant managers and employees of that unit directly report to their unit operations manager. The unit operations managers are critical to implementing extraordinary operations because most of the behavior changes needed to achieve extraordinary operations occur among employees who report to the unit operations managers.

Unfortunately, in most companies, the role of the unit operations manager has been defined in vague, gray terms. Without a clearly defined, appropriate focus, it is difficult for the unit operations manager to lead their unit to achieve extraordinary operations and even more challenging to maintain extraordinary operations.

Let me illustrate how pervasive the problem is of defining the role of the unit operations manager in vague, gray, ambiguous terms. As part of our McClaskey Excellence Institute classes, we have asked thousands of unit operations managers and organization leaders the following question: "How is the role of the unit operations manager described in your company?" Each company can list dozens of descriptions it actually uses for this role. Some of the more common answers include customer satisfaction, training, hiring, orientation, coaching, discipline, accountability, productivity, labor scheduling, controlling to budget, maintenance and repairs, fiscal management, order supplies, approachability, improvement, filling out reports, setting a role-model example, team development, clear communication, setting an upbeat tone, uphold standards, handle customer complaints, handle employees last minutes schedule changes, crisis management, personally work a station to get the product out, recruitment, purchasing/ordering, developing assistant managers.

To illustrate how vague their current descriptions of the role of their unit operations managers are, we asked managers and leaders from the same company to rate their entire list of how their company describes the unit operations manager's role on a 1 to 10 clarity scale; 1 is crystal clear, and 10 is extremely vague. The average rating, based on thousands of companies, is around 7, which indicates substantial ambiguity. We rarely get a rating lower than 4. Companies that rate their list as a 1 or 2, crystal clear, are usually those companies that have attended our Achieving World-Class Results class and are already achieving extraordinary operations.

It is critical for achieving extraordinary operations that the role of one of the most essential positions is clearly defined to achieve and maintain operations excellence. The goal is to rate your company's definition of the role of operations and the unit operations manager on the clarity scale, with 1 or 2. This level of clarity is a key component of the work environment that sets the conditions for extraordinary operations to be achieved and sustained.

We have used the following three-step process in our classes to help thousands of companies develop a crystal clear, concise, and meaningful definition of the role of the unit operations manager.

Step 1: Have managers in the company ask the following question: "How is the role of the unit operations manager described in your company?" Give managers in your company 5-10 minutes to make a list using words and phrases actually used within your company. Usually, the result is a list of 10-20 items.

Step 2: After creating a list of the roles based on how the unit operations manager's role is currently described, ask the same managers to rate their entire list on a 1 to 10 clarity scale: 1 is crystal clear and 10 is extremely vague.

Step 3: Either provide a definition or ask managers to create a simple description of the unit operations manager's role that rates a 1 or 2 on the 1-10 clarity scale. A rating of 1 or 2 represents a crystal-clear definition. The definition has to be clear, concise, measurable, and unambiguous. It also has to reflect the essential role that operations play in meeting the KCRs, namely providing products, services, and customer experience that meet 100% of the brand requirements.

The following definition rates a 1 or 2 on the clarity scale and meets the other criteria by explicitly stating the operations' essential role in providing products, services, and customer requirements that 100% meet the brand requirements. This definition is used by organizations that have achieved extraordinary operations. It has also been rated by thousands of managers as a 1 or 2 on the clarity scale. We highly recommend you use this definition or something very similar.

> *The role of operations and the unit operations manager is to deliver the products, services, and customer experience 100% to the brand requirements, 100% of the time, under 100% of the conditions.*

In this definition, customer experience includes any key aspect of an operation that influences the customer's perception of the interaction with the organization beyond the products or services. Common factors included under the term customer experience in the definition include cleanliness, employee appearance, uniforms, and facilities.

The overall role of operations and the unit operations manager is to deliver the products and services 100% to brand requirements, 100% of the time, under 100% of the conditions. It is a journey that demands an unwavering commitment to meeting every customer's KCRs every time by delivering the products and services 100% to the brand requirements every time.

This definition requires a paradigm shift, a bold step where executing products and services 100% to brand requirements, every time, using the organization's approved processes and consistent with its values, becomes the standard for what it means to be a high-performing unit operations manager.

This transformation is not just about processes and systems but also about the hearts and minds of the people who bring them to life. Achieving extraordinary operations requires a fundamental shift in mindset, a willingness to embrace change, an understanding of the factors that drive employees' behavior, and the ability and desire to use the tools as the unit operations manager to influence employees' behavior. The McClaskey° Triple 100° Path to Excellence pillars and elements will provide a proven path and tools to achieve the roles of operations and the unit operations manager. This is a path other companies have used and can be used by you.

Steps to Operationalize the Role of the Unit Operations Manager

After establishing a clear, unambiguous definition of the unit operations manager that rates a 1 or 2 on the clarity scale, carry out the following steps to operationalize this definition:

1. **Communicate and Implement the Definition:** Share the revised role definition of the operations and the unit operations manager with all unit operations managers to ensure they understand and internalize their responsibilities. Provide training and support to help them fully and effectively implement their clearly defined role. Communicate the clearly defined role of operations and the unit operations managers to everyone in the company.

2. **Monitor and Evaluate Progress:** Regularly assess and measure the impact of the updated role definition on operational performance. Gather managers' feedback to identify areas for improvement and refine the definition. The key measure for each operations unit is the percentage of the products, services, and customer experience produced or delivered by that unit, which is 100% to the brand requirements. The target is 100%. Create a culture that values and rewards delivering the products, services, and customer experience 100% right every time. Recognize and celebrate the efforts and progress of leaders, managers, and their workforce to consistently deliver extraordinary operations. Make the achievement of this role a key element of performance evaluations, coaching, feedback, rewards, and measures of overall operations and the operations of each unit.

By following these steps, you can establish and implement a clear, concise definition of the role of operations leaders and managers within your organization. This foundation will support the company's efforts to drive extraordinary operations.

Another Look at Pal's Sudden Service: A Testament to Operational Excellence

As we revisit the tale of Pal's Sudden Service, let's appreciate the lessons offered. In a world where speed and efficiency often come at the expense of quality, Pal's stands as a shining example of what can be achieved when a company refuses to compromise on quality and does so in a way that also delivers role-model hospitality, accuracy, cleanliness, speed, and efficiency.

When examining the story of Pal's Sudden Service, it becomes evident that the role of the store operations manager, whose title is Owner-Operator, is pivotal in maintaining the company's renowned standard of service. The success of Pal's can be attributed to its culture of extraordinary operations, meticulously cultivated by its leadership. In this context, the Owner-Operator is the guardian of brand integrity, the champion of consistency, and the implementer of excellence. The Owner-Operator is the manager who implements Pal's culture, processes, and excellence at the store level. They are the managers who implement extraordinary operations to 100% by creating a culture that creates and maintains the behaviors and actions that support that level of performance every second the store is open. As a result, the KCRs are consistently achieved, and the customer is delighted in a way that creates loyalty. The Owner-Operator achieves these results through empowering the assistant managers and crew and setting up a work environment where they are able to execute their processes 100% right, 100% of the time, even when they are not in the store. The Owner-Operator is the one who creates and maintains the store's culture of excellence.

During my 6 weeks as a crew member at Pal's, I witnessed how the Owner-Operator created and maintained the store culture that set everyone up for 100% success and ensured that all KCRs were met for every customer, every time. The result is that every customer is delighted in a way that creates loyalty because Pal's meets every customer's key requirements every time. They meet the mission and fulfill the KCRs by carrying out their primary responsibility of ensuring that all products and services meet the brand requirements 100% of the time. This is operation's responsibility, and Owner-Operators are held accountable to ensure their store delivers this.

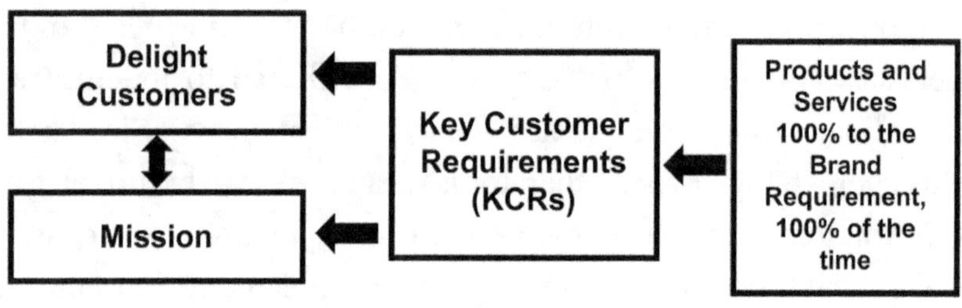

Pal's commitment to executing 100% to brand requirements, every time, is a testament to the Owner-Operator's unwavering focus on executing to 100%. As the guardians of brand integrity, they ensure every aspect of Pal's experience, from the iconic teal and red-colored building scheme to the speed and efficiency of its service, remains true to the company's standards.

As the champion of consistently delivering products and services that meet the brand requirements, the Owner-Operator is responsible for fostering a work environment where employees are empowered to deliver products that meet 100% of the brand requirements, 100% of the time. This dedication to 100% operations sets Pal's apart from its competitors, establishing it as a benchmark for quality and customer experience in the fast-food industry.

As the implementer of excellence, the Owner-Operator implements systems and processes that enable the Pal's team to achieve extraordinary operations and exceptional results. Each Owner-Operator supports the company's pursuit of extraordinary operations, ensuring that their Pal's location upholds the high standards that define the brand.

The story of Pal's Sudden Service highlights the critical role of the unit operations manager in shaping a company's success. Their commitment to brand integrity, consistency, and excellence embodies the leadership necessary to drive extraordinary operations and elevate the organization to be a role-model in the restaurant industry.

The Elements of Focus Excellence and the Role of the Unit Operations Manager

This is the last element in the **Focus Excellence** Pillar. The preceding elements focus and align everything on the company's mission and KCRs. The operations unit cannot achieve extraordinary operations and conduct its role unless everyone focuses on achieving the same mission or purpose.

Note to Unit Operations Managers. As a unit operations manager, this role is pivotal in guiding your organization toward extraordinary operations. The path may be challenging, but the rewards are immeasurable, impacting the bottom line and the lives of those you supervise. To achieve greatness, you must be willing to question the status quo, be committed to a standard of products and services meeting 100% of the brand requirements, make tough decisions, and drive transformation.

Take a moment to assess your organization's operations. Ask yourself what percentage of the time your unit delivers your products, services, and customers' experience 100% to the brand requirements, 100% of the time.

Remember, extraordinary operations is not a destination. It is a never-ending journey where you keep getting closer and closer to 100% right, 100% of the time. You get as close to 100% as you can today and then find a way to get better tomorrow. Embrace a commitment to learning, experimentation, and the pursuit of producing and delivering products, services, and customer experience 100% to the brand requirements, every time.

As a unit operations manager, leadership is essential in navigating this path. Once the company commits to driving and achieving extraordinary operations, you will become a key leader of the transformation, shaping a future where excellence is not just a distant dream but an achievable reality.

A culture of extraordinary operations can propel the organization to new heights and unlock its full potential. The journey may be long, but the satisfaction and rewards are great, and the impact on customers, employees, and the organization is incredible.

Call to Action

1. Develop a clear definition of the unit operations manager.

   A definition we suggest that has worked well for companies that have achieved extraordinary operations is to deliver the products, services, and customer experience 100% to brand requirements, 100% of the time, under 100% of the conditions.

2. Monitor and Evaluate Progress: Regularly assess and measure the impact of the updated role definition on operational performance. Gather managers' feedback to identify areas for improvement and, if needed, refine the definition.

3. Assess the unit operations manager's performance against the definition of their role.

Key Takeaways for Chapter 9: The Unit Operations Manager's Role

1. Unit Operations managers are key to implementing extraordinary operations in their units. They are the leaders essential to achieving and maintaining extraordinary operations within the unit they manage.

2. As the manager responsible for extraordinary operations in their unit, their role must be clearly defined in unambiguous terms.

3. A clear, black-and-white definition of the role of the unit operations manager is to deliver the products, services, and customer experience 100% to brand requirements, 100% of the time, under 100% of the conditions. They must do this using the approved processes and be consistent with the organization's values.

4. All the other tasks and responsibilities associated with the unit operations manager are there to enable the unit operations manager to deliver the products, services, and customer experience 100% to brand requirements, 100% of the time, under 100% of the conditions.

By embracing extraordinary operations, companies across industries can drive customer loyalty, employee satisfaction, and financial success, ultimately elevating their performance and securing a prosperous future.

The Next Pillar

We have now finished the first two pillars of the McClaskey® Triple 100® Path to Excellence. The organization only accepts meeting the KCRs for all customers every time, and everything the organization does is focused on the best way to accomplish the mission and the KCRs. The next pillar, Pillar 3: Process Excellence will enable our processes to be designed and documented to 100%, used everywhere applicable, and systematically improved.

PILLAR 3

PROCESS EXCELLENCE

"You do not rise to the level of your goals.
You fall to the level of your systems."

James Clear

Get Your Path 100% Right

As we go through the McClaskey® Triple 100® Path to Excellence, Pillar 1, Think Excellence, instills in leaders the 100% mindset of an extraordinary leader, and gives you a standard of excellence, EVERY instead of most. Pillar 2, Focus Excellence, creates an organization where everyone is focused and aligned with the organization's mission and KCRs. Focus Excellence also establishes that the role of operations and the unit operations manager is to deliver the products, services, and customer experience 100% to the brand requirements, 100% of the time, under 100% of the conditions.

McClaskey® Triple 100® Path to Excellence
Think and Focus Excellence

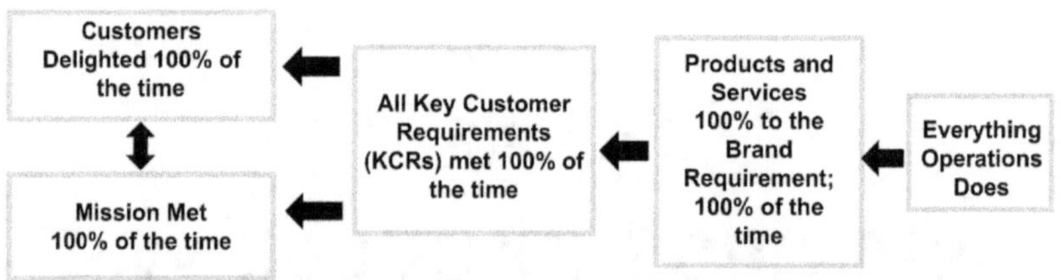

We now turn our attention to the third pillar: Process Excellence.

In this pillar, the goal is to show how to design, standardize, and continuously improve the processes that underpin your operations, ensuring a proven path that delivers your products and services 100% to your brand requirements every time.

Many organizations struggle with inconsistent performance, repeatedly battling the same issues and failing to consistently deliver on their promises. Through Process Excellence, I'll show how to create processes that, when combined with the Pillar 4, People Excellence, make extraordinary operations the norm rather than the exception. I will demonstrate how to build processes that, when followed precisely, consistently, and efficiently, deliver the desired outcome: products and services that are 100% to brand requirements, 100% of the time, under 100% of conditions.

This pillar will examine three elements of Process Excellence, each with its own chapter. The three elements are Element 1: Design and Document Processes to 100%; Element 2: Standardizing Processes; Element 3: Improve Processes.

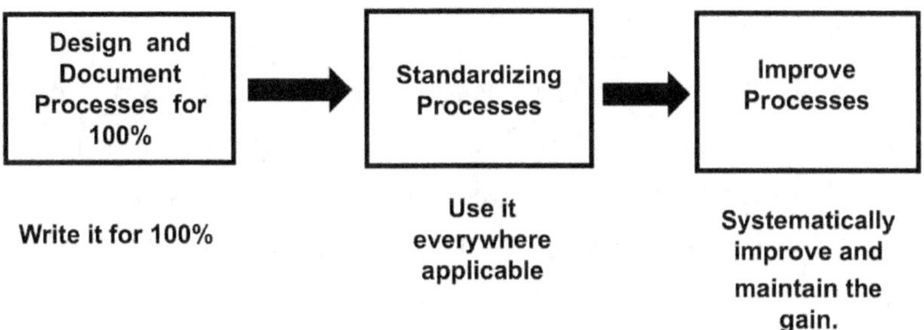

Element 1: Design and Document Processes for 100%: Learn how to design and document processes that are the current, best-known way to effectively and efficiently deliver the output that fully meets the output requirements, every time. Processes are designed and documented to 100% when a trained person precisely follows the process steps, the process consistently delivers outputs that meet 100% of the output requirements, and the process does so in an efficient manner.

Element 2: Standardizing Processes: It does little good to have the best-known way and latest improvements if they are not being used. It is also very wasteful to use the best-known way to perform a task only sometimes, or only in some of the places where it is applicable. The role-model practice is to standardize. Develop policies and practices that make it binding that the approved process for a given task is the process that will be followed everywhere applicable. Standardizing approved processes is critical to maintaining and using the latest improvements. Using the approved process ensures consistency in the products and services and helps to control unauthorized variations and practices.

I will discuss overcoming resistance to standardization, preventing unauthorized changes to standardized processes, and creating a culture that values using the approved processes to deliver outputs.

Element 3: Improve Processes: Over time, better ways and refinements are developed for just about any process. It is challenging for people to use the current, approved, and standardized process when a better way exists. The remedy is a continuous improvement process that regularly refines and improves your processes using a systematic, data-based improvement process. During the improvement process, best-known practices and potential changes will be identified, and the improvements will be verified. Once improvements are verified, they go into the Design and Document Processes for 100% element, so they are effectively designed, documented, approved, and incorporated into the appropriate processes. Then, the approved processes containing the improvements are standardized, using the Standardized Processes element, for use everywhere applicable. As part of a culture of improvement, encourage all employees to suggest process improvements for consideration in the organization's systematic improvement process.

This pillar emphasizes the crucial interplay between Process Excellence and People Excellence. Process Excellence is a necessary element to establish People Excellence. You'll see how well-designed processes enable and set your team up to perform consistently at their best. It is management's job to provide and verify the best-known process for every task your employees perform.

By mastering Process Excellence, the goal is to create an organization where extraordinary performance isn't left to chance. Processes will be in place to consistently deliver excellence when precisely followed.

When processes are designed for 100%, it frees your team to focus on performing the processes rather than firefighting and problem-solving.

Prepare to revolutionize how your organization operates. Learn to design and document processes that make excellence the default, not the exception. The path to extraordinary operations continues here, where precision meets passion, precise meets concise, the best proven way replaces our way, and systems drive success.

CHAPTER 10

DESIGN AND DOCUMENT PROCESSES FOR 100%

"If you can't describe what you are doing as a process, you don't know what you're doing."

W. Edwards Deming, author, Guru of the Quality Movement

A Reliable Process Gets the Desired Results Every Time

Picture every process in your company consistently delivering perfect results. One of the reasons your customers are so happy is that errors, inconsistencies, and inefficiencies are virtually nonexistent, which is why you and your customers would make the McClaskey® $1,000 Bet on your products and services, as they always meet your brand requirements. The next step in making this vision a reality is meticulously designing processes that drive operational excellence.

Consider the analogy of a GPS. It provides clear, step-by-step directions to ensure reaching the desired destination and doing so in an efficient manner. In the same way, well-designed processes serve as a roadmap for achieving flawless execution. Each step brings you closer to the ultimate goal: an output that meets 100% of the requirements, every time.

The interplay between the Process Excellence and People Excellence pillars of the Path to Excellence is essential in this journey to extraordinary operations. Process Excellence involves designing processes so that when the steps of the process are precisely followed, the desired output is efficiently produced every time. People Excellence sets the employees up so they will choose to precisely follow the steps of the approved process every time. Combining these two pillars results in process steps that are precisely followed every time. When this happens for every process, the products and services are delivered 100% to the brand requirements, 100% of the time, under 100% of the conditions.

If the product or service does not 100% meet the brand requirements, there are only two causes: (a) the process steps were incorrect or (b) the performer did not precisely follow the process steps. This assumes the process steps will include ensuring that only the correct inputs are used.

In this chapter, I will cover a design and documentation process that will ensure that the process steps written in the approved procedures will reliably and efficiently deliver the process output 100% to the brand requirements, 100% of the time under 100% of the conditions. The People Excellence section of the book will cover eliminating or reducing the second cause of performers not precisely following the approved process by establishing a work culture in which employees choose to precisely follow the process steps every time. When these two causes are eliminated, you have the correct process steps, and they are precisely followed every time. When this occurs for every process, you have a company with extraordinary operations. By the end of this chapter, you will possess the knowledge and tools to transform your own processes so they are designed for 100% and unlock the true potential of your organization.

Using the GPS example to illustrate this, Process Excellence is the steps the GPS provides that need to be followed to reach the desired destination, and People Excellence is the driver precisely following those steps. When both of those things happen, you arrive at the desired destination every time. If you and others are going back and forth between the same starting point and destination many times, precisely following the same instructions will ensure everyone reaches the desired destination. This is directly parallel to what operations do to produce your brand's products and services 100% to the brand requirements, every time. Just precisely follow the verified, designed to 100% steps.

The Necessity of Flawless Process Design and Documentation

In today's competitive landscape, organizations must continually strive for operational excellence to stay ahead. One of the most critical components of achieving this goal is designing processes that consistently deliver their output 100% to the output requirements. This chapter presents a process for designing processes that will efficiently deliver outputs that meet 100% of the requirements, 100% of the time, under 100% of the conditions when the process steps are precisely followed. The chapter delves into the significance of process design, highlighting its impact on quality, efficiency, and overall performance.

The GPS analogy powerfully illustrates how well-crafted processes can guide organizations toward their desired outcomes. By investing in both Process Excellence and People Excellence, organizations can create an environment where products and services are delivered 100% to the brand requirements, 100% of the time. This is not just an aspiration but an achievable reality.

The Strategic Role of Process Design

Arthur W. Jones, a renowned management consultant, once said, "All organizations are perfectly designed to get the results they get." This profound statement encapsulates the essence of this chapter: redefining how we view process design. Rather than seeing it as a mere operational necessity, we must recognize designing processes to 100% as a critical, strategic tool essential to elevating an organization from good to great.

Ordinary to Extraordinary Process Design: the 15% Change

The transformation we seek is not about reinventing the wheel but about refining the processes that mostly already exist. It's about taking processes that currently deliver products and services to brand requirements most of the time and honing them to deliver 100% to brand requirements, 100% of the time, under 100% of the conditions. For existing processes that are already producing the product or service right most of the time, a 15% change to the process design and documentation is all that is required for the process to be designed for 100%. I will provide a checklist to help you achieve that 15% change by identifying and filling gaps.

You Already Know the Definitive Path, Write it Down

We find that for a company's routine products and services, the knowledge needed to write the process steps to 100% is known within the company. It is about getting that knowledge written down so you have a clearly defined process that, regardless of which trained employee performs it, the output will be 100% to the brand requirements. From our interviews with leaders of thousands of service companies, it is clear that many service companies under actual operating conditions deliver their products and services 100% to their brand requirements at least 75% of the time. If your current process can deliver the output 100% to the brand requirements 75% of the time, we have found that it only takes a 15% change to the process documentation so it can deliver the output 100% to the brand requirements, 100% of the time if the steps are precisely followed.

In this chapter, I will provide and show how to use a checklist that we use in our classes to identify the 15% changes you need to make to your existing processes. Our Designing and Documenting Process to 100% checklist will give you some excellent guidance to identify the gaps in your current process, so you can focus on the changes needed to upgrade your current process to be written to 100%.

The checklist works well for processes where the company knows the steps that reliably deliver a product or service that meets 100% of the brand requirements, every time. As we previously stated, this is the case in almost all products and services a company routinely produces. But what about processes where the company does not know the steps that will lead to the process output meeting 100% of the brand requirements? This is often the case for management, HR, administration, design, marketing, and other similar processes. In this case, the process steps will be the best-known process for delivering the output, even if following the steps does not meet the output requirements 100% of the time.

Case Studies on Improving Existing Processes to Deliver Near 100%

1. Intravenous Catheter Insertion: A Life-Saving Transformation

In hospitals across the United States, central line-associated bloodstream infections (CLABSIs) were once a common and deadly occurrence. These infections, often resulting from the insertion of intravenous catheters, posed a significant risk to patients' lives and increased healthcare costs. However, a remarkable transformation occurred when hospitals redesigned their catheter insertion process.

By implementing a simple five-step checklist that included:

(a) Hand washing, (b) using full-barrier precautions, (c) cleaning the patient's skin with chlorhexidine, (d) avoiding femoral sites for insertion, and (e) removing unnecessary catheters, hospitals saw dramatic results. For instance, a study in Michigan ICUs found that this redesigned process reduced catheter-related infections by up to 66% over an 18-month period, saving an estimated 1,500 lives and $100 million in the first 18 months alone.

This example demonstrates how a seemingly minor process change—following a standardized checklist—can lead to near-perfect execution and significantly improved patient outcomes.

2. Joint Replacement Surgery: Engineering Out Infections

Knee and hip replacement surgeries have become increasingly common procedures, once carrying a high risk of postoperative infections. These infections could lead to prolonged hospital stays, additional surgeries, and, in severe cases, life-threatening complications. However, by meticulously redesigning the surgical process, hospitals dramatically reduced infection rates.

Key changes included (a) standardizing preoperative antibiotics administration, (b) implementing stringent sterilization protocols for surgical equipment, (c) redesigning operating room airflow to minimize contaminants, and (d) optimizing wound closure techniques. As a result of these process improvements, infection rates following joint replacement surgeries plummeted. For example, a study at NYU Langone Health showed that their infection rate for total joint replacements dropped from 1-2% to just 0.3%, a reduction of 80%, after implementing a comprehensive infection control protocol.

3. Clean and Reset the Table

All full-service restaurants want their tables cleaned and reset after each use. One of our consulting customer's cleaning and resetting the table process had many errors and required frequent rework to correct the errors. To reduce mistakes, they observed the process and studied what was written in the process procedure. The root cause of the errors was unclear or gray language in the procedure, which could be reasonably interpreted in ways that did not meet the standard. Two of the issues identified were water streaks and the position of the salt and pepper shakers. The step just said to wipe the table. The step changed to wipe the table and leave no visible water streaks. The position of the saltshaker was supposed to be 1" from the edge of the table. When the bussers and wait staff who cleaned the tables were asked what a 1 inch was, the answers varied from ½ inch to 3 inches. The instructions in the procedure were changed to place the salt and pepper shakers one thumb-width from the edge of the table. The result was that errors became a rarity.

4. Precision in Pet Care: Designing Out the Gray

Even in our daily lives, redesign can lead to 100% execution. Consider the example of feeding a dog. Many pet owners struggle with consistently providing the correct amount of food, leading to overfeeding or underfeeding. By redesigning the feeding process to eliminate ambiguity—or "gray areas"—we can achieve perfect execution.

For instance, I did not realize I had been overfeeding my dog Watson for over a year. The instructions were to "Give one cup of dry food in the evening." I used a 1-cup measuring scoop and always used the correct measuring scoop. However, I was using a heaping scoop, whereas the intention was a level scoop. Watson was getting about 25% more food than the desired amount. The impact was a happy, but a little overweight, dog.

Once the process instructions were changed to use a level cup, I delivered 100% of the correct amount from then on. One scoop is a gray term that can reasonably be interpreted more than one way, whereas a one-cup level scoop is a precise term. This simple change removes the guesswork and provides instructions enabling Watson to receive the exact amount of food required for his target weight every time.

These examples illustrate a crucial point: whether in high-stakes medical procedures, ordinary service tasks, or everyday tasks, precise process design and language are essential to eliminating errors, reducing risks, and leading to consistent, 100% execution that delivers the desired results every time. By identifying potential areas of ambiguity or design flaws in our processes and systematically correcting them, we can set up the 100% execution that this chapter advocates for.

The Benefits of Operational Excellence

The impact of operational excellence through process design is profound. Consider these compelling statistics and insights: (a) written processes give consistently better results, (b) training operators with Standard Operating Procedures (SOPs) ensures a significant reduction in errors, and (c) companies with well-designed processes are 25% more likely to exceed their annual financial goals.

These numbers speak for themselves. Processes designed for 100% are not just a nice-to-have; it's a necessity for any organization that seeks to achieve extraordinary operations and stay ahead of the competition.

Checklist for Designing and Writing a Process to 100%

To truly understand the power of process design, we must first define what it means to design a process to 100%. A process is considered designed to 100% when any trained person precisely performs the steps of the process, and the process delivers the product, service, or customer experience 100% to the brand requirements, 100% of the time, under 100% of the conditions, and in the most efficient manner possible.

To achieve this level of process design, we have developed a checklist that, when followed, provides a roadmap for designing processes for 100%. You can get a copy of this checklist on our website at McClaskeyExcellence.com/100customerdelight .

The McClaskey® Triple 100® Checklist for Designing and Writing a Process to 100%.

The three major sections of the checklist are:

A. **OUTPUT:** the required output and the starting inputs

B. **STEPS:** that convert the inputs to the output that meets 100% of the requirements every time, and

C. **SELF-MANAGEMENT:** to Ensure Desired Output is Obtained

Section A: OUTPUT: the required output and the starting inputs

Section A: Output: identifies the desired output or end result and the inputs that are converted to the output.

The four checklist items under this section are;

1. List the outputs of the process.

2. List the requirements for the process output.

3. List the KCRs impacted by the process.

4. List the inputs to the process that will be converted to the outputs and the requirements for each input.

For example, the output of the GPS process is that you arrive at the destination. The requirements of the output are that it is the correct destination and that the route used to get there was both safe and efficient. The KCRs impacted are safe, timely, and correct destination. The input is the address of your desired destination, and the requirement is that the address is correct.

Section B: STEPS: that convert the inputs to the output that meets 100% of the requirements every time

The second section, "The steps that deliver the output that meets 100% of the requirements every time", lists the steps of the process that, when precisely followed, get you from the starting point of the process to achieving the process output that meets all the process output requirements.

The 9 checklist items under this section are:

1. They are written.
2. They are based on the best-known and most effective way to achieve the output that 100% meets the requirements 100% of the time.
3. When the steps are precisely performed, the process output meets 100% of the output requirements, 100% of the time, under 100% of the conditions.
4. The steps are the most efficient way possible that delivers the output 100% to the output requirements, 100% of the time. Eliminated inefficiencies to the extent possible.
5. Have a step that ensures the inputs meet the requirements before they are used, and if not, how to correct them.
6. Each step includes the level of detail needed for excellence.
7. Each step is stated as a behavior that must be performed.
8. For each step, there is only one way to reasonably interpret what is written. (No Gray)
9. Whenever possible, the performer can determine if the step was performed correctly and then correct it if not.

In the GPS example, the steps are the directions that lead from your starting point to your destination. The GPS process meets all nine criteria.

Section C: SELF-MANAGEMENT: to Ensure Desired Output is Obtained

The third section, "SELF-MANAGEMENT to Ensure Desired Output is Obtained", enables the process performer to determine if the output meets all the output requirements after completing all the steps. If not, they are empowered to correct the output until it meets the requirements.

The checklist items under this section are:

1. The performer can assess if the process output meets all the requirements. To carry out this checklist item, the process performer must know what the process output is, what requirements the output must meet to be fully satisfactory, and how to assess whether the output meets all the requirements. The output and requirements are the first two checklist items provided under the "output" section.

2. List the actions the performer is empowered to take to correct or reroute the output if all the process output requirements are not fully met. Actions can include empowering the performer to correct, divert, inform, or destroy any output that does not fully meet the output requirements.

In the GPS process, after all steps have been followed, the driver can check whether the actual destination they are at matches the desired destination. If not, the driver is empowered to take corrective action until they arrive at the desired destination. Some possible actions the driver is empowered to take include checking whether you have the correct address for the desired destination and whether it was entered correctly into the GPS system; if the address was entered incorrectly, the driver is authorized to enter the correct address.

Self-Management is such a universal process. Building it into just about every process is necessary to deliver products and services to 100%. A personal example was when I was working as a crew member at Pal's making french fries; one of the product requirements was that no fries were served if they were more than 5 minutes old. When the fries were made, a timer was started for each batch. When the timer showed 5 minutes, I was required and empowered to throw out any remaining fries from that batch. Through self-management, I ensured that all french fry requirements were met for every bag sold.

By following the McClaskey® Triple 100® Checklist for Designing and Writing Processes to 100%, organizations can design and document processes that deliver the products, services, and customer experience 100% to the brand requirements, 100% of the time, under 100% of the conditions when the process steps are precisely followed.

Overcoming Challenges in Process Design

Despite the overwhelming evidence favoring designing for 100% execution, some skeptics may question the practicality of designing error-free processes. Let's address these common doubts head-on.

- **Common Doubt**: "The actual processes used are too vague and not always clear."
  - **Counterpoint**: Processes are steps to achieve a goal. They need to be clearly defined to precisely guide every action to the desired output by eliminating ambiguity. The key is to design processes with little to no vagueness or "gray," leaving no room for unreasonable interpretation by someone trained in the process. This clarity eliminates a significant cause of errors.

- **Common Doubt**: "I am the only person who understands this job."
    - **Counterpoint**: Processes allow delegation and scaling. They capture the best practices and essential knowledge, enabling others to perform tasks to the same standard. Organizations can break free from the tyranny of individual expertise by designing processes that anyone with the proper training can follow. Written, approved processes that capture best practices ensure that knowledge does not leave the company when the expert leaves.

Key Insights: The Power of Consistent Process Design

Processes designed for 100% provide proven steps that, when precisely followed, will effectively and efficiently deliver the product 100% to the brand requirements, 100% of the time, under 100% of the conditions. This is essential to achieving extraordinary operations.

Some of the benefits of designing processes to 100% include:

- Reliable delivery of products and services is essential for meeting the organization's KCRs and achieving its mission.
- Consistently and reliably delighting current and future customers, which is essential for repeat business.
- Sustainability and growth. Written processes designed for 100% enable reliable business expansion and better start-ups of new units.
- Capturing the collective wisdom, best practices, and knowledge from both within and outside your organization ensures that products and services are reliably delivered to brand requirements using the best-known methods.

There are two types of knowledge within your organization: personal knowledge and organizational knowledge. Most leaders do not make this distinction until it's too late.

- **Personal knowledge** is knowledge not documented in the approved process. It exists only in the minds of individuals and follows the person when they leave the organization.

- **Organizational knowledge** is knowledge written in the approved process and can be passed on, built upon, and used throughout the organization. By capturing knowledge and best-known practices in processes and documenting approved processes in Standard Operating Procedures (SOPs), organizations can ensure their best-known practices are available to their operations, support future employee training, and scale growth. This eliminates the problem of your best-known practices being available only when certain people are present and prevents knowledge from leaving the company when an employee leaves.

A Roadmap for Designing and Documenting Processes for 100%

The roadmap starts by designing your processes for 100% and documenting them in your organization's approved procedures. The McClaskey® Triple 100® Process Implementation Steps provide a roadmap for this journey:

1. **Identify Critical Processes:** Start by identifying the processes that have the most significant impact on your key results and your KCRs. These are the areas where standardization will yield the greatest returns. We suggest standardizing your processes a few at a time. Trying to standardize too many processes at once usually overloads an organization's ability to manage change, leading to failure.

2. **Flow Chart Current State:** For each critical process, use a flow chart to show how it's currently performed across your organization. Look for variations, inconsistencies, and best practices.

3. **Design the Process Around Best Practices:** Engage process owners and top performers in defining the best-known method for each critical process. The best-known process may also come from sources outside your organization, so identify who is the best at the process you are standardizing, no matter where they are. Document it in clear, step-by-step terms. Use visuals and examples to make it easy to understand and follow.

4. **Design and Write the Process to 100%:** Design and write the process so it includes components that ensure the process output meets brand requirements 100% of the time. The McClaskey® Triple 100® Checklist for Designing and Writing a Process to 100% lists the components that need to be designed and written into a process for the process output to meet the brand requirements 100% of the time.

5. **Develop 100% Training for the Process.** This will be covered in the People Excellence pillar.

6. **Pilot the Process and Revise the Written Steps:** Piloting the process ensures it is designed and written for 100% execution by carefully testing under actual operating conditions. Based on the pilot, revise the process until when the process steps are precisely followed, as written in the process documentation, so that it delivers the process outputs that meet the brand requirements every time. Another purpose of piloting is to identify and revise the process to remove inefficiencies and non-value-adding activities. Pilot the process under the various conditions in which the process will operate. This helps to ensure the procedure, as written, will deliver the process output to brand requirements every time, under 100% of the conditions.

7. **Have Process Approved as the Standard**: After the process has been verified to deliver an output that meets the requirements every time under operating conditions, document, review, and officially approve it as the standard process.

8. **Document and Approve all Process Changes:** All changes to approved processes will be documented in writing, reviewed against the Checklist for Designing and Writing a Process to 100%, and approved for use.

9. **Standardize the Use:** Once processes are approved for use, they will be standardized to be used everywhere applicable. This will be covered in the Standardize Processes element in Chapter 11.

10. **Regularly audit** to ensure standardized processes are the processes provided to employees to follow, and not an unapproved variation of the standardized processes.

By following these steps, organizations can systematically redesign and document their processes to achieve 100% of the process output requirements 100% of the time, under 100% of the conditions. This ensures that every process delivers the desired output every time when the steps are precisely followed.

Take the Next Step Toward Operational Excellence

The path to extraordinary operations begins with a shift in mindset. It requires organizations to overhaul their process design thinking, aiming not just to deliver products and services that meet brand requirements most of the time, but to get it right every time and make the process efficient. Excellence is always in the details, and it's time for organizations to embrace this truth. An essential component of ensuring that the organization's products and services are delivered to its customers correctly every time is to ensure that all processes used are designed and documented to 100%.

I challenge you to take a hard look at your processes. Are they designed for 100% or are they merely adequate and designed for most? Do they deliver your products, services, and customer experience 100% to your brand requirements, 100% of the time, under 100% of the conditions? If not, it's time to make the necessary refinements. It's time to design your processes for 100%.

Remember, 100% in process design isn't an aspiration; it's a necessity for those who aim for excellence. It's essential to unlocking your organization's full potential and creating a legacy of reliable excellence that will stand the test of time.

Call to Action

1. Develop a plan to have all your operations processes designed for 100% in 1-2 years.

2. To start, select 1-3 processes to design for 100%.

3. For each process, design the process for 100% by following the steps listed earlier in this chapter under the title: "A Roadmap for Designing and Documenting Processes for 100%"

4. To have a personal guide through designing your initial processes for 100%, select your process and join a McClaskey Excellence Institute AWCR class, or contact us for consulting on Designing Processes for 100%. The class will guide you through the Design for 100% process, providing both structure and coaching from the instructors. After you have done a few, your management team will be able to design and write processes for 100%. You can always selectively reach out for help as needed.

Key Takeaways for Chapter 10: Design and Document Processes for 100%

1. Processes are designed and documented to 100% when the steps of the written process are precisely followed, it will deliver the product, service, or customer experience 100% to the brand requirements; 100% of the time; under 100% of the conditions, and this is done in the most efficient manner possible.

2. All processes need to be designed and written for 100%, documented as a process, approved, filed in a procedure system, and made securely available when needed to all authorized to use it.

3. A process designed and documented for 100% will include the following three sections: (a) output of the process, (b) steps that deliver the output that meets 100% of the requirements every time, and (c) self-management to ensure the desired output is obtained.

The Next Chapter

With a clear understanding of how to design and document processes for 100%, we now turn our attention to the next critical step: standardization. In the next chapter, I will explore how to standardize these approved, 100% designed, and documented processes so they must be used everywhere the process is applicable. It does little good to have processes designed for 100% if no one is using them. Standardization will enhance your organization's reliability, consistency, and scalability, taking your operational excellence to new heights.

CHAPTER 11

STANDARDIZING PROCESSES

"Goals are good for setting a direction,
but systems are best for making progress."

James Clear

Standardization Turns Pockets of Excellence into Excellence Everywhere

In the annals of business excellence, an unsung hero quietly powers the world's most successful organizations. It's not a flashy new technology or a charismatic leader, but a simple, profound principle: standardization. This often-overlooked principle is the secret sauce that enables organizations to replicate their successes, scale their operations, and deliver consistent quality every time, everywhere. Standardization turns pockets of excellence into excellence everywhere. It's the foundation upon which the skyscrapers of business greatness are built.

The Chaos of Inconsistency: A Strategic Liability

In my over five decades of working with organizations of every stripe—from global giants to local mom-and-pops—I've seen the transformative power of standardization. I've also witnessed the chaos and mediocrity that ensued in its absence. Too often, organizations operate like a collection of fiefdoms rather than a unified empire. Each location, each department, and each team does things their own way, often with vastly different results. A pocket of excellence emerges in one corner of the kingdom, while subpar performance persists in another. The castle is divided against itself. In many cases, even after it is known that one part of the kingdom does it better than other parts, the best practice is not adopted because the improvement was "not invented here."

This inconsistency isn't just a minor annoyance—it's a major strategic liability. It leads to uneven quality and inefficient resource use, makes training, coaching, and capturing improvements difficult, and results in constant reinvention of the wheel. Inconsistency also makes effective scaling and improvement almost impossible.

The antidote to this chaos is standardization.

We are very familiar with product standardization. Almost every electric appliance for a given country will plug into the electric outlets. Why? Because the electrical plugs in that country are standardized. Can you imagine needing a different adaptor for every appliance because electrical plugs weren't standardized? Almost every product you have at work or at home has been standardized. Standardization makes our lives much simpler and removes a lot of complications.

I am specifically addressing process standardization in this Path for Excellence element. Standardization of processes requires enforcing that the approved process is used everywhere applicable. These are the steps of the process, and they will be followed unless an approved exemption is in place. In the GPS example, it is precisely following each step of the directions to get you from where you are to where you want to go. The result of process standardization is that using the approved process everywhere it is applicable is the norm, not the exception. Standardization is not about intention; it is about actual use everywhere applicable. If the preceding Design and Document to 100% element of the Path to Excellence is fully carried out, the approved process will be the best-known way to perform each process. Standardization will then get this designed and documented to 100% process approved to be the company standard, that is required to be used everywhere applicable, unless there is a written exception. That way, a company maximizes the impact of every improvement.

Standardization in Action: The Chick-fil-A Way

Chick-fil-A has become renowned not just for their chicken sandwiches but also for their exceptional and consistent customer service across more than 3,300 locations. This consistency is no accident—it results from rigorous standardization and a commitment to operational excellence.

At the heart of Chick-fil-A's approach are its "Core 4" service standards:

- Create eye contact.
- Share a smile.
- Speak with enthusiasm.
- Stay connected.

These simple yet powerful standards are drilled into every employee, creating a uniform experience whether you're in Atlanta or Anchorage.

Chick-fil-A's standardization goes far beyond customer interactions. Every aspect of their operation, from food preparation to restaurant layout, is meticulously specified and consistently implemented. Their cooking processes are precisely timed and temperature-controlled to ensure every chicken sandwich is perfectly crispy on the outside and juicy on the inside. Even their lemonade is made fresh daily following a standardized recipe.

Another example of Chick-fil-A standardization is its current use of the term: "My Pleasure." This is how Chick-fil-A associates respond to customers in all their stores. This term came from benchmarking The Ritz-Carlton Hotel company, which had used that term as part of their standardized processes for responding to guest requests.

This commitment to standardization allows Chick-fil-A to maintain quality as it has rapidly expanded. At this time, Chick-fil-A generates more revenue per restaurant than any other fast-food chain in the United States. Its standardized processes achieved a level of effectiveness, efficiency, and consistency that directly translates into the bottom line.

Moreover, Chick-fil-A's standardization extends to its rigorous selection and training of franchisees. Unlike many fast-food chains, Chick-fil-A is highly selective about who can open a franchise, ensuring that every owner-operator aligns with their standards and values. This careful standardization of leadership helps maintain consistency even as the brand grows.

The result? A brand that's become synonymous with quality, reliability, efficiency, and customer satisfaction. Chick-fil-A's devotion to standardization enabled them to deliver a consistent product and experience across thousands of locations, turning a simple chicken sandwich into a cultural phenomenon and a model of operational excellence in the fast-food industry.

Common Reasons for Lack of Standardization

If an owner has 30 stores of the same type, I would ask if one or a few of the stores deliver the products and services to the brand requirements more often than others. Usually, the answer is yes. If the stores, products, and services are basically the same, why aren't all the stores using the processes that best deliver the products and services to the brand requirements rather than the ones they currently use?

Let us look at what commonly causes similar units NOT to use the best-performing processes. When one store improves a process, it is common for the store that made the improvements to be the only one to use the improved process. The other stores either do not know about the improvement or do not use it because they want to do it their way. Sometimes, this is referred to as the "not invented here" problem. If I did not invent it, I would not use it.

The owner of the 30 stores now has one store consistently using the proven best way and 29 stores using processes that do not get as good of results. This causes a loss of effectiveness, efficiency, or both. The remedy is first to change the approved process to incorporate the best-known practices and then standardize the approved process across all 30 stores.

When customers have favorite stores within a brand, or when a brand has stores that consistently perform better than others with similar business opportunities, the leading causes are often either that processes are not standardized or that the standardized processes are not precisely followed.

You improve effectiveness when the standardized, approved process contains the best-known way to deliver the process output. You improve efficiency by reducing complexity and variation by having only one process for accomplishing a given task rather than several or many.

Before a process is standardized, its effectiveness should be verified over time and across the many possible environments in which it will be applied. This is usually done during the Design and Document Process for 100% element. In some cases, exceptions to parts of the standardized process must be approved when the standardized process does not apply to a specific situation. For example, if a standardized process was written for a specific type of equipment. All but one of your stores has this equipment, but one does not. The one store that does not have this equipment would need an exception. Exceptions to standardized processes should have a high barrier based on proven need.

The Checklist Revolution: How a Simple Tool Saved Lives

In 2006, Dr. Atul Gawande, a surgeon at Brigham and Women's Hospital in Boston, faced a vexing problem. Despite having some of the world's best-trained surgeons, his hospital still experienced an unacceptable rate of complications and infections from surgery. Dr. Gawande realized that the problem wasn't a lack of skill or knowledge, but a lack of consistency. Even the best surgeons occasionally forgot a step or deviated from best practices. These small variations added up to big problems. His solution was as simple as it was profound: a checklist. By standardizing the essential steps of safe surgery—from handwashing to counting sponges—and putting them into a simple checklist, Dr. Gawande and his team ensured that every surgery followed the same rigorous protocol. The results were staggering. After introducing the checklist, major complications fell by 36% and deaths fell by 47%. The checklist spread to hospitals around the world, saving countless lives and demonstrating the extraordinary power of standardizing best practices. Using checklists to standardize process execution is a role-model practice used by most organizations.

The Numbers Don't Lie: The Measurable Impact of Standardization

The impact of standardization isn't just anecdotal—it's rooted in rigorous data. A Harvard Business School study of over 600 organizations found that firms with standardized processes had, on average, 30% better quality performance than those without. Standardized work practices are a key to eliminating human errors in production and service processes. Programs like Training Within Industry (TWI) can be highly effective for standardizing work processes. According to the American Productivity & Quality Center, top-performing procurement teams, which are presumed to have highly standardized processes, average five hours or less for their PO cycle time, a dramatic improvement over the two days averaged by bottom performers.

Standardization Beneficially Impacts Many Aspects of an Organization

Having just one approved way to do any given task, particularly when that one approved way is the best-known process, yields the best results with the least complexity. This helps just about every aspect of operations.

Standardization frees up mental energy for higher-order thinking. When people don't have to reinvent the wheel or constantly wrestle with unnecessary variability, they can focus on precisely performing the steps of the approved process.

The highest levels of skill can be achieved in the least amount of time when the process is standardized, with infrequent changes and few exceptions. Every time there is a change, it disrupts the speed at which skills can be obtained. This is one reason why just about every sport is highly standardized. Sports also minimize changes to rules, and exceptions to rules are carefully thought out. That is because changes and exceptions are highly disruptive to skill obtainment and cause added complexities and complications. The same is true for every process used within a company. To maximize skill development and minimize complexity, the process should be highly standardized, changed only when there is verified improvement or need, and exceptions carefully considered and granted only upon sufficient proof of need.

Training and coaching are two management activities that profoundly impact employee performance. Both activities are much simpler and can be done more effectively if the operations processes are standardized. For example, standardization facilitates coaching by line managers since there is only one standardized way to perform the process steps. This makes it easier for the manager to identify any variation from the standardized process and provide corrective coaching. It also makes it easier to detect when each step of the approved process is performed correctly so that the manager can give positive coaching or feedback.

Standardization also makes training and onboarding easier. Instead of each new employee learning a different way of doing things, they can be quickly trained to the approved standard. This accelerates productivity and reduces errors. Perhaps most importantly, standardization creates a culture of discipline and excellence. When adherence to standards is an inviolable expectation, people rise to the challenge. They take pride in upholding the standard and in the consistently excellent results it produces.

But standardization isn't just about effectiveness, efficiency, and consistency—it's also a powerful enabler of learning and improvement. When you standardize a process, you create a baseline for measuring and improving. You can spot deviations and errors more quickly and test new ideas against a controlled standard to determine if the new idea is or is not an improvement over the existing standardized process.

Addressing the Critics: Common Objections to Standardization

Of course, standardization is not without its critics or challenges.

Counterpoint 1: Some argue that standardization stifles creativity and innovation, leading to bureaucratic rigidity. They worry it will turn employees into unthinking robots, mindlessly following scripts.

Response: However, these fears fundamentally misunderstand the nature and purpose of standardization. Standardization, done right, is not about blind conformity but about using the approved, proven, best-known practice to accomplish the outcome everywhere applicable.

During the design of the approved processes, the best-known practices and processes documented in the approved processes came from experience and from the best practices used by your organization and other organizations. It's about taking these best ideas and proven practices, reviewing and piloting them to ensure they work in your operation, approving them, documenting the processes in the organization's standard operating procedures (SOPs), and then requiring the documented, approved processes in the SOPs to be used everywhere applicable. The key is everywhere applicable. Exceptions should be authorized when the facts clearly demonstrate the need for an exception from the SOP. Standardization results in the best-known ways being used throughout the company.

Moreover, standardization and innovation are not mutually exclusive—in fact, they're mutually reinforcing. Standardization provides a stable foundation for innovation to flourish. It frees up mental bandwidth for creativity and provides a clear benchmark against which to measure new ideas. The most innovative organizations in the world, from Apple to Amazon, are also some of the most standardized. These companies understand you can't scale the benefits of innovation without standardization. When creativity results in an improved, best-known method, you want it used everywhere applicable. Standardization is the discipline that enables that.

A consultant friend of mine, Deb Owens, told me that she effectively conveyed to others that standardization not only does not interfere with innovation and creative thinking, but actually supports them. She asks the leaders what they are thinking about as they drive to work. They are often thinking about their first meetings, what they need to do that day, upcoming meetings, and possible solutions to current issues. What they are not thinking about is driving. Why? Because driving is highly standardized, it allows us to think about these other topics.

Counterpoint 2: It does not apply to my location or store because we are not exactly like the store or location using it now.

Response: While no two locations are identical, standardization focuses on best practices proven effective in a variety of environments. Appropriate adaptations and exceptions can be made for local nuances when it is demonstrated that they are needed.

Counterpoint 3: The performers of the process know the best way for them and resent having to use processes they did not create.

Response: Standardization allows the best-known way to do any process to be used everywhere applicable. Without standardization, the best-known ways of achieving outcomes would not have a guaranteed way to reach the very people who need to use those processes to create the desired outcome. Managers and employees are encouraged to suggest possible improvements to test, and any verified improvements to the existing standardized process can be integrated into the standard process.

Counterpoint 4: Our current way works, so leave it alone.

Response: This is a variation of the saying: "If it isn't broke, don't fix it." While current processes may work, standardization ensures the best possible method is used consistently across all applicable locations, improving overall performance, reducing variability, and simplifying operations.

What should you do if a store or unit's process is equal to the standardized process? Part of the rationale for using the standardized process everywhere applicable is that it reduces the complexity of having multiple processes produce the same output, even if those processes are identical. Having a single process as the standardized way to produce an output reduces complexity in training, coaching, and implementing improvements.

Counterpoint 5: It is not worth the hassle to get managers to change their current process.

Response: The initial effort to standardize may seem daunting, but the long-term benefits of increased effectiveness and efficiency, reduced errors, and improved customer satisfaction far outweigh the initial hassle. Once standardization is the norm in the culture, it requires very little additional energy and time and eliminates unnecessary complexity.

Counterpoint 6: We are not able to sustain standardized processes. Managers change the process whenever they feel like it.

Response: With the right systems and culture, any organization can achieve a high degree of standardization. Organizations with a high degree of standardization have established a system and culture in which the steps of approved processes are followed consistently, even by managers. In Process Excellence, we are getting the best-known processes approved and standardized. In the People Excellence pillar, the key people-related elements are what organizations use to ensure everyone precisely follows the standardized processes. It does little good to have approved processes if they are not going to be followed.

Another important aspect of standardization is preventing unauthorized changes to approved processes. Unauthorized changes, at a minimum, increase variability and complexity but could also lead to disastrous outcomes for the company.

Standardization helps ensure that customers get what the company promised them every time. Standardization eliminates the need for everyone to figure out the best way. Using the best-known process everywhere it applies maximizes productivity, ensures consistency, reduces waste, and saves the company money.

Counterpoint 7: Standardization means our processes will be too rigid and fail to allow the flexibility needed.

Response: Standardization is to the verified, proven, approved process. The approved processes can and should include the flexibility needed and when that flexibility can and cannot be used. It also notes the limits of flexibility, beyond which the employees cannot go as part of the standardized process. For example, a distribution company allows its drivers to only drive as fast as is safe. The standardized process also limits how fast drivers can go by prohibiting speeds exceeding the posted speed limit.

From Pockets of Excellence to Excellence Everywhere: The True Power of Standardization

The real power of standardization lies in its ability to turn pockets of excellence into excellence everywhere. It takes the best practices of top performers and makes them the default for the entire organization. Think about it: some individuals or teams consistently outperform their peers in every organization. They've figured out a better way of doing things, whether through trial and error, insight, or sheer tenacity. The problem is that, too often, these pockets of excellence remain just that—isolated pockets. Their superior practices aren't replicated across the organization. Their insights aren't captured and codified in the organization's approved procedures, nor are they required to be used everywhere applicable.

Standardization changes all that. It provides a mechanism for identifying and scaling excellence, ensuring that the best way to do a process becomes the only way to do it. Standardization is implemented whenever multiple locations need to use the same best practice. Certainly, the required level of flexibility is built in as part of the piloting and approval process.

Here's a key insight: standardization is not a one-time event, but an ongoing process. The world doesn't stand still, and neither can your standards. As new best practices emerge, as technology evolves, and as customers' needs change, your standards must evolve in tandem. The most successful organizations are those that have mastered the art of dynamic standardization—continuously identifying, verifying, and then systematically integrating new best practices into their standards. They've made standardization not just an operational tool, but a core competency and competitive advantage. Improving and sustaining process improvements will be discussed in Chapter 12.

Implementing Standardization: A Step-by-Step Guide

How can you harness the power of standardization in your organization?

1. **It Starts with a Shift in Mindset:** Much like in the first pillar, Think Excellence, significant change begins with a shift in mindset. You must change how you view standardization. As a company leader and manager, you need to view standardization not as a bureaucratic burden but as an operational advantage and a requirement for sustained excellence. There are no examples of sustained excellence that do not involve standardization. It is a necessity if your organization is going to achieve extraordinary operations that consistently deliver the products and services to the brand requirements. It is also necessary if you want to expand your business into other units or franchise your brand, because standardized, approved processes are needed to operate new units successfully. You must make it a leadership priority and a key part of your organization's culture.

2. **Have a Policy that Requires and Enforces Standardization:** Have a company policy that requires processes to be standardized and that standardized processes must be used and followed everywhere applicable. The policy must be enforced.

3. **Control the Rate of New or Revised Processes Being Standardized:** It is important not to overwhelm the company's capacity to handle change. Part of standardization is timing the implementation of new or revised processes so as not to overwhelm the operation's ability to absorb them and maintain them at 100%.

4. **Develop Approved Processes:** The approved processes will be developed as part of either the Design and Document for 100% element described in Chapter 10 or the Improve Processes element described in Chapter 12.

5. **Train to the Approved Process Procedure:** Roll out the new or revised process to all relevant employees. Provide training and require a demonstration of mastery. Training to 100% will be one of the elements covered in the People Excellence pillar. Adherence to the standard is a core job expectation.

6. **Monitor and Enforce:** Hold every manager using a standardized process accountable for their unit precisely following the steps of the standardized process. Implement regular process audits to ensure the steps of the standardized process are being precisely followed 100% of the time. Use observation, positive and corrective coaching, checklists, audits, and performance data to identify and correct deviations and compliment employees and managers whose units execute the standardized process 100% correctly. Hold managers accountable for 100% adherence to the standardized processes in their areas of responsibility.

7. **Continuously Improve:** The Systematically Sustain and Improve Process element of the Path to Excellence, described in Chapter 12, establishes a process for continuously improving your standardized processes: Encourage employees to suggest improvements to the processes and use your improvement process to rapidly test and integrate verified new best practices into the organization's standardized processes. Make standardization a living, breathing part of your operational rhythm.

8. **Celebrate Successes:** Recognize and reward managers, teams, and individuals who exemplify excellence in following and improving standardized processes. Frequent positive coaching is a key method for providing positive feedback for adherence

to standardized processes. How to do this is covered in the "Coaching to 100%" element of the People Excellence pillar. Share success stories widely to reinforce the importance and impact of standardization.

9. **Emphasize the Importance of SOP Adherence:** Standardized processes are frequently documented in Standard Operating Procedures or SOPs. Ensure the approved SOPs are accessible to all operating units and employees who need to use the standardized process. Also, ensure your SOPs are secure to prevent unauthorized access, use, or changes. This may involve using secure digital platforms or controlled physical access to documents. Communicate clearly that deviations from standardized processes are permitted only with approved, written exceptions.

10. **Leverage Leadership:** Encourage leaders to identify areas in their operations where standardization can lead to significant improvements. Begin by focusing on high-impact processes that directly affect customer satisfaction and operational efficiency. By starting small and demonstrating success, leaders can build momentum and buy-in for broader standardization initiatives.

Conclusion: The Quiet Force of Operational Excellence

Standardization may not be sexy, but it's the unsung hero of operational excellence. It's the quiet force that turns pockets of excellence everywhere. Embrace it and watch your organization soar to new heights of quality, consistency, and continuous improvement. Standardization helps calm the chaos and stress of operations while reducing complexity and errors. Standardization is the secret ingredient that allows excellence to be replicated and maintained. It sets your organization up for reliable growth and expansion. Having your approved processes that incorporate the best-known practices used everywhere applicable is one of the best and most cost-effective ways to achieve and sustain rapid improvement with minimal risk. It also fosters a culture of discipline, which is essential for achieving excellence in any field.

Make Standardization Your Competitive Edge

My challenge to you is simple but profound: make standardization your secret weapon. Embrace it not as a necessary evil but as a strategic imperative to gain a competitive advantage through operations excellence. Start small, but start now. Pick one critical process or one simple process and standardize it. Have your organization experience the benefits of standardizing processes designed for 100%, then scale it across your organization. Build momentum and buy-in by celebrating the results.

Over time, make standardization a core part of your operational DNA. Make it a source of pride and a pillar of your culture. Weave it into your training, your performance management, and your continuous improvement efforts. Remember, operational excellence isn't about heroic feats of individual brilliance. It's about consistent, collective adherence to precisely following your approved processes, based on known best practices, designed for 100% execution, and standardized throughout your organization. It's about doing ordinary things extraordinarily well, every time.

Call to Action

1. Develop a plan to have all your processes standardized in one to two years.

2. Start by standardizing the 1-3 processes you designed for 100% as part of Chapter 10. Then select other processes you are currently using and standardize them until you have all your processes standardized.

3. For each process you standardize, follow the steps listed earlier in this chapter under the title: "Implementing Standardization: A Step-by-Step Guide."

Key Takeaways for Chapter 11: Standardization Processes

1. Standardization requires that approved processes be used everywhere applicable.

2. Standardization needs to be an organizational policy required and reliably enforced to maintain best practices and improvements. Precisely following the standardized process needs to be part of your company's culture.

3. There can be exceptions to using the standardized process when the standardized process is not applicable. Exceptions should be approved.

4. Only allow authorized and approved changes to standardized processes

5. There are many benefits to standardizing your organization's approved processes. They include:
   a. Enabling organizations to replicate their successes, scale their operations, and deliver consistent quality, every time, everywhere.
   b. Maintain consistently excellent operations. There is no model of sustained operations excellence that does not involve standardization.
   c. Enables the use of the approved best-known processes everywhere they are applicable.
   d. Removes the ambiguity of which process to follow by having an enforced policy that requires the use of the approved process everywhere it is applicable.
   e. Enables brands to consistently fulfill their promise to their customers by consistently delivering their products,

services, and customer experiences to the brand standard every time. Standardization of processes is essential for this to happen.

f.   Reduces complexity since there is only one authorized way to produce a given product or service, rather than many ways that can randomly change. This reduced complexity and stability help many aspects of operations run more effectively and efficiently, including training and coaching.

g.   Turns pockets of excellence into excellence everywhere. It takes the best practices and makes them the default for your entire organization.

h.   Provides a systematic method that allows all areas to benefit from verified improvements discovered in one area by incorporating them into the approved process, which is then standardized for use in all applicable areas.

i.   Helps maintain improvements since there is only one approved way to deliver any output, and that one standardized way is enforced through methods like company policy on standardization, audits, coaching, job performance ratings, and clear management expectations.

j.   Makes process improvement much more straightforward and easier to get the change both made and accepted since everyone is using the same process rather than dozens of variations, each of which has to be adjusted to enable improvement to occur.

The Next Chapter

Designing and documenting processes for 100% and standardizing these 100%-designed processes so they are used everywhere applicable are two of the three elements of Process Excellence. But things change. Customer requirements shift, new knowledge about better ways to produce the output is gained, and people have ideas for improving the current approved process. If the processes are not kept as the best-known way to deliver the outputs, they will no longer be a source of competitive advantage. The next chapter covers how to systematically improve your processes and sustain improvements.

CHAPTER 12

IMPROVE PROCESSES

"Unless you have 100% customer satisfaction, you must improve."

Horst Schulze

The Never-Ending Quest for Excellence

This chapter will cover the third element of Process Excellence: Improve Processes.

In the heart of every truly exceptional organization lies a simple yet profound truth: the pursuit of excellence is never complete. It's a journey without end, a relentless quest to be better today than yesterday, and even better tomorrow. This is the essence of continuous improvement – the unwavering commitment to identifying and seizing every opportunity to enhance, refine, optimize, and maintain the gain.

A Cycle of Continuous Improvement Using the Three Process Excellence Pillar Elements

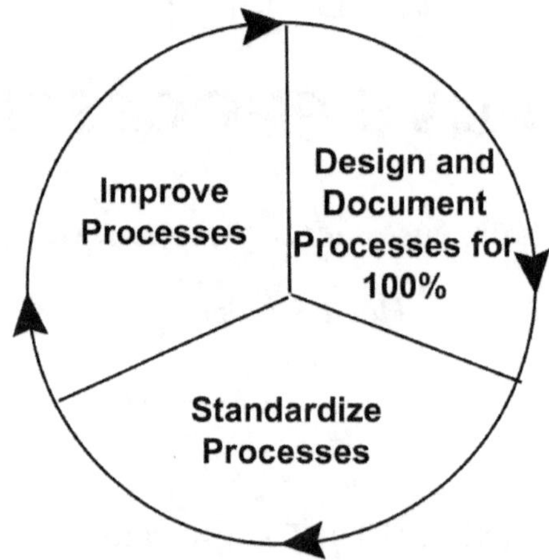

The three elements of the Process Excellence pillar, design process to 100%, standardize processes, and improve processes, work together to create a continuous improvement cycle. At some point, after processes have been designed for 100% and standardized, there will be better ways to accomplish almost any process. The third element of the Process Excellence pillar, Improve Processes, now comes into play.

Companies need to relentlessly seek out and improve their processes. A systematic, data-based improvement process should be used to identify possible process improvements and determine which changes to incorporate. As a result of the Improve Processes element, once you have verified and approved changes to a process, you need to standardize the change so it can be used everywhere it applies and be maintained.

This is where the first two elements of Process Excellence come back into play. For verified improvements, the Design and Document

Processes for 100% element is used to incorporate them into the appropriate processes. Then the Standardize Processes element is used to get the improved process used everywhere applicable. Incorporating improvements into the appropriate processes and then standardizing the improved process are essential to maximizing the benefits of the improvement.

Importance of Regularly Improving Processes

There are several reasons processes must be regularly improved. The obvious ones are that the improved process will either improve its effectiveness, yielding better results, or improve its efficiency, increasing speed and productivity while reducing waste, errors, rework, and costs. Keeping your processes up to date will improve your company's competitiveness.

Another very impactful reason for regularly improving your processes is one that many people do not consider. It is challenging for people to use the current, approved, and standardized process when they know there is a better way. This increases the temptation for employees to avoid following the approved process. If we go back to our GPS analogy, you might precisely follow the GPS directions if you do not know any other way to get from where you are to where you want to be. But if you know a better way to get from where you are to where you are going, then you might ignore all or part of the GPS directions.

Two Basic Types of Improvement

Joseph M. Juran, one of the most impactful quality management gurus of the 20th Century, noted there are two basic types of improvement. A company should use both types of improvement in its continuous improvement culture. The two types of improvement are breakthrough and incremental.

Breakthrough Improvement

Breakthrough improvement is making improvements through major changes to a process. These significant changes come from large improvement projects that often require substantial dedicated resources for a limited period. Breakthrough improvement projects are usually selected by management and carefully chosen for their impact on accomplishing strategic objectives, on KCRs, and/or on the efficiencies they might yield. The Pareto Principle, which states that 20% of the improvements account for 80% of the impact, is often a consideration in selecting these projects. Breakthrough projects require more in-depth study by a diverse team that often includes professionals and employees who perform the process.

Some of the people involved in the breakthrough improvement projects may be dedicated full-time to the project until it's complete. Breakthrough projects identify the root causes of problems and implement major changes to processes that result in significant improvement. In some cases, the project results in a partial or complete redesign of the process. Breakthrough projects often incorporate new technology as part of the process redesign. Breakthrough improvements are generally harder to implement, more expensive, and more likely to fail or not be sustained because they involve a greater degree of change to the existing process.

Kodak and Fujifilm: A Tale of Making and Not Making Breakthrough Improvements

In the late 20th century, Kodak was the undisputed king of photography. With a century-long legacy, the company dominated the film market and seemed poised for continued success. Yet, within a few short years, Kodak found itself in bankruptcy, a victim of the digital revolution it had helped to pioneer. They did not make the breakthrough improvements necessary to survive the technological changes in photography, going from print to electronic.

Contrast this with Fujifilm, Kodak's main rival, which made successful breakthrough improvements to create new products. Faced with the same disruptive forces, Fujifilm adapted and evolved. They invested in R&D, developing innovative new products and services. They diversified their business by pivoting into new areas, including cosmetics and medical imaging. In short, they embraced breakthrough improvement, and it paid off. Today, Fujifilm is a thriving, multibillion-dollar company, while Kodak is a cautionary tale.

Incremental Improvement

As Mark Twain wisely observed, "Continuous improvement is better than delayed perfection."

Incremental improvement involves making many minor refinements or incremental changes to a process. In many, but not all, cases, these improvement ideas may come from the workforce performing the processes.

The most successful organizations understand that waiting for the perfect moment, the ideal plan, or the perfect product is a fool's errand. Instead, these leaders embrace the power of incremental progress, knowing that many small, consistent steps forward can add up to significantly higher-performing processes.

Incremental Improvement in Action: The 1% Doctrine: How Marginal Gains Revolutionized British Cycling

In 2003, the British Cycling team was in a rut. Despite a proud history, they had become also-rans on the world stage, rarely contending for top honors. Enter Dave Brailsford, a former professional cyclist with a radical philosophy.

Brailsford believed in the power of marginal gains – the idea that if you improved every aspect of performance by just 1%, the cumulative effect would be massive. He applied this principle to every facet of the team's operations, from the obvious (training regimens, nutrition plans) to the obscure (pillows for optimal sleep, paint for aerodynamics).

The results were staggering. Over the next decade, British cyclists dominated the sport, winning a staggering 178 world championships and 66 Olympic and Paralympic gold medals. They went from underdogs to unbeatable, and much of it was thanks to the power of 1% improvements.

This story illustrates a powerful truth about incremental improvement: no gain is too small. No matter how seemingly trivial, every enhancement contributes to the larger whole. It's the cumulative impact of marginal gains is one way to transform the ordinary into the extraordinary.

Continuous Improvement

Role-model companies use a combination of both breakthrough and incremental improvements to drive their continuous improvement efforts. A company's continuous improvement has a greater impact and flexibility when it combines the benefits of breakthrough improvement projects featuring single, significant enhancements with the cumulative effect of countless minor improvements over time. The improvement culture needs to promote and support both types of improvement. Investing in a highly effective continuous improvement effort has been shown to give steady, high returns. In many cases, it is what enables businesses to remain competitive over the long term.

The Toyota Way: Lessons from the Master of Continuous Improvement

Few companies embody the spirit of continuous improvement quite like Toyota. Toyota has had a culture of continuous improvement for decades. The Japanese automotive giant has become synonymous with quality, efficiency, and innovation, and much of this success can be attributed to its unwavering commitment to continuous improvement, encompassing both incremental and breakthrough improvements.

At Toyota, continuous improvement isn't just a slogan; it's a way of life. Every employee, from the factory floor to the executive suite, is empowered and encouraged to identify opportunities for enhancement. They're trained to spot waste, to question inefficiencies, and to propose solutions." They are also restricted from making changes to approved processes unless the proper reviews and approvals have been obtained.

This culture of continuous improvement has yielded remarkable results. Toyota has consistently set the standard for automotive quality with vehicles renowned for their reliability, durability, and performance. They've pioneered revolutionary production systems, like Just-In-Time manufacturing and the Toyota Production System, which have become the gold standard in the industry.

But perhaps most impressive is Toyota's resilience. When faced with challenges – from quality issues to supply chain disruptions – Toyota doesn't just weather the storm; it emerges stronger. This is the power of a continuous improvement culture. It's not just about avoiding problems but about turning problems into opportunities for growth and learning.

The Numbers Don't Lie: The Impact of Continuous Improvement

The power of continuous improvement isn't just anecdotal; it's backed by hard data. Studies have consistently shown that organizations with a strong culture of continuous improvement outperform their peers on a variety of metrics.

For example, a study by the Aberdeen Group found that companies with best-in-class continuous improvement programs achieved 48% higher profit margins and 37% higher customer retention rates compared to laggards. Another study by Deloitte found that companies with mature continuous improvement capabilities were 2.5 times more likely to outperform their industry in revenue growth.

These numbers are compelling, but they shouldn't be surprising. After all, continuous improvement is fundamentally about optimizing operations, enhancing quality, improving efficiency, and delivering more value to customers. It's a recipe for business success in any industry.

The lesson here is clear: in a world of constant change, continuous improvement isn't optional; it's essential. Companies that rest on their laurels and become complacent with the status quo are doomed to obsolescence. It's only through a relentless commitment to continuous improvement that organizations can hope not just to survive but thrive.

Systematic, Data-Based, Improvement Process

Your systematic, data-based improvement process is the engine that drives both breakthrough and incremental improvement. Improvement processes can also be referred to as problem-solving processes. This path or process guides you step by step from the problem to an effective, implemented, and maintained solution. There are many excellent systematic improvement processes. You need to choose one or several that work well for your company's culture.

Some popular improvement processes at this time are Plan, Do, Check, Act (PDCA); Lean; Kaizen; A3 Structured Problem Solving; and Six Sigma, which uses DMAIC – Define, Measure, Analyze, Improve, Control as its improvement process. It would be beyond the scope of this book to enable you to use the various improvement processes. Fortunately, you can learn as much depth as you want about these improvement processes, including how to actually apply them, on the internet, in other books, classes, and from consultants. I will briefly describe three improvement processes that are simple, logical, easy to learn, and applicable to a wide range of problems. I would certainly recommend that you consider them. The three are PDCA, Lean, and the SimpleEXCELLENCE® Improvement Process.

PDCA

Plan-Do-Check-Act is a wonderful improvement process because it is amazingly simple and applies to just about every type of problem, from simple to complex. It is also straightforward and very intuitive. Its weakness is that the guidance is very high-level, offering a general path, but you need to figure out how to do it specifically. Here is a summary of PDCA, along with a simple example:

1. **Plan** — determine what you are going to do to solve a problem. For a process, this might be the proposed revision to a process. For example, reduce the no-show rate for virtual one-on-one meetings from 20% to 5% or less by adding automated email reminders 24 hours before the meeting and automated text reminders 1 hour before the meeting.

2. **Do** – Try it or carry out your plan; for the example: carried out the plan for the last 25 business days.

3. **Check** – to see if you achieved whatever you were aiming for; for the example: the percentage of no shows was 4% with the changed process. Your target was achieved.

4. **Act** – if you achieved what you were aiming for (your target or goal), then document and standardize what you did and follow the same plan next time you have the same problem. If you did not get what you were aiming for, then ask "why" three to five times to determine the root cause and revise your plan to address the root cause you found. Then repeat the PDCA cycle until you achieve your aim. For the example: the change you implemented worked and was approved as the standardized

process for all one-on-one virtual meetings. Over the next 6 months, the no-show rate averaged 3.5%, maintaining the target level.

Lean:

1. Lean is a methodology that reduces or eliminates non-value-adding activities or waste. There are many lean tools that can be used to do this, and the person or team uses the tools they believe are most appropriate. Lean usually teaches about eight types of waste. There is no standardized list of names of these eight types of waste, but a common way to remember them is with the acronym **DOWNTIME.**

   a. Defects

   b. Overproduction

   c. Waiting

   d. Non-Utilized Talent

   e. Transportation

   f. Inventory Excess

   g. Motion Waste

   h. Extra-Processing

2. Lean can be used at various levels of complexity, from very simple and easy to apply in 10 minutes to fairly complicated lean projects. At its core, it is a simple problem-solving methodology that can be added to any other improvement process or stand on its own.

3. There are many lean tools, varying from very simple to very complicated. On the Internet, you will find lists of lean tools, what they are, how they can be used, and examples of use. We at the McClaskey Excellence Institute have had the pleasure of teaching Lean problem-solving to hundreds of service companies. It is great to see how rapidly companies

can put lean to work, making improvements. The very best make lean improvement part of their culture, with everyone in the company always looking to identify and eliminate non-value-adding activities as they go about their daily work. Some service companies we have worked with have saved over $1 million in annual savings through their lean improvement efforts.

4. An example of using Lean: Motion Waste is the movement of people. In most work environments, people are not productive when walking. Most jobs require you to be stationary to work. So walking, in most cases, is a non-value adding activity that needs to be minimized. A Spaghetti Diagram is a lean tool that helps determine the amount of motion waste. Based on the current process, a restaurant server had to walk from their workstation to the back storage room an average of 17 times during the 2.5-hour lunchtime period to get items needed for the order. Each trip took 1 minute. A lean technique called point-of-use storage was used to move 20% of the items, which caused 80% of the trips to the back storage room to be near the order-taking station. This change reduced trips to the back storage room to four per 2.5-hour lunch period. Total time savings were 14 minutes per 2.5-hour lunch time period. The one-time cost was less than $100 for some storage units.

SimpleEXCELLENCE® Improvement Process

This improvement process is one I developed over 35 years ago by combining the best elements of over half a dozen improvement processes, while keeping it simple. This improvement process, like the others I mentioned, has stood the test of time and can be used for almost any type of problem. I recommend it to all our consulting clients.

The second purpose of sharing the SimpleEXCELLENCE® Improvement Process is to illustrate a list of criteria you can use to evaluate various improvement processes and select an effective one for your company. The SimpleEXCELLENCE® Improvement Process does meet all the criteria.

Here are the criteria for evaluating and selecting a systematic improvement process:

1. It can be used on a wide range of problems and levels of complexity, from simple to very complex.
2. Relatively simple and intuitive.
3. The problem is defined as a gap between the current level of performance and the desired or targeted level.
4. Contains the Plan, Do, Check, Act flow and process, but gives more guidance on how to flow through PDCA.
5. It contains the Diagnostic Journey from symptom to root cause (Steps 1-3) and then the Diagnostic Journey of Root Cause to Remedy (Steps 4-6). To learn more about the Diagnostic and Remedial Journeys, see the Quality Management Handbook by Joseph Juran. Dr. Juran was a global educator and executive consultant who advanced and conveyed the quality sciences worldwide. I was lucky enough to learn about quality directly from Dr. Juran early in my career, and his handbook will help you acquire some of that same knowledge.
6. The root cause of the problem is determined before coming up with solutions.
7. Multiple solutions are considered before selecting the best solution.
8. Use facts and data to form conclusions.
9. Has a specific step related to maintaining the verified improvement as part of the improvement process.

Here are the 8 Steps of the SimpleEXCELLENCE® Improvement Process, along with an example of each step:

Step 1: Select an Improvement Opportunity Area to Improve. This is often the process selected for improvement or a statement of a result wanted. Example: A restaurant serves both sweet (brewed with sugar) and unsweet (no sugar) iced tea. The opportunity is to reduce customer complaints resulting from the wrong type of iced tea being served.

Step 2: Select a Problem and State it as a Gap Between the Current and Targeted Results. Reduce iced tea complaints about the wrong type of tea being served from 26 per month to 0.

Step 3: Determine and Verify the Root Cause of the Problem. This is done by asking "why" three to five times.

- Why was the wrong type of tea served?
    - Because the server pouring the iced tea misunderstood what the order taker said as to the type of tea the customer wanted.
- Why? Because sweet and unsweet sound similar
- Why? Because that is what the customers say when ordering iced tea from the restaurant
- Why? The root cause was that 'sweet' and 'unsweet' were how the menu listed the two types of iced tea.

Step 4: Select the Best Solution that Addresses the Root Cause. The names on the menu for the two types of iced tea were changed from sweet and unsweet to sweet and plain; the order taker would use the term plain tea to refer to unsweet tea.

Step 5: Implemented the Selected Solution. The solution was first implemented in one restaurant and then, after proving successful, in all 20 restaurants of that brand.

Step 6: Did the Solution Solve the Problem and Close the Gap Stated in Step 2? The complaints due to the wrong type of tea being served dropped from 26 per month to 0. Target achieved.

Step 7: Maintain the Gain. The term "unsweet tea" was dropped from employees' vocabulary, and they always referred to it as "plain tea." The menu, procedures, and training were all changed to reflect this change. Iced tea complaints due to the incorrect type of tea being served stayed at zero.

Step 8: List Lessons Learned from Solving this Problem. The restaurant looked at other words that sounded similar but had different meanings and found alternative words that were very distinct.

Principle Building Blocks of a Continuous Improvement Culture

While an improvement or problem-solving process is essential to a continuous improvement culture, other elements are also needed. What does it take to build a culture of continuous improvement? While the specifics may vary from organization to organization, several key principles underpin success:

Leadership Commitment: "Continuous improvement must be a top-down priority. Leaders need to support the philosophy and actively champion it, modeling the behaviors and mindsets they wish to see in their teams." Leaders must foster a culture and provide the resources necessary for systematic improvement.

Employees Engaged in Improvement: "Continuous improvement can't just be the domain of managers and consultants. At every level, every employee must feel engaged and empowered to identify and suggest enhancements. This requires investment in training, getting everyone focused on the company's mission, KCRs, and job expectations, and a willingness to listen to employees' ideas."

Data-Driven Decisions: "Facts, not feelings, should guide continuous improvement. Organizations need robust systems to measure performance, track progress, and identify areas for improvement. Decisions should be based on hard data, not hunches, to the extent possible." The use of a systematic, data-based improvement process is the engine that drives data-driven continuous improvement.

Use of a Systematic Improvement Process: An improvement process that meets the criteria outlined in this chapter.

Standardization and Maintain the Gain: Improvements are only valuable if used and sustained. Verified process improvements must be written into the appropriate processes, approved, be required to be used everywhere applicable, and sustained over time.

A Learning Culture: "Continuous improvement is, at its heart, about learning and applying what you learn. Organizations must foster an environment where authorized piloting of promising improvements is encouraged, where failures are seen as opportunities for growth, and where best practices are eagerly shared."

A Belief that There is Always a Better Way—we need to find it: Many companies have an ingrained belief that if it is not broken, don't fix it. While there is utility in the "not broken, don't fix it" philosophy, it can lead to a culture that only reacts to problems rather than seeking best practices. This can give your competitors a competitive advantage.

Provide Reinforcement for Continuous Improvement: Continuous Improvement consists of both making value-adding improvements and maintaining them. Both parts are equally important and should be recognized and rewarded equally.

Overcoming Obstacles: Addressing Challenges in Continuous Improvement

The path to continuous improvement is not without its challenges. Sustaining a culture of continuous improvement requires significant effort, resources, and commitment. It can be tempting, especially in times of success, to become complacent and believe that the current way of doing things is good enough.

Moreover, change is hard. Even when improvements are clearly beneficial, there can be resistance from those comfortable with the status quo. Overcoming this inertia requires strong leadership, clear communication, accountability, and a willingness to push through discomfort.

Yet, the alternative – stagnation – is far worse. In today's fast-paced, hypercompetitive business environment, standing still is tantamount to moving backward. Organizations that fail to continuously improve are not just missing opportunities; they're inviting obsolescence.

As the legendary CEO of General Electric, Jack Welch, once said, "If the rate of change on the outside exceeds the rate of change on the inside, the end is near." Continuous improvement is how organizations ensure that their internal rate of change keeps pace with the external world.

Two Dangers to Avoid: Two dangers related to the Improve Processes element are failing to consistently improve your processes and uncontrolled changes. Not consistently improving processes will make you non-competitive sooner or later. In the meantime, this lack of improvement will cost you each year in terms of higher costs and lower quality than you would have had if your processes had been improved. Uncontrolled changes can be as dangerous as little to no improvement at all. It is highly detrimental to allow or authorize everyone in your company to implement and try any change they can think of. This can easily lead to inconsistent quality, delivery, and costs, making your products and services worse and preventing you from identifying when changes are improvements and when they are not. In some cases, unauthorized changes can have such a disastrous impact that they lead to a company going out of business."

The consequences of unauthorized changes can be severe. In extreme cases, they can even lead to a company's downfall. Therefore, a structured, systematic approach to improvement with controls and approvals is essential. This ensures that changes are beneficial, consistent with organizational goals, aligned with the organization's values, approved as a company-authorized change to a process, implemented in a controlled manner that maintains quality and reliability, implemented everywhere applicable, and sustained. It also ensures that you learn from failures.

In essence, the Path to Excellence through continuous improvement requires careful navigation. It demands a delicate balance between fostering a culture of improvement and maintaining the improvements. Organizations that can strike this balance not only position themselves to survive but thrive in an ever-changing business landscape.

Why Extraordinary Organizations Get More Impact From Their Improvement Efforts

The Path to Excellence is based on the practices of extraordinary companies that make their operations excellent compared to those of ordinary companies. I have found that most ordinary companies' continuous improvement efforts place a lot of emphasis on the number of improvements, and much less on ensuring the improved processes are actually used everywhere applicable and maintained so that they can create value over the long term. Extraordinary companies do just the opposite. They put more importance on maintaining and standardizing the improvements than on the number of improvements they make. As a result, they rarely fail to standardize and maintain the improvement. Because of this, they get much more impact from every change they make. Because they make fewer changes, they are much more careful about the improvements they select. They also never start an improvement project that they do not intend to maintain. One way they incorporate this emphasis on maintaining and standardizing improvements is by adopting the Triple 100° Sustainable Change Speed Limit: "Only Improve as fast as you can maintain the gain."

This Triple 100° Sustainable Gain Speed Limit is a remedy to one of the major causes of many improvements not being maintained. One of the primary reasons for the failure to maintain the improvements is that as soon as the improvement is demonstrated in one area, the company almost immediately diverts its improvement resources to the next improvement. As a result, the previous improvement is not maintained over the long term.

The best practice is to keep your company's resources and focus on the current improvement until it becomes the established norm. I have found this generally takes between 1 to 3 months. The old saying "21 days a habit makes" is not true for many improvements.

A good way to see when your company has a process that is fully used and maintained is to ask the following McClaskey® $1,000 Bet question of managers or employees involved in the process: "Would you bet $1,000 of your money that the next time the process used, the steps of the process will be precisely followed exactly as written in the approved process?"

If you get a yes to the first question, then ask the second question: "Will you bet that the process is used everywhere and every time applicable?" When the answer is yes to both questions, it indicates the improved process is standardized and maintained. Remember, part of the continuous improvement process takes the verified improvement through the Design and Maintain Processes to 100% and Standardizing Processes elements to set up maintaining the improvement. The Triple 100° Sustainable Gain Speed Limit does not mean you wait until all processes are working at 100% before starting your next improvement project. It does say to be cautious about starting the next improvement project if it means you are taking resources away from maintaining processes at 100% execution. When you do not sustain improvements and keep processes at 100%, you have mostly wasted the effort that went into making the improvement. You only make sustainable improvements that benefit the company when the gains are maintained. Suppose one of your metrics for operations is the percentage of processes maintained at 100% operation, and that measure shows deterioration. In that case, it indicates that adequate resources are not being dedicated to maintaining the gain.

The Transformative Power of the Improvement Mindset

At its core, continuous improvement is about a mindset, a way of looking at the world. It's about rejecting the notion of 'good enough' and always striving for 'better.' It's about understanding that there is always a better way; we just need to find it.

When truly embedded into an organization's DNA, this mindset is transformative. It turns every employee into an innovator and every process into an opportunity for enhancement. It creates a self-reinforcing cycle of learning, growth, and adaptation. However, this only systematically and sustainably improves the organization when there is a disciplined process for learning; if the change is an improvement, incorporate it into approved procedures and standardize it so it is used everywhere applicable and maintained. The systematic improvement process provides a disciplined approach to evaluating an improvement idea, testing it, and, if verified, incorporating it into the approved procedures so it can be standardized, used at all applicable locations, and maintained.

The Chinese philosopher Lao Tzu stated, "The journey of a thousand miles begins with a single step." Continuous improvement is about taking that step, day after day, always moving forward, always striving for better. The systematic and sustainable improvement process verifies whether the change is an improvement, incorporates the improvement into the approved procedures, and standardizes it for use everywhere applicable.

From Theory to Practice: Implementing Continuous Improvement

1. **Secure Leadership Buy-In:** Ensure that continuous systematic and sustainable improvement is a cultural norm and a clear strategic priority championed by the highest levels of leadership.

2. **Establish Clear Metrics:** Define key performance indicators (KPIs) that will be used to measure progress and identify areas for improvement. These measures can also verify whether improved processes lead to better results.

3. **Train and Empower Employees:** Invest in training programs that equip employees with the skills and knowledge to drive continuous improvement in their daily work.

4. **Comply with the Triple 100˚ Sustainable Gain Speed Limit:** Only improve as fast as you can maintain the gains.

5. **Use Data-based Systematic Improvement Processes:** Adopt structured approaches like PDCA, Lean, Six Sigma, and/ or SimpleEXCELLENCE˚ Improvement Process to guide improvement efforts.

6. **Authorize Improvements and Don't Allow Unauthorized Changes:** The improvement process uses authorized pilots for improvement and not uncontrolled experimenting and process changes. Only verified improvements are incorporated into new or revised processes.

7. **Celebrate Successes:** Regularly recognize and reward successful improvements and maintain the gain, no matter how small, to reinforce the importance of continuous enhancement.

8. **Standardize and Sustain:** Ensure that improvements are integrated into standardized processes, are used everywhere applicable, are standardized, and are maintained over time.

9. **Continuously Reassess:** Regularly review performance data and adjust improvement priorities as needed. Review the

organization's improvement processes, ability to standardize and maintain the gain, policies, results, culture, and support systems to determine what can be done to improve the overall organization's ability to achieve improved results through continuous improvement.

The Key Practices and Policies Related to Continuous Improvement

- Reject the notion of "good enough" and always strive for 'better.'

- Engrain in policy and practice the Triple 100° Sustainable Gain Speed Limit: Only improve as fast as you can maintain the gains.

- Regularly schedule processes to be systematically reviewed and improved at a rate consistent with the Triple 100° Sustainable Gain Speed Limit.

- Improve processes by using a data-based, systematic improvement process. The systematic improvement process should include: stating the problem as a gap; conducting root cause analysis; proposing a solution that addresses the root cause; piloting to determine whether the proposed solution effectively addresses the root cause and resolves the problem; and taking appropriate steps to maintain the gain.

- Pilot changes to be sure they deliver the desired result under various on-the-job conditions, are improvements that are worth the cost, are reasonably efficient, and the process is designed and written for 100%.

- Prioritize the improvements to processes that will most significantly impact your KCRs.

- Every employee, at every level, should feel encouraged and empowered to identify and suggest enhancements.

- Foster an environment where authorized piloting of promising improvements is encouraged, failures are seen as opportunities for growth, and where best practices are eagerly shared and adopted.

- Have enforced policies that limit employees from making unauthorized changes to processes. Experimenting with possible improvement ideas should be conducted only when authorized, so learning from these experiments can be maximized and risks minimized.

- Improvements should be based on best practices from within and outside your organization.

Your Role in the Excellence Journey

As leaders, embrace the power of incremental enhancement and breakthrough improvement. Empower your employees to improve. Build a culture that prizes learning, adaptation, and progress. Require all changes to use the organization's continuous improvement process, which authorizes the changes, provides a systematic process to determine whether the change is an improvement, and, if it is, whether it is worth the cost of change, incorporates the improvements into the appropriate procedures, and standardizes and sustains the change everywhere applicable.

To the individual contributors: Look at your work with a critical eye. Question the status quo. Propose ideas, no matter how small. Your efforts, compounded over time, can transform your organization." Welcome new or revised processes and put in the extra effort to make them work. Change always requires some extra effort.

Continuous improvement is not a destination, but a journey. It's a commitment to being better tomorrow than you are today. It's a recognition that there's always room for growth, an opportunity to learn, and a chance to evolve.

Embrace this mindset, and you'll unlock a world of potential. You'll build an organization that doesn't just adapt to change but creates it. You'll foster a culture of excellence, innovation, and unrelenting progress.

In the race for excellence, there is no finish line. The only true competition is with the version of yourself from yesterday. Embrace continuous improvement, and you'll ensure that you're always leading the pack.

Call to Action

1. Establish a process where all processes in your company are systematically improved over a specific period of time.

2. Select a systematic improvement process to be used by your company and have it approved as the official or preferred improvement process to be used.

3. Select a few processes to systematically improve over the next month using the systematic improvement process you selected.

4. Systematically review all processes over time and, based on the review, make the desired improvements.

Key Takeaways for Chapter 12: Improve Processes

1. Processes need to be systematically improved to ensure they are current and contain the best-known practices.

2. The best practices should be obtained from inside and outside the company and incorporated into the process using your systematic improvement process.

3. After process improvements are determined and verified, the improvement enters the Design and Document for 100% element. In this element, the improvements are designed into the overall process and maintained by being documented

in the correct procedure. The documented, improved, and approved process is then standardized using the Standardized Processes element for use everywhere appropriate.

The Next Pillar

With a robust, continuous improvement culture in place, your organization will be well-positioned not just to weather the storms of change, but to harness them. It is not enough to have the best-known processes designed for 100%. To achieve organizational greatness, you must also engage and empower your most valuable asset: your employees. The processes must be followed to have an impact. The processes must be improved, or they will no longer be the best-known processes.

We have now completed three of the four pillars. In the next pillar, People Excellence, we'll explore how to build a culture of excellence where every employee is motivated and set up for 100% success every day. In the People Excellence pillar, I will show you the proven process used by role-model companies to create an organization where every employee chooses to precisely perform the steps of 100% designed and standardized processes and, as a result, produce products and services that are 100% to the company's brand requirements. Get ready to take your excellence journey to the next level.

PILLAR 4

PEOPLE EXCELLENCE

"Nothing of significance was ever achieved by an individual acting alone. Look below the surface and you will find that all seemingly solo acts are really team efforts."

John C. Maxwell

Introduction to Pillar 4: People Excellence

In the relentless pursuit of operational excellence, organizations often focus on perfecting processes, implementing cutting-edge technologies, or optimizing resource allocation. While these elements are undoubtedly crucial, there's a fundamental aspect that can make or break even the most well-designed system: human performance. Throughout this book, we've explored various facets of operational excellence. Now, we turn our attention to a critical pillar that binds all these concepts together and brings them to life through the actions of every individual in your organization: People Excellence.

The result of the entire people excellence pillar is that all products and services delivered are 100% to the brand requirements, every time. When every customer's KCRs are met every time, the customer is delighted, tells their friends, and because they know their KCRs will be met every time, they return. They know you will not disappoint them.

The primary purpose of the first three pillars of the Path to Excellence is that they are necessary conditions for establishing people excellence. If you have not fully achieved the first three pillars, you are unlikely to fully achieve the human performance component of people excellence. That does not mean you have to implement the four pillars in order. You can work on any aspect of any pillar, and it makes your organization better. But to get to 100%, you need all 4 pillars fully implemented.

Having discussed Think Excellence. Focus Excellence, and Process Excellence, we now turn our attention to the most vital asset of any organization – its people. This section of the book will guide you through the transformation from ordinary to extraordinary operations by mastering the art of People Excellence. We have found that the People Excellence pillar is the one that gets the most interest among the many leaders and managers we have trained and consulted with.

People Excellence is achieved when every individual in your organization is enabled and chooses to precisely perform each step of the approved process, every time, even when no supervisor is present, and they 100% comply with your Conditions of Employment. It's about creating a culture where excellence isn't just expected; it's ingrained in your organization's DNA.

At the heart of this concept is a fundamental shift in management thinking. As we always emphasize, "You don't manage people. You manage people's on-the-job behavior." This distinction is crucial as we explore the nine elements of People Excellence. Each element has its own chapter.

Throughout this section, I'll challenge you with thought-provoking questions. For instance, what percentage of your team can perform their job 100% correctly when set up for success? Since most companies answer this question with a high percentage (95% or higher), this pillar establishes conditions that ensure employees are set up for 100% success. When this happens, your current employees will choose to perform the job 100% right.

I will also delve into the concept of "gray" in management, a critical and pervasive obstacle to achieving People Excellence. As we have previously discussed, gray is defined as anything that can reasonably be interpreted in more than one way. Gray cannot be managed, so you have to design it out. Your company created the gray and thus your company can remove the gray. Gray can come from many sources, including:

What is written.

- What is said.
- If your actions are not consistent with your words (Do what you say.)
- Inconsistent accountability that can come from many sources, like seeing and ignoring actions that are not consistent with the approved process.
- Understanding and eliminating gray areas is essential for creating an environment of clarity and consistency. This is crucial for achieving People Excellence.

The ultimate goal of People Excellence is to create a win-win-win situation where all three major operations stakeholders – customers, employees, and the organization – are all delighted:

- **The customer** is delighted because they receive the organization's products, services, and customer experience 100% to the organization's brand requirements, 100% of the time, under 100% of the conditions.
- **The employee** is delighted because they are engaged in their work, feel valued and essential, are set up for 100% success, and feel respected.

- **The organization** is delighted because they experience high customer satisfaction leading to repeat business and positive recommendations, high levels of employee retention and productivity, increased revenue and profitability, as well as low levels of avoidable costs due to errors and employee turnover.

As one of the three principles of the Path to Excellence, everything we do to achieve People Excellence will be done in a win-win manner among the three primary stakeholders: customers, employees, and the company. All three win without trade-offs. All the other stakeholders, like shareholders and the community, will win when the three primary stakeholders do.

As we embark on this exploration of People Excellence, prepare to transform your approach to managing your team. You'll learn how to create an environment where excellence isn't just expected, it's the natural state of being. I'll guide you through each of the nine elements, showing you how to implement them in your organization to achieve extraordinary results.

This journey will challenge your preconceptions about management and employee engagement. It will provide you with practical tools and insights, based on proven practices, to elevate your team's performance to unprecedented levels. By the end of this section, you'll have a comprehensive understanding of how to cultivate People Excellence in your organization, setting the stage for sustainable success and a truly extraordinary workplace.

Welcome to the transformative world of People Excellence – where ordinary becomes extraordinary and the full potential of your organization and its people is unlocked. Where you set your people up for 100% success. Let's begin this crucial and final pillar of your journey to organizational excellence.

CHAPTER 13

SELECTING THE RIGHT EMPLOYEES FOR OPERATIONS

"If we get the right people on the bus, the right people in the right seats, and the wrong people off the bus, then we'll figure out how to take it someplace great."

Jim Collins, author, "Good to Great"

Selecting the Right Operations Employees is a Critical First Step

Selecting the right employees is crucial to pursuing extraordinary operations. Imagine investing in cutting-edge technology and state-of-the-art equipment only to be let down by an inexperienced driver. Your employees are the ones steering your organization towards success or failure.

Consider this eye-opening statistic from the Society for Human Resource Management (SHRM): a bad hire can cost up to five times their annual salary. A single hiring misstep could cost your company tens of thousands, if not hundreds of thousands, of dollars. Now, envision the transformative impact of consistently making stellar hiring decisions. How would your organization advance if every new hire were not merely competent but exceptional?

Getting the Right People on the Bus: The Key to Excellence

In the realm of extraordinary operations, the importance of selecting the right employees cannot be overstated. Hiring is a vast topic. To give you something you can use, I am going to cover only one specific and important aspect of hiring in this chapter: selecting the right hourly team members for operations jobs.

It's important to note that the material applies only to hiring hourly team members in operations. For most businesses, this is the most common type of hiring. The advice provided may or may not be relevant to other types of hires. For example, I know that some of the advice I will share in this chapter does not apply and should not be used when hiring knowledge workers, managers, or professionals.

Hourly operations jobs require a set of characteristics, primarily centered around two critical factors:

- The ability to precisely perform the steps of the processes, 100% of the time, even when no supervisor is watching.
- 100% complying with the Conditions of Employment, which include reliably showing up for work as scheduled.

These might seem like basic requirements, but they're surprisingly unusual and incredibly valuable. Throughout this chapter, we'll explore how to identify and hire individuals who excel in these two crucial areas.

Hiring by the Numbers

The significance of effective hiring practices extends far beyond anecdotal evidence; compelling data substantiates it. This data reveals how crucial role-model hiring practices are for businesses.

A study conducted by The Boston Consulting Group found that companies that prioritize strong recruiting practices experienced 3.5

times the revenue growth and 2 times the profit margin. These findings emphasize the tangible rewards of investing in superior hiring strategies.

Gallup research shows that highly engaged teams are 21% more profitable, underscoring the indispensable role of hiring in building such teams. These results serve as a testament to the significant impact of selecting the right candidates.

The consequences of poor hiring decisions are equally striking. According to the Harvard Business Review, a staggering 80% of employee turnover can be attributed to bad hires, emphasizing the high cost of selection mistakes.

Fortunately, there's a solution. The Society for Human Resource Management (SHRM) reported that comprehensive hiring practices can reduce turnover by up to 50%. This statistic underscores the potential of implementing robust selection strategies, ultimately protecting your bottom line.

These insights collectively underscore a critical point: hiring is not merely an HR function; it's a fundamental business process with direct, substantial implications for your organization's success. An organization's operations, HR, and other functions must be involved in designing and executing the best employee selection process.

Key Principles for Hiring

1. When it comes to hiring for extraordinary operations, there are key principles and best practices you should follow:
2. Know the objective of the hiring process for operations employees.
3. Hire employees who will:
   a. Precisely follow the process, every time
   b. 100% comply with the organization's Conditions of Employment

    c.   Reliably show up for work as scheduled

4.   Hire First for Character Attributes:

    a.   Look for candidates who, based on their character and past performance, will be predicted to precisely follow processes every time, 100% comply with the Conditions of Employment, and will reliably show up for work as scheduled.

    b.   The idea of value-based employee selection isn't new. Companies known for their excellent employees, like Pal's Sudden Service, the Ritz-Carlton, Walt Disney Company, have long used values-based hiring to ensure they bring in individuals who not only have the necessary skills but also possess character that aligns with the two critical factors, as well as the company's culture and values. This approach recognizes a fundamental truth: while you can teach skills, you can't easily change someone's core values

5.   Screen for Cultural Fit and Trainability:

    a.   Skills can be taught, but values and character are ingrained. Hire for fit, not just skills. A candidate who aligns with your organization's culture is more likely to thrive, excel, enjoy their job, and stay long-term.

6.   Don't Hire a Known Poor Fit:

    a.   Do not compromise on quality. Extraordinary organizations have found it is better to work short-handed than to hire a candidate who is determined to be a poor fit during the interview process. A bad hire can damage your organization's reputation, culture, and work ethic, while being short-staffed is a temporary stress that doesn't compromise your standards.

7.   Act Quickly and Decisively:

    a.   Swift hiring processes give you the best chance of securing top talent. When you find the right candidate, don't hesitate. Make the hiring offer as fast as possible.

8. There is No Perfect Hiring Process:

    a. At this time, no hiring process will not sometimes hire an employee who is a bad fit. You want to use the hiring process that best works for your organization. You can determine whether the hiring process is precisely followed by the percentages of great hires and poor hires. To have a great hiring process, you need to keep improving it by learning from experience and studying the role-model practices of others. It also means there will be hiring mistakes that will have to be corrected.

    b. Netflix's Culture Deck: Netflix emphasizes hiring only "stunning colleagues" through its famous culture deck. It implements the "keeper test," in which managers are repeatedly asked whether they would fight to keep an employee. If not, that person is let go with a generous severance package. This approach ensures that every team member is not just competent but exceptional — a key factor in maintaining extraordinary operations.

9. Learn and Adapt:

    a. Your hiring process should evolve based on experience. Continuously learn and refine your approach based on your hires' performance. When you have hired an employee who did not work out, find the root cause by asking "why" three to five times. Adjust your hiring process based on the causes you have identified. Also, determine the root cause when you have hired a terrific employee, and use that information to enhance your hiring process and training.

10. The best-known predictor of future performance is relevant past performance:

    a. Use a Multi-faceted Approach. Consider the candidate's past (resume, employment history, and education), present (interview performance, appearance, and personality), and potential future performance (attitude assessments).

By following these principles and best practices, you can build a strong team that will drive extraordinary operations in your organization.

From Principles to Actions

To put these principles into action, follow these detailed steps:

Step 1: Define Key Attributes:

Focus on hiring employees you predict will precisely follow processes every time, 100% comply with the Conditions of Employment, and reliably show up for work when scheduled.

Step 2: Define the Must-Haves:

Identify and list your non-negotiable characteristics or conditions (the "must-haves") for your operations employees.

For example, some organizations consider being available at least one weekend day and having reliable transportation a "must-have" to be employed. Identify your must-haves.

Step 3: Develop a Comprehensive Selection Process:

a.   Review Resumes and Job Histories:

Look for employment gaps and advancement patterns. Gaps may signal unreported work history, while advancement can indicate strong performance in prior roles. Ask open-ended follow-up questions to evaluate these two key factors (precisely follow the steps of the process every time, comply with Conditions of Employment, which include showing up when scheduled), and inform candidates that you may contact their previous employers for verification. Mentioning the possibility of reaching out to previous employers often encourages candidates to give more honest answers about their past employment.

b. Conduct Structured Interviews:

Focus on questions that evaluate the two key factors. Be clear about "must-have" characteristics and ask open-ended questions to gain deeper insights into candidates. Make sure that by the end of the interview, you know whether they meet all the "must-haves."

c. Use Values-Based Assessments:

Create test questions to assess cultural fit, and have applicants complete an "Attitude Survey" to compare their responses to those of top employees. Some organizations can provide questionnaires to help determine whether a candidate possesses qualities similar to those of employees who are a good cultural fit for your organization.

d. Conduct Work Simulations:

Observe how candidates handle everyday tasks and challenges. Whenever possible during the selection process, have candidates perform activities to demonstrate their core job skills. For example, use dexterity tests for jobs that require high dexterity, or have candidates read a children's story to assess their friendliness and communication skills for potential customer-contact roles.

Following these steps ensures a thorough, effective hiring process that supports extraordinary operations.

Step 4: Train Your Interviewers:

Ensure that everyone involved in the hiring process understands the two critical hiring factors and how to use the process to effectively assess candidates against them. Proper training will enable your interviewers to use the hiring process effectively, make informed decisions, and maintain consistency throughout the process.

Step 5: Implement a Rapid Decision-Making Process:

Establish clear decision-making criteria and rate candidates on their predicted ability to precisely follow process steps and to 100% comply with the conditions of employment, including reliably showing up for work on time. Identify any red flags or "must-haves" that would disqualify a candidate. Remember, candidates who do not meet all the "must-haves" should not be considered for the position. When you find a suitable candidate, make the offer quickly, as outstanding candidates won't stay on the job market for long.

Once a "red flag", like a must-have condition, has been confirmed about a candidate, that person is off the selection list unless you feel the "red flag" condition can be resolved before employment.

Step 6: Utilize Technology:

Consider using hiring software that includes assessment tools, automated workflows, and Artificial Intelligence (AI). This can help streamline your process and provide valuable data-driven insights. For instance, you can use technology such as a computer-based phone interview scheduling tool created by an AI application assessment. Leverage technology to expedite decision-making, enabling you to quickly make an offer when you decide to hire a candidate. Technology can also help you drop candidates who do not meet your criteria from further consideration, thus saving time and effort.

Incorporating these strategies into your hiring process will enhance efficiency, maintain high standards, and secure top talent for your organization.

Step 7: Drop Poor Fits:

Implement a trial period of employment for all new hires and carefully evaluate their performance during this time. Recognize that no hiring process is perfect; even the best selection methods can lead to hiring mistakes. When it becomes evident that a hiring mistake has been made, address the situation promptly.

Usually, this involves letting the employee go, since continuing with a poor hire only makes the mistake more costly. Be respectful during this process, acknowledge the mistake, and express hope that the individual will find a better-suited job. This benefits the company, its customers, and the new hire, as people cannot take pride in jobs they cannot perform well. Give them a chance to find a position where they can feel pride in their work.

Jeff Offutt, President of CNW Management, has operated numerous restaurants and systematically tested various hiring practices to identify which are most effective. He discovered that quickly recognizing and dismissing poor hires as soon as they are identified is essential. His managers can usually spot poor hires for operational roles within the first seven shifts, sometimes even during the first or second shift. To motivate managers to find and address poor fits, Offutt implemented a policy requiring new hires to be evaluated during each of their first seven shifts. After each shift, managers ask themselves: "Knowing what I know now, would I rehire this person?" If the answer is "no," they must immediately terminate the employee. You wouldn't do that if the issues were fixable by the manager. However, poor hires are often unfixable or require disproportionate effort and expense to correct because the person hired isn't the right fit for the role. Of course, you should continue to question whether the new hire is a poor fit after the first seven shifts and take action if it is. Catching and fixing hiring mistakes early is vital to creating a positive work culture and achieving people excellence.

By quickly addressing poor hiring decisions, your organization can uphold high standards and maintain an engaged, productive workforce with high retention who take pride in their work.

Step 8: Continuously Improve:

Routinely assess new hires' performance against your established hiring criteria. Use these insights to improve your hiring process over time. Examine successful hires and poor fits, seeking to understand the hiring-related factors contributing to each outcome. Ask "why" three to five times to find the root cause. Use the identified root cause to improve your process.

Identify the steps or questions in the selection process that helped you recognize and hire top talent. In future interviews, focus more on those key questions and indicators, as well as any missed opportunities or additional questions that could have prevented poor hiring decisions. Use your experience to improve and refine your selection process.

Organizations that excel at employee selection succeed by systematically learning from their recruitment experiences and adapting their processes accordingly. This commitment to continuous improvement allows you to make more successful hiring decisions and build a strong, high-performing team for extraordinary operations.

Why It's Better to Hire Well

Some may argue that a rigorous hiring process is too time-consuming and costly, especially for small businesses or in tight labor markets. They might suggest that filling positions quickly and providing on-the-job training is a more practical approach.

This short-term view can cause long-term problems. The expense of a poor hire goes beyond just salary. It includes lost productivity, lower team morale, the loss of some of your top employees, potential customer dissatisfaction, and the time and resources spent replacing employees who don't fit well.

Furthermore, while working short-staffed can be difficult, it's often better than lowering your standards. A dedicated, aligned team usually performs better than a larger one with mismatched members. Remember: Never sacrifice quality; it's wiser to work short-handed until you find the right person who fits your organization's values and standards.

The Compounding Effect of Good Hires

The true power of an effective, high-performing hiring process isn't just about avoiding bad hires; it's about creating a ripple effect of excellence. When you consistently bring the right people on board, you're not just filling roles; you're cultivating a culture of excellence. Each excellent hire elevates the entire team, motivating others to perform at their best.

Over time, this creates a virtuous cycle, or self-reinforcing loop, where your company attracts more of the right candidates and employees. Top performers attract other top performers. As your reputation as an employer that hires mainly top-performing employees, or what are sometimes called "A Players," improves, it becomes easier to recruit exceptional talent. It is often said that "A Players" do not like to play with "B Players." B Players are less skilled than A Players in their roles. Having A Players in a company fosters a culture that A Players want to join. By hiring candidates who consistently follow the process and fully comply with the Conditions of Employment, which include reliably showing up for work when scheduled, your operations become more effective and efficient, your customers are more satisfied, and your business becomes more profitable.

This is the often-overlooked secret of exceptional companies. Their success isn't just about products, processes, or even strategies. It's about people. Get the people right, and everything else tends to fall into place.

Raise the Bar on Hiring

It's time to elevate your hiring process from a necessary evil to a strategic advantage. Start by critically assessing your current approach. Are you selecting employees who consistently follow the process, comply with the Conditions of Employment, and reliably show up for work? Are you compromising your standards in the face of pressures to fill positions?

Challenge yourself and your team to elevate standards. Create a selection process that emphasizes the significance of this vital business function. Dedicate the time and resources needed to do it correctly. Part of the process involves not only identifying best practices but also learning from experience about when you make the right hire and when you don't. Adjusting your selection process based on these lessons is essential for developing an excellent hiring approach.

Exercise: For each of your recent hires, evaluate them on the two critical factors you are hiring for:

- Do they precisely follow the steps of the process, every time?
- Do they 100% comply with all the Conditions of Employment, including reliably showing up for work when scheduled (consider both absenteeism and tardiness)?

Use this evaluation to refine your hiring process. Where are you succeeding? Where do you need to improve?

Action Steps:

1. **Review your job descriptions.** Do they clearly emphasize the importance of precisely following processes and complying with the Conditions of Employment, which includes reliable attendance?

2. **Create a list of interview questions specifically aimed at assessing these two key factors.**

3. **Implement a trial period and evaluate if you will continue their employment** as part of your hiring process to observe candidates' on-the-job behavior. In most cases, assess the new hire within the first three weeks to determine: "Would you rehire the individual?" If not, acknowledge a mistake was made and respectfully dismiss the person. Do not tolerate the problem once it is clear that the new employee is a poor fit.

4. **Create a selection scorecard to evaluate candidates based on the two critical factors and other key attributes of your organization.** This will help you quickly determine during the selection process whether you want to extend an offer to a candidate. Speed in making a job offer is critical, but it must also be a high-quality decision. Be able to quickly gather all your facts and make a decision based on the data.

5. **Establish a system for regularly evaluating new hires' performance** based on the two critical factors and other criteria. Use the trial employment period to confirm the right hiring decision, and if necessary, make corrections.

Find Game Changers and Play to Win

Your employees are critical to your organization's success. Choose wisely, for in their hands lies the future of your organization. Remember, the right people are not just your greatest asset; they are your company's destiny.

Call to Action

1. Integrate the best practices from this chapter into your hiring process to improve it. Key sections to review for these practices include: Key Principles for Hiring, From Principles to Actions, and Action Steps.

2. Test the improvements in your hiring process to see which ones add value. Standardize the improvements that help you hire employees who are good fits. Ensure everyone uses these enhancements as part of your standardized hiring process.

Key Takeaways for Chapter 13: Selecting the Right Employees for Operations

Note: This chapter and the key takeaways are solely focused on hiring hourly operations employees. Some of the best practices being shared may apply to other types of hires, but others may not.

1. Know what you are hiring for. Hire individuals who have the necessary skills and character that align with the two critical factors when hiring operations employees, and ensure they also fit with the company's culture and values.

   a. The ability to precisely follow the processes 100% of the time, even when no supervisor is watching.

   b. 100% compliance with the Conditions of Employment, including dependability in showing up for work as scheduled.

2. Hire first for fit. Factors that can help you determine fit with your organization's culture include: values, character, and past performance.

3. A candidate who matches your organization's culture is more likely to succeed, perform well, enjoy their work, participate actively, be productive, and remain with the company long-term.

4. The most reliable predictor of future performance is relevant past performance. Use a comprehensive approach to evaluate this. Consider the candidate's past (resume, employment history, education), present (interview performance, appearance, personality), and potential future performance (attitude assessments).

5. Avoid Hiring Known Poor Fits: It is better to be short-handed than to hire a candidate who you already know is a poor fit during the interview process. A bad hire can harm your organization's reputation, culture, and work ethic, while being short-staffed is a temporary issue that does not compromise your standards.

6. Act Quickly and Decisively: Fast hiring processes increase your chances of securing top talent.

7. When you have a bad fit, fire the employee: There is no perfect hiring process. Even the best hiring methods can sometimes result in hiring a poor fit. Correct the mistake as soon as it is identified. The earlier in employment this happens, the better. Make it a priority during the first few weeks to determine if the employee is or isn't a good fit for the job you hired them for.

8. Learn and Adapt: Your hiring process should evolve based on experience. Continuously learn and refine your selection process based on the performance of your hires. When you have hired an employee who did not work out, find the root cause by asking "why" three to five times. Adjust your hiring process

based on the causes you have identified. Also, determine the root cause when you have hired a terrific employee, and use that information to enhance your hiring process and ensure the most effective hiring criteria are a key selection factor. Share what is being learned with all of your hiring managers.

The Next Chapter

In the next chapter, you will take another step toward building a culture of extraordinary operations, starting with a new hire joining your team. I will introduce an important part of the onboarding process: how to clearly communicate your company's Conditions of Employment to your new employee and secure their full commitment to complying with these conditions 100% of the time.

CHAPTER 14

THE POWER OF CRYSTAL-CLEAR CONDITIONS OF EMPLOYMENT

"The most common reason that employees fail to meet performance expectations is that those expectations were never made clear in the first place.

Paul L. Marciano, author, a leading authority on employee engagement and respect in the workplace

An Important Component of Setting Employees Up for Success is Clearly Conveying the Conditions of Employment

Let me share a hypothetical story that illustrates the transformative power of clear expectations.

With high hopes, Sarah, a talented marketing professional, joined a mid-sized tech company. Her first day was a whirlwind of introductions, paperwork, and a brief overview of company policies. She left feeling excited but somewhat overwhelmed and unsure of what was expected of her.

Fast-forward three months, and Sarah is struggling. She works long hours but feels she isn't meeting her manager's expectations. The problem is that she isn't sure what those expectations are. The vague "do your best" and "work hard" mantras aren't effective. Frustrated and stressed, Sarah considers leaving.

Compare this to Tom's experience at a company that had clear employment conditions. On his first day, Tom met with his manager to review the company's Conditions of Employment. These weren't vague statements but specific, actionable expectations written in clear, behavioral language.

For each condition, Tom's manager explained what was expected and why it was necessary. Tom had the chance to ask questions, making sure he fully understood each point. At the end of the discussion, Tom signed a document agreeing to follow these conditions 100% of the time he was working.

The result? After three months, Tom was thriving. He knew exactly what was expected of him and how his work contributed to the company's success. His productivity was high, and he felt a strong sense of belonging and purpose.

These two stories highlight two fundamental truths. Setting clear expectations is key to employee success and satisfaction, and these expectations must be communicated, understood, and committed to from the very start of employment.

The Triple 100® Approach to Conditions of Employment

This element of People Excellence will set expectations that strongly influence how successful the employee will be in delivering your products and services 100% to the brand requirements and in effectively contributing to meeting the KCRs. I have labelled this set of requirements ' Conditions of Employment'.

Conditions of Employment: The specific requirements and expectations that an employee must meet to keep their position within an organization. Conditions of employment are "must do's". These are not suggestions or optional. Anything that is optional is not a condition of employment. If it is not going to be consistently and uniformly enforced, it is not a condition of employment. Either you follow the conditions of employment, or you don't work here. Some common conditions of employment include: being on time for work, wearing the proper uniform, not bringing guns to work, not bringing illegal drugs to work, not being under the influence of drugs or alcohol, and not stealing money.

Now, let's dive into how you can implement this powerful approach in your organization. I call it the Triple 100° Approach to Conditions of Employment:

Step 1: 100% Written in Black and White.

Step 2: 100% Communicated for Understanding.

Step 3: 100% Committed to by the Employee.

Step 1: 100% Written in Black and White

The first step is to have your conditions of employment written down in clear, unambiguous terms. Here are the key practices:

- **Concise:** Your conditions of employment should be as brief as possible but still include all the "must-dos" if you are going to work here. Usually, you write the subject of each condition of employment, for example, "On Time," and then put bullet points under it explaining the details. The list of subjects will usually fit on one to two pages.

- **List One Strike Conditions of Employment:** Identify which employment conditions would result in immediate termination even if committed only once. These are typically behaviors the company has "zero tolerance" for. A typical example is theft of cash. Separate these on the checklist because they are highlighted during the employment conditions discussion.

- **Black and White:** Eliminate all "gray areas" that could be reasonably interpreted in more than one way. If three people observe the employee, they will all reach the same conclusion whether the employee met or did not meet a specific employment condition. If there is a split decision, then the condition of employment is too ambiguous and requires further clarification.

- **Behavioral Terms:** Describe each condition of employment in employee-based behaviors, not abstract concepts. This is a behavior you can observe.

- **Create a Conditions of Employment Checklist:** There are two versions of the checklist. The manager version has each condition of employment listed with the details of that condition listed under each condition. Usually, that is 3-5 bullets. The employee version of the checklist lists only the conditions of employment, without details. Usually, the employee version is one to two pages long and provides a place for the employee to either initial or check off each condition as they agree that they understood and agreed to 100% compliance while they are working.

Instead of saying, "Be punctual," you might say, "Clock in no earlier than 5 minutes before your scheduled start time and no later than 5 minutes after your scheduled start time. If you clock in 6 minutes or later past your scheduled start time, you are late." This is an example of taking the "gray" out because it is concise, in clear black-and-white terms, and behaviorally based.

Step 2: 100% Communicated for Understanding

Having a well-written document is only the first step. The next crucial phase is communication:

- **In-Person:** Conditions of employment should be communicated face-to-face, ideally on the first day of employment. A best practice is for the employee's manager to do the communication through a one-on-one meeting. Hand the employee the one-page checklist containing the subjects of the condition of employment at the beginning of the conversation.

- **Clarity:** Make sure each point is explained clearly, with examples if needed. Encourage the employee to ask any questions for clarification.

- **Consistency:** Implement a uniform process to make sure all employees get the same information, no matter which manager delivers it.

- **Confirmation:** Use questions and observations to verify understanding. Research shows that much of the meaning in face-to-face communication comes from nonverbal cues. The manager observes these cues to detect if the employee has questions, concerns, or needs clarification.

- **You need to discuss the conditions of employment with all employees**, not just new employees. With existing employees, it is usually done in groups over a two to three-week period.

Step 3: 100% Commitment by the Employee

The final critical step, which is very important, is securing the employee's commitment to fully comply with the clearly understood conditions of employment.

- **Verbal and Written Agreement to Commitment:** Have the employee, both verbally and with some written confirmation, like a checkmark or initial on the printed conditions of employment, confirm they understand and commit to 100% comply with each condition 100% of the time they are on the job or clocked in for their shift. The employee and the manager who communicated at the end of the meeting will sign the document after all conditions have been agreed to, indicating their commitment to 100% compliance with all conditions of employment at all times while on the job. Research, reported by Dr. Robert Cialdini in his book Influence, has shown that agreements that are both verbal and written result in a much higher level of compliance.

- **Applies to 100% of the Work Time:** Make it clear that this commitment applies every second they are clocked in for their shift. This is not a most of the time commitment but an every time commitment to the Conditions of Employment.

- **Sets Up 100% Compliance and Accountability:** This understood, no gray, clear, oral, written, and signed commitment to the conditions of employment leads to higher compliance and sets up the conditions for the next People Excellence element, Accountability, which helps maintain 100% compliance.

Case Study: Pal's Conditions of Employment Discussion

Let me tell you, from my experience, what it was like for me to experience Pal's Conditions of Employment discussion. When I worked for Pal's as a crew member, one of the first things that happened on my first day of employment was a thorough orientation that included the conditions of employment. The manager used specific behavioral terms to describe each condition. For example, instead of saying, "Arrive on time," he said, "Clock in at your scheduled time; you will be considered late if you clock in one minute past your scheduled start time, and you cannot clock in before your scheduled time. If your scheduled time is 8:00 am, you cannot clock in before 8:00 am., If you clock in after 8:01 am, you will be late and receive a strike. This clarity was behaviorally based actions with the gray removed, so it left no room for interpretation.

The discussion of each condition went beyond my understanding of the expected behavior. During the conversation, the manager would make sure I understood the why behind each condition. That helped me realize these weren't arbitrary rules. Each one was explicitly tied to KCRs, giving them purpose and weight. The manager would also explain that "If your uniform isn't correct, you'll be asked to fix it before clocking in. This may result in a tardy if it makes you late, which counts as one strike." The discussion for each condition ends with making sure I fully understood the condition of employment and having me confirm that I was committing to comply with each condition, 100% of the time I was working, by checking the line on the orientation form for that condition. When the manager had gone through all the conditions of employment and I had agreed that I understood them and committed to 100% compliance, we both signed the bottom of the orientation form.

As a result of this condition of employment discussion, I not only understood these rules, but I also understood the why behind the conditions of employment, and I was committed to 100% compliance with them every second I was on the clock.

Implementing the Triple 100® Conditions of Employment

Now that we understand the principles, let's look at how to put them into practice:

1. **Draft Your Conditions of Employment:** List all the "musts" for staying employed in the job category you are developing conditions for. Typical examples include being punctual and maintaining proper on-the-job behavior, such as not stealing company property or hitting other employees. Begin by gathering key stakeholders to define what behaviors are "musts" for all employees, regardless of their role. Then add any conditions specific to the relevant job category to the list. Some conditions will apply to specific job categories and may differ for others. For example, employees paid by the hour

might have different conditions related to being on time than salaried employees or managers. Conversely, some conditions, like prohibiting sexual harassment, apply to all employees.

2. **List the Subject of the Condition of Employment and the Detail:** Usually, you write the subject of each condition of employment, for example, "On Time," and then bullet points under it explaining the details. For example, just having a condition of employment that states "be on time" would be gray if it did not have clarifying details to go with it. Details might include: cannot clock in early; if clocked in 5 min. past your scheduled time you are late; you have to be in proper uniform to clock in.

3. **Design out Gray**: Ensure each condition is written in clear, black and white, behavioral terms. You need to remove the "gray." Gray is where what you wrote as the condition of employment could be reasonably interpreted in more than one way. If you say, come to work in the proper uniform, that could be interpreted in many different ways. Add the necessary details until it can be interpreted only one way. For instance, you must wear the shirt provided, but it must be clean and pressed so that there are no visible wrinkles and a crease shows in the shirt sleeve. Test it by giving the actual wording to three or more knowledgeable people, along with some examples of the behavior, and see if all agree whether the behavior did or did not meet the condition of employment. Keep refining until all key conditions of employment are listed and stated in black and white terms. You also want to eliminate all unneeded detail and communicate it in the most intuitive way possible. Sometimes pictures are better than words.

4. **Create a Commitment Document:** Develop a checklist form where employees can confirm their understanding and full commitment to comply with each condition.

5. **Train Your Managers**: Ensure all managers understand the importance of this process and how to conduct the Conditions of Employment conversation effectively.

6. **Schedule the Conversation**: For new employees, make this a priority on their first day. For existing employees, it is usually scheduled in convenient groups over a 2- to 3-week period after the Conditions of Employment list is created or substantially updated. The process for existing employees is the same as for new employees. For conditions of employment to be effective, all new and existing employees must agree and commit to the same list of conditions of employment.

7. **Conduct the Discussion**: Go through each condition, explaining the details and their importance, and answering any questions. Do this until the employee understands the condition and agrees to it.

8. **Gain Commitment**: Have the employee verbally and in writing, by checking or initialing that condition on the checklist, commit to complying 100% of the time they are on the job with each condition. Once all employment conditions are agreed upon, the employee and the manager who conducted the discussion will sign the document. The document will be filed in the employee's personnel file. Employees who cannot commit to 100% compliance with all the conditions of employment generally can't work for you. If a condition of employment is not truly a condition of employment, it should be removed from the list.

9. **Follow-up:** Consistently reinforce these conditions and address any deviations promptly using your accountability process. Some conditions of employment will result in termination if violated even once.

Overcoming Objections

You might encounter some resistance when implementing this approach, particularly from existing employees who were hired before you precisely stated your conditions of employment. Let's address common objections:

1. **Managers feel: "We don't have time for this."** This investment pays for itself many times over. Consider the time and cost of replacing an employee who leaves because of misunderstood expectations. The entire idea is to set the employee up for 100% success from Day 1, so conditions of employment are not violated.

2. **Everyone feels: "These are just common sense."** What's common sense to you may not be to others, especially across different backgrounds and generations. Clarity leaves no room for misunderstanding.

3. **Managers feel: "We'll scare people off."** Clear expectations make employees feel valued and set up for success. It's the lack of clarity that drives people away and leads to misunderstandings that result in inappropriate behavior.

4. **Long-term employees often think, "I have been working here for years. I don't need this discussion."** However, all employees need to understand and commit to 100% compliance with the current version of the conditions of employment. Every current employee has some level of commitment to certain employment conditions, but it's usually not true that they are aware of or have committed to the entire current set of conditions. In our experience, most companies did not have a written list of conditions of employment before starting the Path for Excellence. When these conditions are documented, they are discussed, modified, clarified, and refined. This process often represents the first detailed, holistic, in-depth review of employment conditions, leading to modifications—even if 75%

of the conditions remain the same. Frequently, it is the first time they've been clearly written down and ambiguities removed. Officially listing, reviewing, and approving these conditions as a written company policy helps ensure stricter enforcement. In the past, enforcement was often inconsistent. It's crucial to get everyone—both new and existing employees—committed to the same, current conditions of employment to achieve 100% compliance and accountability. These points clearly illustrate why it's essential to hold a discussion about conditions of employment with all employees, so everyone commits to the current requirements. Additionally, new employees often look to more experienced staff for guidance on how to act. We want experienced employees to serve as good role models, which is more likely if everyone is aligned and committed to the same conditions of employment.

The Payoff: A Foundation for Excellence

Implementing this approach does more than increase compliance with the conditions of employment. It sets the stage for a culture of excellence by being a key part of setting the employee up for 100% success with your company:

- Employees feel respected and valued.
- Significantly improves compliance.
- Managers have a transparent and fair basis for coaching, feedback, and consistently applying the accountability process.
- Misunderstandings and conflicts are reduced.
- Significantly reduces workplace drama due to people getting different consequences for the same infraction of the conditions of employment.
- Productivity increases as everyone knows what is expected.
- A foundation of trust is established from day one.

Your employees should understand what's expected of them as clearly as they know their compensation. Anything less sets them—and your organization—up for failure.

Are you ready to transform your onboarding process and set your employees up for 100% success? The choice is yours. Will you continue with vague, assumed expectations, which set employees up to fail, or will you commit to crystal-clear communication and unwavering employee commitment?

Clarity isn't just nice to have in organizational excellence—it's essential.

Call to Action

I challenge you to take these steps:

1. Draft or refine your Conditions of Employment using the Implementation Steps described earlier in this chapter.
2. Assess how well your current employees understand and commit to your current Conditions of Employment.
3. Implement the Conditions of Employment with all current employees and, moving forward, with each new hire. This can be done over 1-4 weeks. Usually, you do this on the first day for new hires. Implementing the Conditions of Employment means having a clear, unambiguous list; communicating it so every employee understands each condition; ensuring every employee commits to complying with 100% of the Conditions of Employment during their work time; obtaining their acceptance both verbally and in writing; and strictly enforcing compliance. One effective way to communicate and secure full compliance is for the manager to have a one-on-one discussion with the employee, focused solely on this.
4. Use your accountability system, the next element in People Excellence, to enforce 100% compliance with your Conditions of Employment.

5. Monitor the results, looking at metrics like rate of compliance with conditions of employment based on audits and personal observations, early (first 1 to 6 months) turnover rates, non-compliance rates, and employee satisfaction scores. Use this information to provide coaching and feedback to your managers and to adjust your conditions of employment process, including adjustments to the conditions of employment.

Key Takeaways for Chapter 14: The Power of Crystal-Clear Conditions of Employment.

Implement your conditions of employment with all of your existing employees and in the future with all of your new hires. Usually, you do this on the first day for new hires. Some companies do it as part of the hiring process. To be most effective, your conditions of employment need to be:

- 100% Written in Black and White: The first step is to have your conditions of employment written down in clear, unambiguous terms. Remove the gray.

- 100% Communicated for Understanding: Ensure the employee clearly understands each condition of employment before committing to it.

- 100% Committed to by the Employee: Verbal and Written Agreement.

The Next Chapter

Now that you've clearly communicated the conditions of employment and gained your employees' commitment, what's next? In our next chapter, we'll explore how to handle situations when these conditions of employment aren't met. I will discuss accountability, including best practices for progressive discipline, ensuring that your commitment to excellence is maintained long after the first day on the job.

CHAPTER 15

ACCOUNTABILITY: PROGRESSIVE DISCIPLINE

"Executives owe it to the organization and to their fellow workers not to tolerate nonperforming individuals ..."

Peter Drucker

Great Employees Stay Because Rules are Fairly and Reliably Enforced

As we explore the Accountability element, you'll recognize familiar names and understand how the accountability practices at Pal's Sudden Service and the Ritz-Carlton support and improve every other aspect of their operations. By showing examples of these companies across many elements of the Path to Excellence, I have demonstrated that each element is implemented within the same company.

Furthermore, I will present new examples and case studies, such as the U.S. Navy's nuclear submarine program, that demonstrate how these principles of accountability are applied across various industries and settings. By the end of this chapter, you will understand how to establish a top-tier accountability system in your organization.

Let's revisit Pal's Sudden Service, where my six-week immersion challenged everything I thought I knew about managing people.

The Accountability Dilemma

Before we dive back into the Pal's story, let's address the elephant in the room. Many managers I've worked with feel trapped between two unpalatable choices:

1. Strictly enforce rules and suffer high turnover.
2. Be lenient on rule enforcement, tolerate violations, and as a result have inconsistent quality and lots of problems, but will have average turnover.

This dilemma has plagued managers for generations. But what if I told you there's a third option? What if you could enforce rules 100% of the time, achieve near 100% compliance, do so in a way that keeps your best employees, and have lower turnover than most of your competitors? This isn't a fairytale – it's the reality at companies that implement extraordinary operations.

The Science of Accountability

Pal's has more rules, more strictly enforced than those of any service company I know, and their employees stay twice as long as the employees of their competitors. Their system of accountability has this impact because of how it is designed, implemented, and integrated with the system of setting clear, committed to Conditions of Employment.

The Conditions of Employment and Accountability elements work together to foster the desired behavior, increasing engagement and decreasing turnover. First, conditions of employment are clearly explained and committed to. How Pal's does this was described in Chapter 14, The Power of Crystal-Clear Conditions of Employment. Then, accountability enforces clearly prescribed violations of the conditions of employment. Let's break down why this system works so effectively:

1. **Clear Communication**: During orientation, the conditions of employment are explained in unambiguous, black-and-white terms. All the gray is designed out, leaving no room for misinterpretation. Each employee understands and commits to complying with the conditions of employment

2. **Consistent 100% Enforcement of the Accountability System:** Rules apply equally to everyone, from the newest hire to the most experienced employee. There are no favorites and no exceptions. If you violate a rule, the manager will immediately enforce the consequence dictated by accountability every time. The rules are enforced promptly at 100%, providing immediacy and certainty that employees can rely on, which promotes the right behaviors.

   Turnover Rates: Regardless of the industry's average rate, Pal's, with its strict enforcement, maintains a turnover rate that is less than half, sometimes only one-third, of that average while offering comparable pay. Having clear, consistently enforced rules fosters an engaged, stable, reliable, and experienced workforce.

3. **Progressive Nature of Discipline**: The "4 strikes" progressive discipline is the primary accountability and discipline approach. This approach allows employees to learn from mistakes. It's not about punishment; it's about providing consequences that shape behavior over time. You want employees who 100% comply with the rules and continue to work for you. You do not want to trade off between those two factors; you want both at the same time.

   Metaphor: The Sculptor. Think of this approach like a sculptor chiseling a block of marble. Each strike of the chisel is a step towards revealing the masterpiece within. Similarly, each strike in the progressive discipline system helps refine and shape the employee's behavior towards excellence.

4. **Purpose-Driven Rules**: Every rule is tied directly to Pal's mission of "delight customers in a way that creates loyalty" and to one or more of their KCRs, which are quality, hospitality, accuracy, speed, cleanliness, and value. This linkage and alignment give meaning and purpose to even the most minor compliance details.

    Example: Uniform Policy. Pal's strict uniform policy isn't just about appearances. It's an important factor in how customers perceive cleanliness. Clean, proper uniforms help prevent contamination and project a professional image that reassures customers about the quality and safety of their food.

5. **Fairness in Action**: The system is perceived as fair because it is applied consistently to all employees. Employees know exactly what to expect and that they won't be singled out. Exceptions are rare and granted in accordance with an exception policy.

6. **One-Strike Rules**: Pal's employs a one-strike policy for the most serious infractions. The one-strike offenses were explained during the Conditions of Employment discussion. This policy clearly shows a zero-tolerance stance for certain behaviors, emphasizing the importance of all rules. A one-strike rule means that if you violate it even once, you are fired. During the 20 years I was with Pal's, there were a few violations of these rules, which is exactly the behavior you want to see.

The Pal's Way: 4 Strikes and You're Out

Their "4 strikes and you're out" progressive discipline system is at the heart of Pal's approach. It sounds harsh at first glance, but its implementation is nothing short of brilliant.

What amazed me most wasn't the strictness of the rules, but how rarely they needed to be enforced. Because the conditions of employment were clearly described, committed to during orientation, and enforced every time, nearly everyone followed them meticulously. The clarity of the conditions of employment and the certainty of accountability created an environment where everyone knew what to do, leading to full compliance even when managers weren't watching.

Metaphor: The Traffic Light System

Think of Pal's accountability system as a highly efficient traffic light system. In a well-designed traffic system:

- Rules are clear and visible (green means go, red means stop).
- Enforcement is consistent (running a red light always has consequences), particularly if a camera system records 100% of the rule violations and results in a traffic ticket 100% of the time.
- The purpose is understood (traffic lights exist for safety and efficiency).
- Everyone follows the rules, even when no police are present. If someone does violate the rules, there are consequences.

Just as a sound traffic system allows for the smooth flow of vehicles without constant intervention, Pal's system creates a smooth-running operation where everyone knows and follows the rules, thanks to a clearly defined, 100% enforced accountability system. As a result, customers are delighted because the products and services are always 100% delivered to the brand requirements.

Let us dig a little deeper into the scientific basis for why Pal's and the accountability system that is part of the Path for Excellence work so well. Research and practice by the American psychologist Dr. Aubrey Daniels, as outlined in his book Performance Management, state that consequences that are both immediate and certain have the greatest impact on driving behaviors. Dr. Daniels coined the phrase Performance Management to describe a scientific approach to managing behavior rooted in the field of behavior analysis, which is a way of getting people to do what you want them to do and like it. My good friend Russell Justice, who Aubrey Daniels personally mentored, taught both me and Pal's how to apply performance management effectively in the workplace. Thom Crosby, Pal's CEO, has applied performance management principles at Pal's to such an extent that Pal's is a role-model for their application in the workplace.

Pal's Accountability Process

Once the conditions of employment are understood and committed to, Pal's managers implement the accountability system whenever there is a violation.

1. When a violation of the conditions of employment is identified, the accountability system is applied consistently and fairly. A strike is issued every time. Most violations are handled through the progressive discipline part of the accountability system. This means the consequence depends on which of the four strikes is applied. If it is a one-strike violation, then the individual is fired immediately.

2. Because the consequences are immediate and certain for violations of agreed-to conditions of employment, and the entire process is conducted with respect, accountability drives the desired behavior to occur in a way that also reduces turnover.

The Counterintuitive Results

Now, you might be thinking, "Sure, but at what cost? Surely, this level of strictness must be driving away good employees." This is where Pal's story gets truly fascinating.

Remember that Pal's has half the average turnover rate of its competitors. It's not despite the many strictly enforced rules—it's because of them. When rules are clearly communicated, committed to, and the accountability system is designed and enforced consistently and fairly, they lead to higher employee engagement, increased productivity, and lower turnover.

Let me share a personal story about how the conditions of employment discussion and the accountability system affected my behavior when I worked for Pal's as a crew member. I had very few violations of any rules during my entire time working as a crew member for Pal's. Even more importantly, there were very few violations among my fellow crew members. The system was designed to be reasonable, rational, and logical, encouraging compliance with the rules, which is why almost everyone, including myself, followed them nearly every time. The key takeaway is that having rules that are clearly understood and committed to, combined with an accountability system that enforces those rules 100% in an immediate, certain, and fair manner, creates an environment where employees choose to do the correct behavior every time. This also fosters feelings of respect and encourages staff to stay. My fellow crew members and I experienced increased job satisfaction because the rules we understood and were committed to were fairly and consistently enforced.

During my 6 weeks as a Pal's crew member, I observed firsthand the effects of their orientation, accountability, and other people excellence systems.

- Employees moved confidently, assured of their understanding of expectations.

- Managers spent less time policing minor infractions because there were very few of them and more time coaching and developing their team.

- Customers raved about the consistency of their experience, which delighted them every time. Pal's customers say: "You don't have to look in the bag because you know it is right."

- The workplace atmosphere was built on mutual respect and a shared commitment to excellence. It's what I imagine it would be like to be on an Olympic team. You felt like you were part of a team of superstars, all working together to delight every customer.

Statistics that Defy Conventional Wisdom

Let's look at some numbers that challenge our assumptions about strict accountability chasing good employees away from their employers:

1. **Turnover**: Pal's turnover has been half the industry average or lower for over a decade while paying comparable compensation

2. **Productivity**: Pal's drive-through speed is 18 seconds per car, which is about four times faster than the industry average of 1 to 2 minutes. Yes, I did say 400% faster.

3. **Quality:** Pal's has one complaint per 3500 orders, while the industry average is one mistake in every 15 orders. If we assume a long-standing statistic that customers generally only complain about 1 in 10 mistakes they experience, Pal's accuracy rate will be more than 10 times better than the industry average.

4. **Customer Satisfaction**: Pal's overall satisfaction or delight is the benchmark when compared by third parties to their competition.

These statistics paint a clear picture: strict accountability, when implemented correctly as part of a larger system of setting employees up for 100% success, drives performance to extraordinary levels. What a track record! Pal's is 1,000% more accurate year after year while going four times faster. Training to 100% and strict discipline to precisely follow the process are key to making this possible. Pal's carries out accountability in a way that promotes employee retention and lowers turnover.

Case Study: The Ritz-Carlton's $2,000 Employee Empowerment and Lateral Service

We've talked about the Ritz-Carlton's dedication to service excellence before, but its approach to accountability adds a new layer to its success story. Their policy famously lets any employee spend up to $2,000 per incident to resolve a guest issue without managerial approval.

This policy may appear risky, but it is supported by thorough training and clear accountability. Employees are expected to record every instance of this empowerment and explain their reasoning for it. The result? Employees feel trusted and empowered, guests receive exceptional service, and the policy is rarely misused.

Another example of the Ritz-Carlton culture is the concept of lateral service. Each employee is empowered to act when they see a guest has a need or problem: "You should break away from your regular duties to address and resolve the issue." After resolving the issue, they return to their regular duties. Ritz-Carlton employees are authorized to do this without needing supervisor approval. That makes every Ritz-Carlton employee part of a role-model customer-delight system.

These examples show that when high accountability is paired with training and clear empowerment with a mission and customer focus, the results are transformative. It's not just about enforcing rules, but about creating a culture where employees are empowered and accountable for delivering excellence.

Case Study: The Nuclear Navy

To understand the power of strict accountability, let's look at a high-stakes environment: the U.S. Navy's nuclear submarine program. Admiral Hyman Rickover, known as the "Father of the Nuclear Navy," implemented a system of unwavering accountability that resulted in over 60 years of safe nuclear reactor operation without a single radiological incident.

The Navy's nuclear program enforces strict zero-tolerance policies, similar to Pal's. No matter how minor, there is strong accountability for following every procedure precisely. The result? An unmatched safety record in the energy sector and a culture of excellence.

If such strict accountability can work in environments as diverse as fast food and nuclear submarines, it can work for you and your business, too.

Implementing Your Own Accountability System

Here's a step-by-step guide you can use to bring this level of accountability to your own organization:

1. **Design Your Progressive Discipline System**:
    - Determine the number of "strikes" or "violations" before termination (3-5 is typical).
    - Set a timeframe for violations to expire. A progressive discipline process requires a certain number of violations before termination. It also needs a policy stating that, after a set number of months, violations no longer count. For example, if you have a 4-violation policy that fires an employee after the fourth violation, it wouldn't make sense to fire someone who received three violations in the first 2 months and then gets a fourth violation a year later. The process should specify that if four violations happen within, say, 3 months, the employee is terminated. You choose the number of violations and the time period after which violations expire to make your progressive discipline process effective.

2. **Pilot the Program**:
    - Start with a small department or team.
    - Gather feedback from the people piloting the process and refine the process based on the input.

3. **Train Your Managers:** Make sure they understand and can use the accountability process across a wide range of situations. This includes practicing applying the process in everyday scenarios. It's crucial to stress the importance of consistency and fairness in how the accountability process is used.

   - Teach them how to communicate conditions of employment clearly and enforce rules fairly and consistently according to the accountability process, with only rare exceptions. Even the rare exceptions should be in accordance with a carefully developed policy of when to grant exceptions.

   - Practice scenarios to prepare for various situations, including unusual situations.

4. **Implement Company-Wide:**

   - Roll out the system. Since the accountability system will apply to all employees, not just new ones, part of the rollout will include a strong communication plan for current employees, similar to the one for new employees, usually delivered in groups. A good plan is to launch the conditions of employment, covered in the previous chapter, and the accountability process at the same time.

   - Provide resources for employees to understand the new system.

5. **Coach and Audit:**

   - Check regularly to ensure that all managers follow the accountability process 100% of the time. Provide positive coaching and feedback when precisely following the accountability process with no unauthorized exceptions, and corrective coaching when not.

   - I have found that it is very common for general managers to be inconsistent in enforcing the consequences outlined in the accountability system. This inconsistency in executing the accountability system leads to many justified employee issues and problems. Employees often interpret these inconsistencies as evidence that managers are unfair, playing favorites, or selectively targeting certain employees.

6. **Evaluate and Improve**:

   - Collect data on the system's effectiveness.

   - Be open to refinement based on real-world applications.

An effective accountability system, like the one described, is key to creating a work environment where employees are highly engaged, choose desired behaviors that align with exceptional performance, and experience low turnover. Accountability systems work best when the consequences are both immediate and certain.

Sample: Progressive Discipline Framework

Here's a sample framework of a 4-violation progressive discipline you might use as a starting point:

1. **First Violation:** Verbal warning and retraining on the specific rule violated.

2. **Second Violation**: Written warning and meeting with a supervisor to discuss an improvement plan.

3. **Third Violation**: Final written warning and one-day suspension.

4. **Fourth Violation**: Termination.

You determine the appropriate consequence for each violation that will best motivate compliance with the rules. Remember, violations clear after a certain period (usually 2-6 months) to allow for improvement and learning, but don't expire too quickly, so each violation still influences future behavior.

Overcoming Resistance

As you implement this system, you'll likely face some pushback. Here are some common objections and how to address them:

1. **"One size doesn't fit all"**: While flexibility is important, a standardized system actually ensures fairness and reduces confusion. The consequence must depend on the accountability system, not on which manager sees the infraction.

2. **"Strict accountability will drive employees away"**: When implemented correctly, this kind of policy actually does the opposite. Employees appreciate clear conditions of employment and fair treatment, preferring to work at a company where rules are consistently enforced. As a result, operations run more smoothly. Think about a system you deal with every day—driving your car. Don't you get frustrated when someone breaks rules that could affect safety, and no one does anything about it? This is how many employees feel when rules aren't enforced or, worse, when enforcement is inconsistent or unfair.

3. **"Every situation is unique"**: While contexts may differ, maintaining a consistent framework ensures fairness and minimizes perceptions of favoritism. Most policies include provisions for exceptions to address truly unique cases, but such exceptions must be used with good judgment about when to apply them. Exceptions can obscure the true nature of the rule and affect how fairness is perceived.

Metaphor: The Sports Rulebook

Think of your conditions of employment and accountability system as the rulebook for a sport. In basketball, for instance:

- Rules are clear, understood, and apply to all players equally.

- Referees enforce rules consistently, regardless of a player's star status.
- Players understand that rules exist to make the game fair, safe, and enjoyable.
- Despite strict rules, players love the game and strive to excel within its framework.

Just as clear rules and consistent enforcement make sports more enjoyable, fair, and competitive, a well-designed system of conditions of employment and accountability will make work more engaging and productive.

The Bigger Picture: The Secret to High Levels of Performance Creates Employee Self-Accountability

What I learned at Pal's goes beyond just a set of rules or a disciplinary system. Pal's creates an environment where excellence is the norm, not the exception. It's about showing employees you respect them enough to be clear about your conditions of employment and to be consistent in your enforcement.

With responsibility and empowerment come boundaries and accountability. Setting people up for 100% success in operations requires clearly defined rules that are consistently, predictably, and fairly enforced. When done right, this approach doesn't constrain employees—it empowers them to consistently deliver the desired behaviors and results.

When we discuss accountability, we often think of managers holding employees responsible for their actions. The key to maintaining high, consistent performance is for the company to foster a work environment and culture in which each employee serves as their own enforcer, responsible for following the rules and job conditions of employment. This concept is known as self-accountability. Managers implementing a well-designed and fully executed system of conditions of employment and accountability are essential to creating a workplace environment that motivates employees to be responsible for their behavior, adhere to the rules, and fulfill their job duties, even when a manager is not present. The main goal of managers enforcing rules is to create a work environment where employees can choose their behaviors so they consistently meet employment conditions and accurately follow the steps of their tasks.

Case Study: Toyota's Andon Cord

Toyota's famous Andon Cord System exemplifies how high accountability can coexist with employee empowerment. If a quality issue is detected, any worker on the production line can pull the Andon Cord to stop the entire line.

This system places immense responsibility on each worker, making them accountable for the quality of the entire production. However, it also empowers them to take decisive action. The result? Toyota's reputation for quality is legendary. Their cars are among the best-selling because they are among the most reliable, and their employees report high job satisfaction.

Key Accountability Principles that Drive Excellence

As we reach the end of our exploration into progressive discipline and accountability, I'm reminded of a profound truth: this chapter is not just about rules and consequences; it's about laying the foundation for a culture of excellence that permeates every aspect of your organization.

Throughout this chapter, we've uncovered key principles that drive extraordinary operations:

1. **Accountability Through Progressive Discipline**: We've seen how a clear, consistently applied, and fair progressive discipline system can shape and reinforce desired behaviors.

2. **Consistency and Fairness**: We've learned the importance of uniform rule enforcement in maintaining trust, fairness, and clarity across the organization.

3. **Employee Self-Accountability:** We've seen that a well-designed accountability system consistently and fairly executed by managers creates a work environment in which each employee is personally accountable for their behavior being consistent with the rules and their job responsibilities.

4. **Accountability Promotes Excellence, Employee Engagement, and Retention:** The common belief that enforcing rules causes higher turnover is not always true. Properly designed and executed accountability systems drive the desired behaviors and increase employee retention and engagement, and reduce turnover. I need to note here that improperly designed and executed accountability systems can have the opposite impact. I have seen that happen too many times.

5. **Positive and Corrective Coaching**: We've explored the delicate balance of corrective feedback and positive reinforcement in encouraging continuous improvement.

6. **Engagement and Empowerment**: We've discovered how setting clear conditions of employment and providing necessary support and boundaries can drive responsible empowerment and higher levels of employee engagement.

These principles don't exist in isolation. They're part of a larger journey towards operational excellence—a journey that encompasses thinking, focusing, processing, and people.

Think about Toyota's Andon Cord System. Toyota didn't just create a quality control mechanism by empowering every worker to stop the production line if they spot a quality issue. They cultivated a mindset and culture where excellence is the standard, not the exception. They focused their entire operation on delivering perfect quality. They designed a process that works 100% of the time. They invested in their people, trusting them with immense responsibility.

As we close this chapter, I challenge you to rethink your approach to accountability. Audit your current practices. Are they clear? Consistent? Fair? With few exceptions? If not, use the principles and steps we've discussed to design a progressive discipline system that drives excellence, fosters engagement, and reduces turnover.

Remember, the goal isn't punishment—it's creating a high-performance culture where every employee understands and is personally committed to the standards of excellence. They know it is their responsibility to ensure that their behavior is consistent with the conditions of employment and precisely perform the steps of the processes.

In the world of extraordinary operations, accountability isn't a punishment – it's one of the key foundations upon which excellence is built, one clear, enforced, expectation at a time.

The path to operational excellence is challenging, but with the right accountability system, you're setting the stage for extraordinary success. Are you prepared to transform your organization?

Call to Action

1. Determine if your company has a progressive discipline system. If not, create one using the guidance outlined in this chapter and get it adopted as the company system.

2. Audit your company's progressive discipline system on a monthly or quarterly basis to determine if it is: fully complied with and effective at getting the desired behaviors.

3. Use the audit results to improve your accountability system. This includes improving the level at which managers comply with carrying out the accountability system.

4. Fully integrate your accountability system with your manager assessments, training, and coaching systems.

Key Takeaways for Chapter 15: Accountability: Progressive Discipline

1. Create an accountability system that encourages employees to fully commit to following the process steps exactly each time, adhere strictly to employment conditions, and follow other rules. Implement this system to help your organization achieve a lower turnover rate than your competitors.

2. A well-designed accountability system offers consequences that are immediate, certain, consistently enforced, and have few exceptions. Effective accountability systems are essential for creating a work environment where employees willingly follow desired behaviors, such as precisely following process steps and meeting 100% of the conditions of employment.

3. The accountability system is a critical element in creating a work environment that makes each employee self-accountable for choosing the desired behaviors for their job responsibilities. High levels of sustained performance require a company to create a work environment and culture where each employee is the primary enforcer and accountable for their own behavior.

4. The common belief that enforcing rules causes higher turnover is not necessarily true. It certainly can be true. But you can design and execute accountability systems that drive the desired behaviors while also decreasing turnover and increasing employee retention, engagement, and productivity. The key is to have a well-designed system for setting clear conditions of employment and holding employees consistently accountable for 100% compliance with those conditions.

The Next Chapter

We have made a good start on the People Excellence pillar. In the next chapter, we will explore how to create an effective, efficient training process that enables your employees to precisely perform each step of your approved processes every time. Even the best accountability system can only do so much if your team lacks the skills to succeed.

CHAPTER 16

TRAINING TO 100%

"We train our employees to do it 100% right, 100% of the time, at 100% volume. Someone asked, What if you spend all that time and money and they leave? I say, what if you don't and they stay."

Pal Barger, Founder of Pal's Sudden Service

There is no Route to 100% Execution that Does not Go Through Training to 100%

Imagine you're about to undergo brain surgery. As you're wheeled into the operating room, you hear the surgeon say to a colleague, "Don't worry, I'm 75% trained on this procedure." How would you feel? Terrified? Ready to leap off the gurney and run?

Now, let me ask you a question that might make you equally uncomfortable: How well-trained are your employees?

The Training Gap: A Silent Killer of Excellence

As part of our Achieving World-Class Results class, I've posed this question to over 10,000 service organization executives, directors, and managers:

"After your company's formal training is completed, what percentage of the steps does the person who was just trained actually perform them precisely as stated in the approved process?"

The results are not only startling—they're alarming. The average? Just 75%. Based on our surveys of over 10,000 leaders, about 90% of the answers fall between 65% and 85%. Let that sink in for a moment. The very people responsible for delivering your brand promise and creating the experiences that keep customers coming back are trained in a way that leaves them doing only 75% of the steps correctly after formal training. This means many products and services won't fully meet brand standards, leading to dissatisfied customers and less repeat business.

Even more shocking? Almost all these leaders know their company isn't training anywhere near 100%, and it seems okay—no alarm bells. No panic. Just a resigned acceptance of mediocrity that delivers incorrect products and services.

Ask yourself: Would you be okay with you if your recently repaired car's brakes did not work some of the time? Of course not. So why do we accept it in our businesses, where the stakes are just as high?

A great place to start is with training to 100%. You can't expect your employees to deliver your products and services at 100% to your brand standard, 100% of the time, unless you train them to 100%. It's not just a nice-to-have—it's a business necessity.

Metro Bank

Consider the story of Metro Bank in the UK. When they implemented 100% training across their customer service processes, they saw complaint rates drop by 56% within 6 months. Their customer satisfaction scores soared, and they were voted "Best for Service" among all UK banks. That's the power of commitment to 100% training.

The 100% Training Revolution: My Pal's Epiphany

To truly understand the transformative power of 100% training, let me take you on a journey—my personal odyssey at Pal's Sudden Service.

As you remember, I stepped out of my consultant shoes and into the role of a frontline crew member making french fries at Pal's for six weeks, so I could personally experience, from an employee's perspective, the impact of Pal's implementation of the People Excellence elements. What I experienced there didn't just change my perspective on training; it revolutionized my understanding of how to effectively implement operational excellence.

From day one, I was immersed in a culture where 100% excellence wasn't just encouraged—it was expected, cultivated, and celebrated. It began with their orientation, where I committed to comply with the conditions of employment for every second I was on the clock. But the real eye-opener came when I was tasked with learning to make their famous "frenchie fries."

Picture this: I'm standing at the fry station, having never made a french fry in my life, when my trainer—a certified trainer as well as the store manager—looks me in the eye and asks, "Can I have your commitment that you will never let a bag of french fries leave this station that doesn't 100% meet all of our standards?"

I was surprised. I didn't yet know how to make fries, and they were asking for this level of commitment? That question set the tone for everything that came after. It wasn't just about making fries; it was about maintaining a 100% standard of excellence in everything I did.

What followed was a masterclass in what I now call "Triple 100° Training":

1. 100% precisely follow the process steps and thus produce the products and services 100% to the brand requirements.
2. 100% of the time.
3. Under 100% of the conditions.

The training method was one-on-one, conducted on the production line, making fries for sale to customers (provided they met all product requirements). Pal's used a method called one-on-one training, which consisted of the following four components for each process step for which I was trained: "Tell, Show, Practice, Evaluate":

1. **Tell:** The trainer told me about a step and explained why it contributed to meeting the product's 100% compliance with the brand requirements.
2. **Show:** Then, the trainer would show me how to do the step, and as he did the step, I watched the details of how it was executed.
3. **Practice:** Next, I practiced the step while the trainer carefully watched me so he could coach for improvements or confirm I was doing each detail of the step precisely right.
4. **Evaluate:** Finally, the trainer assessed my performance on the step and provided immediate feedback. The trainer would correct even minor deviations. I repeated the practice and evaluation steps until I performed each step exactly as written in the approved process. When I got it right, I received positive feedback like "great" or "perfect."

Once I was competent and confident in doing the step 100% correctly, the trainer would start training me on the next step, using the 4-step one-on-one training process until all steps were mastered.

The training process started with the trainer doing all 20 steps of the french fry process. The trainer talked me through each step as he did that step. After watching the entire process, the trainer selected a step for me to perform and began the one-on-one training. For that step, the trainer would Tell me about the step and why it is important; then Show me how to do it as he did it so that I could watch; then I Practice the step; and the trainer would Evaluate and give feedback on my performance of that step.

I started by doing just one of the 20 steps while the trainer handled the other 19. Once I was trained on that step, I was responsible for it every time. When the trainer saw that I was both competent and confident in performing that step correctly every time, including all the details, he would then train me on the next step.

This meticulous, systematic one-on-one training process was repeated for each new step until I could perform all 20 steps flawlessly. I was now making French fries. The entire initial training took about 4-5 hours. But here's the key point that makes this training very cost-effective: once I reached the skill level where I could do all 20 steps exactly as written in the approved process, the trainer left me to work independently, checking in only occasionally. Responsibility for my training then shifted to the assistant manager on my shift. The assistant manager made sure I continued to perform all the steps correctly. The cost of training effectively ended when the trainer left, making this training approach 100% effective and highly efficient.

My training journey wasn't over. What I had achieved was just the first two 100s of the Triple 100˚ Training. I could do each step of the job 100% right, 100% of the time. The third 100%, being able to perform under 100% of the conditions, especially during the lunch rush, took several more weeks to master.

Throughout this process, I adhered to what I now consider the "Triple 100® Speed Limit for 100% Operations":

ONLY GO AS FAST AS YOU CAN DO EACH STEP 100% RIGHT

This isn't just a speed limit for trainees; it's a rule that every Pal's employee follows in every process, regardless of their experience level.

The result? After several weeks, I became certified in french fries, where I had the habit of performing each process step 100% right, 100% of the time, under 100% of the conditions, which included the lunch rush. Every bag of fries I produced met 100% of Pal's brand standards before it left the fry station. I am so sure of this, I would bet $1,000 of my own money that this was the case.

You might be thinking, "That's great for fast food, but my business is different." Stop right there. This isn't just about fries at Pal's—it's about a mindset and a commitment to excellence that can transform any business or industry. In this case, a commitment to training to 100%.

The Hidden Costs of Mediocre Training

Let's talk numbers. During our classes, we have asked thousands of service company managers about the impact of 75% training versus 100% training. The results are staggering:

For Customers:

- **75% Training:** Disappointed, not delighted; aggravated; more negative reviews, come back less often.
- **100% Training:** Delighted customers who come back more often and write positive reviews.

For Employees:

- **75% Training:** Frustrated; increased stress; set up to fail; robbed them of pride in their work; increased turnover and lowered productivity, product quality, and customer satisfaction.
- **100% Training:** Confident, engaged employees who take pride in their work and are more likely to stay with the company.

For the Company:

- **75% Training:** Reduced customer satisfaction; increased complaints; reduced revenue and repeat business; increased turnover; increased negative reviews; increased costs related to fixing errors.
- **100% Training:** Increased customer satisfaction, positive reviews, and repeat business; reduced employee turnover and increased engagement; increased revenue and reduced costs.

Here's where it gets even more interesting. In a survey of over 5,000 service organization leaders and managers, we asked:

"How much more revenue could your company make if 100% of your customers got your products, services, and customer experience 100% to your brand standards 100% of the time, and they knew they could count on it?"

Most answered they would earn 25% more revenue, with some responses exceeding 100%.

Let that sink in. By not training to 100%, you could be leaving 25% or more of your revenue on the table. Can you afford that in today's competitive landscape? You are also giving your competitors an opening to take some of your customers.

The 100% Training Mindset: Principles of Excellence

Now that we've seen the impact, let's dive into the key principles that make 100% training not just effective, but transformative:

1. **100% Training is an Investment, Not an Expense**: Pal Barger, the founder of Pal's, said it best when asked if he was concerned about training costs. His response: "What if you don't train them

and they stay?" Every dollar spent on comprehensive training pays dividends in improved performance, customer satisfaction, more repeat business, and employee retention. The cost to train to 100% can be close to the cost of training to much lower levels with an effective and efficient Training to 100% process, like the one I have outlined in this chapter, and taking into account the decreased training costs from lower turnover levels. When you add the benefits of as much as 25% more revenue and increased repeat business, 100% training is one of the best and least risky investments a company can make.

2. **100% Execution Demands 100% Training**: You cannot expect 100% performance if you're not willing to invest in 100% training. It's that simple.

3. **The Triple 100° Speed Limit for 100% Operations**: Only go as fast as you can get each step of the process 100% right. This principle ensures quality is never sacrificed for speed. This speed limit is not just during training but is universally applied to all operations processes.

4. **Personalized Pace**: One training speed doesn't work for all. Recognize that different individuals will reach 100% proficiency at different rates. The goal is competence and confidence, not speed. Of course, you will go as fast as the trainee can master the steps.

5. **Perfect Practice Makes Perfect**: The adage "practice makes perfect" is a lie. Practice doesn't make perfect; it makes it permanent. Only perfect practice makes perfect. Don't let trainees practice incorrectly. Correct as soon as you see even the slightest detail done incorrectly.

6. **Balanced Feedback:** Use both positive and corrective coaching during training. Reinforce what's done right while immediately correcting what's wrong. Do at least as much positive coaching as corrective coaching, while never passing up an opportunity

to correct a step that is not performed 100% in accordance with the approved process.

Overcoming the "We Can't Afford It" Myth

I can hear the objections now: "We can't afford to train people to 100%." Let's tackle this head-on.

First, consider Pal's Sudden Service. Even if their training cost per person were twice as high as their competitors (which it probably isn't), their annual training costs per person would be the same. Why? Because Pal's has half the employee turnover, so they train half as many people each year as their competitors.

Second, when you're short-staffed, it's tempting to cut corners on training. But this leads to a vicious cycle of errors, unsatisfied customers, rework, employee dissatisfaction, and ultimately, more turnover. Some companies have broken this cycle by temporarily scaling back operations to focus on training. While it might seem counterintuitive, it's often a necessary step to build a foundation for future growth. As we came out of the pandemic, I heard from many store owners that their stores with the best operations during COVID-19 recovered faster and more completely afterward than those with poorer operations.

When you look at the benefits-to-cost ratio for training at 100%, it usually offers an excellent return on investment. It could be one of the best investments you make in your business and your future competitiveness.

Remember, training to 100% isn't just about cost—it's about creating a sustainable, competitive advantage by consistently delivering your products and services 100% to the brand requirements, which will maximize customer loyalty, repeat business, and positive recommendations, all of which impact your revenue.

The 100% Training Roadmap: From Mediocrity to Excellence

Ready to transform your training process? Here's your roadmap to 100% training excellence:

1. **Perfect Your Processes**: Ensure your processes are designed for 100% execution. The Process Excellence section of the book explains how to do this in Chapters 10-12. You can't train to perfection if your processes are flawed.

2. **Design Training for 100%**: Create a training program that develops the skills and knowledge needed to perform each step of the approved process precisely to the approved process, every time, under 100% of the conditions. One-on-one training process, as described in this chapter, is a recommended way to do training for 100%.

3. **Develop Comprehensive Support Materials**: To support the execution of the one-on-one training, create trainer checklists, visual aids, flashcards, and testing materials.

4. **Pilot and Refine**: Test and refine your training program based on results.

5. **Train the Trainers**: Ensure your trainers are equipped and certified to deliver 100% training.

6. **Implement with Rigorous Follow-through**: Schedule training, ensure trainers follow the training process, and verify that trainees achieve 100% proficiency.

7. **Continuous Improvement**: Regularly evaluate and improve your training process.

I challenge you to take the first step towards 100% training in your organization today. Remember, 100% training means your employees have the skills, knowledge, and ability to perform each step of the approved process precisely as written, 100% of the time, under 100% of conditions.

Are you ready to revolutionize your business by leveraging training to 100%? Your organization's future may depend on it. The choice is yours: Will you settle for training to 75% or commit to excellence?

Remember, in the world of business, you're either growing or dying. There's no standing still. 100% training isn't just an option—it's your lifeline to a future of sustainable success.

The path to 100% begins now. You can create transformed processes, delighted customers, and motivated employees. All it requires is your dedication to excellence.

Are you in?

Call to Action: The 100% Training Challenge

Implement Training to 100%. Here is a path to implementing Training to 100% that has worked well as we coach and guide participants in our AWCR class and with our consulting clients to effectively implement Training to 100%:

1. Choose one critical process in your organization.
2. For the process you selected, evaluate and identify the percentage of times the process output currently meets all the requirements. Also, assess the percentage of steps performed exactly as written in your approved process.
3. Design the process you selected for 100%. Chapter 10: Design and Document Processes for 100% outlines a process for this.
4. Implement Training for 100% for this process within the next one to two weeks using the process outlined in this chapter.
5. After implementation, audit and calculate the percentage of times the process output fully meets the requirements. Audit and determine the percentage of steps that are currently performed exactly as written in your approved process. Compare these

results to the measures taken before starting the Training to 100%. Most companies see significant improvement. If not, continue working until very high percentages are achieved.

Once you see the results, and you will see them, expand process-by-process until all process training reaches 100%. Training to 100% is an essential part of achieving extraordinary operations for a process.

Key Takeaways for Chapter 16: Training to 100%

1. You cannot get your employees to deliver 100% unless you train them to 100%.

2. An investment in Training to 100% for your operations employees has a high rate of return. For a small incremental training cost, the company increases revenue because its products and services meet 100% of the brand requirements, 100% of the time, and it reduces costs by less turnover, rework, and waste, since employees are set up for 100% success.

3. After your company's formal training is completed, what percentage of the steps does the person who was just trained perform the steps precisely as written in the approved process? Audit and determine this before you start the Training to 100%. The average answer based on a survey of thousands of service organization managers and leaders is 75%. That is what you get with 75% training. With 100% training, your answer will be 100%.

4. Design your operations training so it gets to the Triple 100° Training level, where the employee being trained can:
   - 100% precisely perform the process steps, every time, and thus produce the products and services 100% to the brand requirements.
   - 100% of the time.
   - Under 100% of the conditions.

5. A standard training method, one-on-one training, can be designed to reach 100% proficiency. For each step, one-on-one training consists of four parts: the instructor explains the step, then the trainer demonstrates it to the trainee. The third part involves the trainer allowing the trainee to practice the step, and the fourth part is the trainer providing feedback. The Practice and Evaluate steps are repeated until the trainee can perform the step perfectly. When the trainee is both competent and confident that they can do the step correctly every time, the trainer moves on to the next step. Once a trainee masters a step, they continue performing it. As trainees practice, they improve their skills, enabling them to perform the steps correctly more quickly.

6. Comply with the Triple 100® Speed Limit for 100% Operations: Only go as fast as you can get each step of the process 100% right. This principle ensures quality is never sacrificed for speed. This speed limit is not just during training but is universally applied to performing all operations processes.

The Next Chapter

Training to 100% is a game-changer, but it must be maintained. In the next chapter, you'll learn how to implement "Coaching to 100%"— the essential follow-up to Training to 100% that helps sustain your training at the 100% level. This way, your investment continues to yield benefits long after the initial training is finished.

CHAPTER 17

COACHING TO 100%: THE CORNERSTONE OF SUSTAINED EXCELLENCE

"Use lots of positive reinforcement with your people. Don't take acceptable work for granted; thank people for it. Praise a person every time you see improvement."

John C. Maxwell

Coaching to 100% is Essential to Achieving and Maintaining 100% Operations

In the first four elements of people excellence: employee selection, commitment to conditions of employment, accountability, and training to 100%, we have set up the employee so they can precisely follow each step of the approved processes involved in their job, and are committed to 100% complying with the conditions of employment. However, just because a person can do something does not mean they will do it every time they are supposed to. This is where the remaining five elements of people excellence come into play. It is the employees' behavior that makes the products and services. It is their behavior that is the focus of people excellence. These remaining five elements set up the work environment so an employee will choose to precisely perform the steps every time and 100% comply with the conditions of employment.

The first and probably the most used is Coaching to 100%.

The Power of Precision: Where Excellence Becomes Second Nature

Imagine stepping into a workplace where excellence isn't just an aspiration—it's the very air you breathe. Picture an environment where every employee, from the newest recruit to the most seasoned veteran, approaches each task with the focus and precision of an Olympic athlete. This isn't a far-fetched utopia; it's the tangible reality in organizations that have implemented all nine elements of People Excellence, including mastering the art and science of Coaching to 100%.

To truly grasp the transformative power of this approach, let's immerse ourselves in the experience of an employee, in this case, me, working at Pal's Sudden Service:

It is incredible to work in an environment of 100% coaching. It was such a pleasure to work in that environment. I imagine it is like being on an Olympic team; only you are serving products and services rather than competing in a sport. Everyone is dedicated to ensuring that every customer is delighted by meeting all their KCRs, every customer, every time. As you will remember, the KCRs are met by delivering the products and services 100% to the brand's requirements. To do that, everyone focuses on using their skills to precisely perform each step of the approved process, every step, every time.

Because I focus on my assigned job, I can recognize when I perform each step precisely as written in the procedure and when I do not. When I am on point, I feel good about producing products that meet 100% of the brand requirements. When I am not, I correct the situation. This is self-management. The proven path is known and written; I just need to follow it. My manager is also watching. At Pal's, most managers coach while working in a production role. Managers can only observe a small sample of the steps any employee performs. Their role is to periodically check if I am performing the steps exactly as the process requires. They also check whether I am self-managing my work and make corrections if my actions don't perfectly align with the process or if the product doesn't meet the brand requirements.

When the manager observes that my self-managing system is not in place, they immediately do corrective coaching. When the manager sees me following every step of the approved process, they provide positive coaching. Implementing the coaching to 100% element is a key contributor to enabling all products and services to be delivered 100% to the brand requirements, which delights customers. Because we consistently delight customers at Pal's, sometimes, they return the same day, but we know it will not be long until we see that customer again. It is a great feeling. You go home energized and can't wait to return to playing your role on the winning team.

This vivid account paints a picture of an organization where excellence isn't just a goal—it's a way of life. How do we bridge the gap between this standard and the reality in most workplaces? Part of the answer lies in understanding and implementing Coaching to 100%.

Decoding Coaching to 100%: The Science of Performance Excellence

At its core, coaching to 100% is a systematic, unwavering approach to helping employees achieve and maintain perfect process execution on the job. It's about creating what we call "People Excellence," a state where every employee, driven by intrinsic motivation and supported by effective coaching, chooses to perform each step of the approved process with precision, every single time, regardless of whether a supervisor is watching.

This might sound like an impossibly high standard, but as we'll see, organizations across various industries have not only achieved this level of excellence but have reaped tremendous benefits as a result.

Coaching to 100% operates on two fundamental pillars, both of which are important:

1. **Positive Coaching**: This occurs when a manager observes an employee performing a task precisely as prescribed. It's not a generic pat on the back, but a specific, immediate acknowledgment of precise performance. This reinforcement is crucial in cementing desired behaviors and motivating continued excellence. This motivates the employee to do this more often, since the way to receive positive coaching is to precisely perform the process steps and conditions of employment as written in the approved process.

2. **Corrective Coaching:** This occurs whenever there is any deviation from the prescribed process, no matter how minor. It isn't about punishment. Its goal is to provide immediate, respectful course correction to ensure that every action fully aligns with established process standards. Imagine every employee is committed to achieving the mission of delighting customers in a way that builds loyalty by fulfilling all the KCRs. In that case, the expected behavior is for the employee to follow the steps of the approved process exactly. When they cannot manage this on their own, they appreciate the extra coaching from the manager to help them do their job correctly and meet expectations. This is why all champion athletes value coaching: to become the best they can be and help the team win. The same applies in business; employees of successful companies value corrective coaching so they can excel at their jobs and deliver products and services that are 100% to the brand requirements.

The power of this approach lies in its consistency and balance. By providing immediate feedback, both positive and corrective coaching, managers create an environment of continuous improvement to unwavering standards of excellence.

Structured Approach to Coaching

Coaching Overview

Coaching is divided into two categories: (a) Positive Coaching and (b) Corrective Coaching.

Positive Coaching Steps

1. Observe no deviation from the standard.
2. Provide positive feedback.

Corrective Coaching Steps

1. Observe deviation from the standard.
2. Provide corrective feedback.
3. Verify deviation corrected.
4. Provide positive reinforcement.

When do you coach?:

As soon as you see it. The phrase "See it; Say it" captures that practice. Another way to say it is "coaching in the moment".

How do you coach?:

Provide both positive and corrective feedback that has all 4 of the following characteristics: sincere, specific, immediate, and personal.

One way to remember these four characteristics is with the first letter of each characteristic: SSIP. When we train, we help managers remember the SSIP acronym by asking them to think about what SSIP spells backwards. After that, they remember it. An example of the use of the four characteristics for positive coaching is: "Sally, that was a great way you just handled the customer complaint with Ms. Jones. You restored goodwill and even had Ms. Jones compliment you on how promptly you addressed and resolved her problem. The empathy you used was terrific." An example using the four characteristics of coaching for corrective coaching is: "Sam, our standard is to speak to guests when we come within 5 feet of a guest. You just passed a guest without even looking at them, and you didn't speak to them. Remember, our standard is to speak to every guest when within 5 feet." When you observed that Sam then greeted the next guest he came within 5 feet of, say, "Great, that is exactly to our standard."

Coaching to Reinforce Following the Process and Conditions of Employment

- Enforce strict adherence to precisely following each step of the approved process and the conditions of employment.

- Positive Coaching when each step is precisely performed, or conditions of employment are precisely followed.

- Corrective Coaching when there is any deviation from precisely following any step (no matter how slight the deviation) or not adhering to the conditions of employment.

- Provide all coaching feedback using SSIP.

These guidelines for Coaching to 100% drive the behavior of adherence to standards, provide immediate, personal, specific feedback for both positive and corrective coaching, and support the behavior of adherence to standards.

The two best practices that make Coaching to 100% more effective than how most managers coach are never to pass up a corrective coaching opportunity, no matter how small, and to have an equal or greater amount of positive coaching than corrective coaching.

The way most managers practice coaching is that they may see many process steps not being performed precisely right, but as long as they are close, they will not provide corrective coaching. The problem with this is that the real standard is what managers see and ignore. When they don't say anything about performance that is not precisely right but close, they make that "almost right level of performance" the real standard. Coaching to 100% provides corrective coaching whenever they see any step in a process not being performed precisely right.

Another way most managers practice coaching that makes it less effective than Coaching to 100% is that most of the coaching provided is corrective, with little to no positive feedback. This results in most of the time managers talk to an employee about their work, it is to correct that employee. Yet in reality, most employees are doing many things right and never get feedback on the good things they're doing. Even the best employees will make some mistakes. What I have found is that what makes extraordinary organizations' coaching so impactful in influencing and maintaining the desired behavior is that they give equal to or more positive coaching or feedback than corrective coaching, while always providing corrective coaching whenever they observe performance not 100% to standard.

The Transformative Impact: Real-World Success Stories

The effectiveness of Coaching to 100% isn't just theoretical—it's been proven time and again in diverse organizational contexts. Let's explore some real-world examples that demonstrate its transformative power:

1. **Coca-Cola Enterprises:** When Coca-Cola Enterprises implemented a coaching program for its executives and high-potential employees, the results were nothing short of remarkable:
   - 88% of participants reported improved relationships with direct reports.
   - 81% noted better relationships with stakeholders.
   - 80% experienced increased productivity.
   - 72% improved their work quality.

   A senior executive summed up the impact: "The coaching program has been transformational for our leadership team, fostering a culture of continuous improvement and excellence." This case illustrates how coaching can enhance not just individual performance, but also team dynamics and overall organizational effectiveness.

2. **Microsoft:** Tech giant Microsoft took a bold step by implementing a company-wide coaching initiative. The results speak volumes about the power of systematic coaching:
   - 10% increase in productivity.
   - 20% improvement in employee engagement scores.
   - 15% reduction in turnover among high-potential employees.

   Satya Nadella, CEO of Microsoft, observed, "Coaching has been instrumental in fostering a growth mindset across our organization, driving innovation and excellence." Microsoft's experience demonstrates how Coaching to 100% can be scaled across a large, complex organization, driving significant improvements in key performance indicators.

These success stories set the stage for understanding why Coaching to 100% is so effective. But to truly harness its power, we need to delve deeper into its core principles.

The Eight Principles of Coaching to 100%: Building a Foundation for Excellence

Coaching to 100% isn't a one-size-fits-all approach. It's a carefully crafted methodology built on eight key principles. Each of these principles plays a crucial role in creating an environment where excellence becomes the norm:

1. **Dual-Faceted Coaching**: The first principle recognizes that effective coaching isn't one-dimensional. It requires both positive reinforcement when employees precisely follow processes or rules and corrective guidance when deviations occur.

2. **Balanced Positive and Corrective Feedback:** Building on the first principle, this principle emphasizes providing at least as much positive coaching as corrective coaching. This balanced approach ensures employees see that managers notice both when they meet and when they fall short of standards. This balance is vital for maintaining morale and motivation, leading to ongoing performance excellence while quickly addressing areas for improvement.

3. **Immediate Corrective Coaching:** This principle emphasizes the importance of addressing deviations as soon as they are noticed. Feedback has the greatest impact on behavior when delivered immediately. The longer you wait after the event, the less influence it has on behavior. By not letting even minor deviations go unnoticed, managers reinforce the importance of accuracy and prevent minor deviations from becoming ingrained habits. Providing positive coaching promptly for correctly following the steps and rules of the process will have the greatest effect on encouraging that positive behavior to be repeated in the future.

4. **Create Certainty that Feedback will be Provided:** When rules and processes are clear and consistently enforced, employees can count on it. This eliminates confusion over expectations

and maximizes the impact that the feedback will drive future desired behavior. This principle ensures that everyone understands what's expected and that these expectations are consistently and uniformly applied.

5. **Self-Management**: This principle empowers employees to monitor their own performance, fostering a sense of ownership, responsibility, empowerment, and accountability. When employees can self-manage, it creates a culture of employees who are responsible and accountable for their own excellence. The basis of extraordinary operations is setting each employee up for 100% success and empowering them to be responsible and accountable, first and foremost to themselves, to deliver work that 100% meets the brand requirements, 100% of the time. The manager's coaching helps ensure employees are self-managing so that they will deliver their work 100% to the brand requirements.

6. **SSIP Feedback Delivery:** All coaching, whether positive or corrective, should be delivered in a way that is sincere, specific, immediate, and personal (SSIP). This method ensures that feedback is meaningful, actionable, and impactful.

7. **Respectful Coaching:** This principle stresses that all coaching, particularly corrective coaching, should be given respectfully. This approach encourages employees to view coaching as a means for development rather than as criticism.

8. **Coaching Through the Hierarchy, Not Around It:** When implementing organization-wide change, it is crucial that training and coaching go through the hierarchy rather than around it. For training, start with the manager or supervisor first so they can effectively coach their direct reports. Coaching through the hierarchy means coaching should be delivered by their direct supervisor or manager, not by their manager's supervisor. Following this approach strengthens and supports each level of the hierarchy. Conversely, coaching around the

hierarchy undermines the authority of their direct supervisor. The exception to this best practice is when there is a safety or critical customer issue. In such cases, anyone who detects the issue should promptly notify the involved employee.

By adhering to these principles, organizations create an environment where excellence isn't just encouraged—it's expected, supported, and consistently achieved. These principles enable excellence in operations using practices that build employee self-esteem rather than creating dependencies.

Coaching Across Industries: Tailoring Excellence to Every Context

While the principles of Coaching to 100% are universal, their application can vary across different sectors. Let's explore how this approach has been successfully adapted in diverse industries:

1. **Healthcare:** In an industry where precision can literally be a matter of life and death, coaching to 100% has shown remarkable results. A study of nursing managers who received coaching revealed a 36% increase in identifying solutions to problems, a 25% increase in taking on more initiative, and a 32% improvement in conflict resolution skills. These improvements translated into better patient care, safer healthcare environments, and more efficient hospital operations.

2. **Financial Services:** When a major bank implemented a coaching program for its branch managers, the ripple effects were felt across key performance indicators: 17% increase in customer satisfaction scores; 12% improvement in employee retention; 15% growth in new account openings. In an industry built on trust and precision, these improvements

demonstrate how Coaching to 100% can enhance both customer relationships and business growth.

3. **Manufacturing:** A global manufacturing company that introduced coaching for its plant managers and supervisors saw significant operational improvements: 22% reduction in workplace accidents; 18% increase in production efficiency;14% improvement in quality control metrics. These results highlight how Coaching to 100% can simultaneously enhance safety, efficiency, and quality in high-stakes production environments.

These diverse examples illustrate a crucial point, regardless of the industry, the principles of Coaching to 100% can be adapted to drive significant improvements in performance, safety, and customer satisfaction.

Overcoming Resistance: Addressing Common Challenges

Despite its proven benefits, implementing Coaching to 100% can face resistance. Let's address some common objections and explore how to overcome them:

1. **"Managers don't have time to coach anything but the big mistakes."** This perspective overlooks the cumulative impact of slight deviations. By consistently addressing minor issues, managers prevent them from escalating into significant problems, ultimately saving time and resources in the long run.

2. **"It's better to let employees learn from their mistakes."** While experiential learning has its place, in many operational contexts, mistakes can be costly, dangerous, or damaging to customer relationships. Coaching to 100% provides a safer, more controlled environment for learning and improvement.

3. **"Managers want to be friends with their employees."** I have heard from many managers that they minimize corrective coaching and do not address many behaviors that are not up to standard because they want to be liked, be friends, and build a positive relationship with their employees. It is essential that all coaching and feedback be done respectfully. When a manager does not provide both corrective and positive coaching as described in Coaching to 100%, they are setting their employees up to underperform, doing a disservice not only to the employees but also to customers and the company. One leader described not doing Coaching to 100% as a "race to the bottom." The employees see how far off standards they can be until the manager says something. When they have found that point, they see how much further they can be off standard before anything happens. Therefore, a "race to the bottom." Unfortunately, some things get so far off that the employee gets fired. The manager set that up.

4. **"Managers do not want to constantly correct and criticize employees."** Effective coaching isn't about criticism—it's about support and development so the employee can do their very best to meet company standards. When done respectfully, corrective coaching demonstrates a manager's commitment to the individual and their team's success and growth. Prompt coaching shows the manager cares about the employee, the customers, and the company, so future, avoidable mistakes are not made. This role-modeling is essential to instilling in employees a mindset of caring for their customers, the company, and themselves by being the best they can be.

5. **"Constant coaching will demotivate employees and increase turnover."** Contrary to this belief, when coaching is based on clear standards and requirements and is balanced, consistent, and respectful, it often increases engagement and retention. Employees value clear expectations, as well as respectful, timely, consistent, and relevant feedback, and growth opportunities.

6. **"Employees don't need positive coaching; they're paid to do their job."** This view underestimates the power of positive reinforcement. Acknowledging good performance isn't just about making employees feel good—it's about reinforcing desired behaviors and motivating continued excellence. Giving both positive and corrective coaching shows that the manager (and the employee) notices when things are going right and when behaviors need correction. It also helps build a better relationship between the manager and the employee, since they hear both the positives and the need for correction, not just the need for correction.

By addressing these concerns head-on and demonstrating the tangible and intangible benefits of Coaching to 100%, organizations can overcome initial resistance and create buy-in at all levels. Since coaching plays such a central role for managers and supervisors, delivering Coaching to 100% should be a requirement for becoming or being a manager or supervisor.

The Leadership Imperative: Coaching from the Top Down

For Coaching to 100% to truly transform an organization, it must be championed by the highest levels of leadership. As Jack Welch, former CEO of General Electric, insightfully noted:

"Before you are a leader, success is all about growing yourself. When you become a leader, success is all about growing others."

Eric Schmidt, former CEO of Google, echoes this sentiment:

"Every famous athlete, every famous performer has somebody who's a coach. Somebody who can watch what they're doing and say, 'Is that what you really meant? Did you really do that?' They can give them perspective. The one thing people are never good at is seeing themselves as others see them. A coach really, really helps."

These insights from industry titans underscore a crucial point: effective coaching isn't just a tool for managing front-line employees— it's a fundamental leadership skill that drives organizational success from the top down.

The role of each level of the hierarchy is to enable the level below them to be effective. For example, a manager who supervises multiple stores, such as a district manager, needs to ensure the store managers who report to them are effective.

Implementing Coaching to 100%: A Roadmap to Excellence

Now that we've explored the principles, benefits, and challenges of Coaching to 100%, let's outline a strategic approach to implementation:

- **Establish a Clear Policy**: Begin by creating a formal policy that outlines the principles and expectations of Coaching to 100%.

- **Set up an initiative:** Enable all unit operations managers to Coach to 100%.

- **Train and Certify Coaches:** Invest in comprehensive training for managers, ensuring they understand both the theory and practice of effective positive and corrective coaching. You want managers to fully understand and embrace Coaching to 100% as a key element in setting employees up for 100% success. It has been very gratifying to hear from managers that their coaching practices have significantly improved because their leaders invested in them by taking our Achieving World-Class Results class. Investing in your managers is truly valuable.

- **Start Small, Scale Gradually**: Begin with one area of processes in a single unit, then gradually expand to other areas and units over 3-6 months.

- **Monitor and Adjust**: Regularly assess the effectiveness of the coaching program, gathering feedback from and direct observations of both coaches and employees to refine the approach.

- **Celebrate Successes**: Recognize and reward both individuals and teams that exemplify the principles of Coaching to 100%.

- **Foster a Coaching Culture**: Encourage peer-to-peer coaching and self-management to create a pervasive culture of continuous improvement.

By following this roadmap, organizations can systematically implement Coaching to 100%, transforming their operations and unleashing the full potential of their managers and workforce.

Conclusion: Coaching to 100% - The Key to Sustained Excellence

As we've discussed throughout this chapter, Coaching to 100% is more than just a management technique—it's a fundamental shift in how organizations view performance, quality, and ongoing improvement. By fostering an environment where every employee is empowered and motivated to perform at their best, organizations can reach levels of excellence once thought impossible.

The journey to implementing Coaching to 100% may be challenging, but the rewards are immense. Organizations that successfully adopt this approach don't just see improvements in metrics and KPIs—they experience a transformation in their culture, where employees are more engaged, skilled, and committed to excellence in everything they do.

As we move forward, remember that excellence is not a destination but a continuous journey. Coaching to 100% provides the roadmap and the tools for this journey, ensuring every step taken is a step toward perfection.

Call to Action

1. Implement Coaching to 100%. Start with one process that has been designed and Trained to 100%. Once Coaching to 100% has been obtained for the first process, systematically expand it to all processes.

Key Takeaways for Chapter 17: Coaching to 100%: The Cornerstone of Sustained Excellence

1. The main objective of Coaching to 100% in operations is to provide feedback that will promote the employee behavior of precisely performing the steps of the process every time and 100% comply with the organization's rules (Conditions of Employment). Coaching to 100% is one of the most effective ways to achieve and maintain 100% performance.

2. There are two types of coaching: positive and corrective. Both types need to be used. To get the best results, you want the amount of positive coaching to be equal to or greater than the amount of corrective coaching. This gives you the maximum impact on shaping the desired behavior. Research shows that a positive-to-corrective coaching ratio of 1:1 or higher is even more beneficial, but we have found it harder to achieve in practice. The one-to-one ratio is sufficient in most cases.

3. Use positive coaching when each step is precisely performed or conditions of employment are 100% met.

4. Use corrective coaching when there is any deviation from precisely following any step of a process (no matter how slight

the deviation is) or when the conditions of employment are not 100% met.

5. For corrective coaching, "See it; Say it" is a role-model practice. When a manager sees a deviation from the process, they should coach immediately, if possible, and, if not, as soon as possible.

6. To effectively deliver both types of coaching, make sure your coaching is delivered using SSIP: sincere, specific, immediate, and personal.

The Next Chapter

In the next chapter, we'll explore how to empower each employee to only pass on work that 100% meets the brand requirements. This step will help maintain 100% quality throughout every stage of your operations.

CHAPTER 18

EMPOWER: EMPLOYEES TO DELIVER CONSISTENT EXCELLENCE

"Leaders become great, not because of their power, but because of their ability to empower others."

John C. Maxwell

The Driving Force: What has to be there before you hold people accountable

A car with two people inside was stopped by the police for speeding. Why did the officer only issue a speeding ticket to the driver and not the passenger? (Both were speeding). This simple question opens up a deeper discussion about responsibility, accountability, and self-management at work. As we explore this chapter, we'll see how this traffic situation directly relates to empowering employees to consistently deliver excellence.

Enabling Employees to Control Operations

In this chapter, I will show you how to manage the outputs of processes. Understanding this helps you identify missing components and add them to each process, enabling them to be managed. Without control over our actions, we produce less, face more bad outcomes, rework, and waste. The core of extraordinary operations is to control a process so it reliably delivers products and services 100% to the brand requirements.

Precision Empowerment: Empowering Employees with Purpose

This chapter focuses on empowering all operations employees in a very specific way. I'm not talking about general empowerment, but targeted empowerment that allows operations employees to precisely follow the steps of the approved processes they perform and to pass on the output only when it fully meets all brand requirements. We enable this by integrating self-management into every operations process. Self-management, which I will discuss later in this chapter, allows employees performing a process or task to determine whether what they are doing, or the process's output, fully meets the brand requirements. If it doesn't, they are empowered to correct it until it does.

This is self-management because we empower operations employees regarding the processes and tasks they perform. We empower the performers so they can get it right every time.

Regarding the McClaskey® Triple 100® Path to Excellence, we specifically focus the recommended empowerment on operations employees who precisely perform the process steps of the approved operations-related processes and deliver the process output that meets the approved brand requirements. Empowerment, as discussed in this chapter, is limited to executing the approved process and does not include modifying it in any way. If a company wishes to broaden the scope of empowerment beyond this, that is a decision for the company and falls outside the scope of what I am recommending or discussing in this chapter.

Peter Drucker, the renowned management consultant, once said: "The most important, and indeed the truly unique, contribution of management in the 20th century was the fifty-fold increase in the productivity of the manual worker in manufacturing. The most important contribution management needs to make in the 21st century is similar to increasing the productivity of knowledge work and knowledge workers."

Although Drucker wasn't specifically discussing self-management in this quote, his emphasis on increasing worker productivity and effectiveness closely relates to the topic. In today's rapidly changing business environment, empowering employees through self-management isn't just a nice-to-have—it's a competitive necessity for delivering your products and services to 100% and thus obtaining a competitive edge over your competitors.

The Power of Ownership: Self-Management in Action

I have spoken with many business leaders from restaurants, convenience stores, hotels, grocery stores, and other service businesses. Before our training class, leaders are usually not confident that the quality of their service business's work will meet 100% of their brand requirements. For example, most service managers and leaders do not expect that the next customer they serve will receive products or services that meet 100% of their business's brand requirements.

Let me compare this to businesses with outstanding operations. They are so confident in consistently meeting their brand standards that they will bet their next customer will also receive products or services delivered 100% to their brand requirements.

What do companies with extraordinary operations do to create such certainty that their products and services will be delivered 100% to their brand requirements? The next element that extraordinary organizations have that ordinary organizations do not is that they empower every employee with self-management.

For example, consider a small but important task for restaurants: preparing toppings like onions, tomatoes, and lettuce for sandwiches. Each topping has specific brand requirements. For instance, lettuce must be a specific thickness and free of brown spots. Restaurants with extraordinary operations, when inspecting their refrigerators where the prepped toppings are stored before use, will find that every container of prepped toppings fully meets these brand requirements. Their managers are so confident in this that they would bet their own money on it. Why? Because the employee responsible for the prep work is empowered with the three components of self-management.

- Knows what the requirements are.
- Knows if what they are doing meets the requirements.
- Has the ability and authority to adjust the output until it 100% meets the requirements for that output.

This real-world example illustrates the transformative power of self-management in ensuring consistent quality and meeting brand standards. Why is this approach so effective? Let's dive deeper into the principles and impact of self-management.

The Three Pillars of Self-management: Knowing, Evaluating, and Adjusting

At the heart of effective self-management lie three crucial components. The performer of the process:

- **Knows the requirements:** This involves having a clear, detailed understanding of the specific standards and specifications for each task or process. For instance, in the toppings prep example, employees must know the precise requirements for preparing each ingredient—the thickness of tomato slices, the size of diced onions, and the absence of brown spots in the lettuce, among others.

- **Knows if their work meets the requirements:** This component focuses on real-time self-assessment. Employees must be able to evaluate their work against established standards while performing tasks and, upon completion, determine whether the product or service fully meets the brand's requirements. For example, they should be able to look at a sliced tomato and immediately decide whether it meets the thickness standard.

- **Has the ability and authority to adjust the output until it 100% meets the requirements:** This is where the employee is empowered. If employees recognize that their output doesn't meet the requirements, they must have both the skills to make corrections and the authority to do so. For instance, if a batch of onions is cut too large, the employee should be able to re-cut them or start over without seeking permission. In some cases, permission is needed to take specific corrective actions, and the employee is empowered to immediately seek that permission.

Empowerment for Excellence: Precision, Authority, and Impact

Empowerment in this context means giving employees the tools, knowledge, and authority to ensure their work meets brand standards. It's not about broad decision-making power but rather the ability to make precise adjustments to meet predefined quality requirements before the output is passed to the next step in the process.

The Self-Managed Workforce: Driving Engagement and Reducing Supervision

When these three components of self-management are built into every operations process, it creates a decisive shift in operational performance:

- **Consistency:** Every output, whether an ingredient that goes into a product or a finished product or service, consistently meets brand standards. This level of consistency allows businesses to confidently guarantee the quality of their products and services.

- **Proactive Quality Control:** Primary quality control is now the employee's responsibility and is an essential part of every process. The employee identifies and corrects errors in real time, reducing waste and boosting efficiency. Employees can learn from their mistakes more quickly because corrections are made as issues occur. Secondary quality control for products and services, typically performed afterward by a third party, will still be conducted periodically to verify that the employee's primary quality control meets 100% of the brand standards.

- **Employee Engagement:** When employees are empowered with self-management, they take greater ownership, responsibility, and accountability for their work. As a result, they learn faster, perform at a higher level, and become more engaged. Higher engagement leads to increased productivity and lower turnover. They don't just follow orders; they actively ensure the quality of their output by strictly adhering to the process. They can be held accountable to only pass on process outputs that 100% meet the brand requirements because they are enabled and empowered through self-management. Empowering employees with self-management reduces dependencies and gives employees more control.

- **Reduced Supervision:** With employees enabled and empowered to manage the quality of their own work, managers can focus on higher-level tasks like training, coaching, employee development, and process improvement.

- **Customer Satisfaction:** Consistent quality leads to higher customer satisfaction. Customers can rely on receiving the same, high-quality product or service that meets 100% of the brand requirements every time. Customers who have 100% confidence in the quality of your products and services lead to significant increases in repeat business and positive recommendations.

Lessons From the Field: Real-World Success Stories of Self-Management

Zappos adopted a holacracy model, removing traditional management hierarchies and enabling employees to self-manage their tasks according to the approved process. This change boosted employee engagement and increased customer satisfaction scores by 30%. The Zappos case study shows how self-management can lead to real improvements in employee engagement and customer satisfaction. By empowering employees to take ownership of their roles and responsibilities, Zappos built a more responsive, customer-focused organization.

The Fundamentals of Self-Management: Building Accountability

Building on the three core components, let's explore some additional principles that underpin effective self-management:

- **Self-Managed Employees:** For employees to be self-managed, all three self-management components must be built into the process. They must know the requirements for the process steps and outputs, know whether what they are doing meets those requirements in real time, and have the ability and authority to adjust the output until it 100% meets those requirements.

- **Clarity of Expectations:** Employees must have a crystal-clear understanding of the brand requirements for their outputs. Clear guidelines enable them to accurately self-assess their work against these standards.

- **Accountability occurs when all three components of self-management are in place:** Employees can be held responsible for the quality of their work if they possess all three parts of self-management. If one or more components are missing, the employee cannot be fully accountable for the overall quality of the output. Self-management encourages a sense of personal responsibility. When employees are enabled to self-manage and held responsible for their results, and when they precisely follow the process steps, they are more likely to take ownership, learn faster, and aim for excellence. Empowered, responsible, accountable employees who are set up for 100% success tend to take pride in their work. Not incorporating self-management into the process reduces employees' ability to deliver the output right 100% of the time, which diminishes their pride in their work.

- **Continuous Feedback:** Establishing a feedback loop allows employees to assess their performance continually. This leads to more rapid and continuous learning. Regular check-ins and constructive feedback help them adjust their actions to meet brand requirements.

- **Empowerment through Training:** Providing training focusing on self-management skills equips employees with the tools they need to succeed independently. This includes decision-making, problem-solving, and time-management skills.

Steps to Empower Employees by Building In Self-Management:

- **Familiarize yourself** with the three components of self-management:
  - Know what they were supposed to do (the standard).
  - Know what they were doing compared to the standard.
  - Empowered to correct if what they did was not what they were supposed to do.

- **Company Policy:** Establish a policy that each employee will be set up, enabled, and empowered through self-management to be responsible and accountable for the output of any process they perform, ensuring that any output they deliver 100% meets the brand requirements. Once fully set up to 100%, employees will be held responsible and accountable for output that meets 100% of the requirements.

- **Examine and Classify Processes:** Go through every process or task in your operation and classify it as either having all three self-management components or not.

- **Redesign Processes:** Redesign processes that lack all three components of self-management to incorporate the missing elements to the extent possible.

- **Integrate Self-Management into Process Development:** When creating or modifying processes, include all three components of self-management as much as possible in the process design. This helps ensure the final output meets all brand requirements.

- **Train Employees:** Provide comprehensive training on self-management and how to apply it in their daily work. Include self-management training as part of the training for each process.

- **Continuous Improvement:** Regularly review and refine processes to ensure they support self-management and meet evolving business needs.

Driving Operational Excellence: The Roadmap to Self-Management Mastery

- **Implement the SDCA Cycle:** Introduce the Standard-Do-Check-Act cycle as a practical tool for employees to apply self-management:

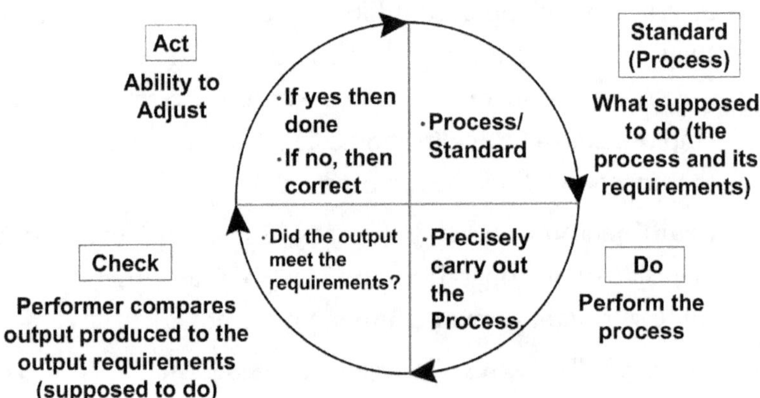

Using the Three Elements of Self-Management Using the Standard-Do-Check-Act (SDCA) Cycle:

- **Standard (Process)**: What you're supposed to do. Establish the standards. The standards usually take the form of a process documented in an approved Standard Operating Procedure (SOP). The requirements for each process output must be clearly stated in black-and-white terms as part of the approved process.

- **Do**: Precisely carry out the process according to the standards (the approved process).

- **Check**: Employee determines if the actual output meets all the brand requirements (the standards).

- **Act**: If the output meets the brand requirements, continue to repeat the cycle, starting with the standard, every time you want the process output. If the brand standard isn't met, ask "why" three to five times to determine the root cause and adjust the process SOP until it does meet the brand standard.

Whenever There is an Error, Check to Ensure the Performer was in a State of Self-Management

Error Handling: Errors occur when the output of a process is passed to the next step without meeting all the brand requirements. When this happens, the first step in the analysis to determine the root cause of the error is to assess whether the employee was in a state of self-management. Determine:

- If all three components were present, hold the employee accountable for their part in the error.

- If any component of self-management is missing, address the deficiency in the process by adding that component to the process.

Overcoming Roadblocks: Navigating Challenges in Self-Management

While the benefits of self-management are clear, implementing this approach can come with its own challenges:

- **Resistance to Change:** Employees may resist self-management due to fear of increased accountability. Organizations can address this by fostering a supportive environment that encourages learning from mistakes.

- **Lack of Confidence:** Some employees may doubt their ability to self-manage. Providing mentorship and coaching can build their confidence and skills.

- **Inconsistent Application:** Ensuring self-management principles are applied consistently across all processes and departments can be challenging. Regular audits and refresher training will help maintain consistency. Make self-management a factor in both positive and corrective coaching, as well as employee and management assessments.

- **Balancing Autonomy and Alignment:** Empowerment and self-management promote and enable autonomy, but this only works within clearly defined and authorized boundaries. Empowerment and self-management do not grant authority beyond what is explicitly permitted and authorized by approved processes and company policies.

Empowering Your Team: The Journey to Continuous Improvement

The implementation of self-management principles can have far-reaching effects on an organization:

- **Increased Process Improvement:** Companies that promote self-management often see higher levels of process improvement. Employees feel empowered to propose new ideas and solutions, leading to continuous improvement in processes and products.
- **Enhanced Customer Experience:** When employees are empowered to make decisions, they can correct products and services that do not meet the brand requirements before the product is delivered to the customer.
- **Cost Efficiency:** When employees take ownership of quality control through self-management and process improvement, organizations see reduced waste and operational costs.

Conclusion: The Path to Operations Excellence

By implementing self-management, organizations will achieve operations excellence, with every output consistently meeting the brand requirements. This approach transforms employees from passive followers of instructions to active guardians of quality, empowered to ensure excellence in every task they perform.

Let's revisit our initial scenario: a car with two people was stopped by the police for speeding. Why did the officer only give a speeding ticket to the driver and not the passenger? (Both were speeding.) The answer lies in the three components of self-management. The driver was in a state of self-management: they knew the speed limit (the standard), could see how fast they were going (compared to the standard), and could adjust their speed (the ability to correct). As a result, the driver could be held accountable and receive the ticket. Meanwhile, although the passenger was traveling at the same speed, they were not in a state of self-management because they could not control the car's speed; therefore, they couldn't be held accountable and did not receive a ticket. This simple analogy captures the core of empowerment and accountability in self-management.

Imagine yourself as the passenger, and the police officer gives you a speeding ticket, too. How would you feel? You might feel as if you were treated unfairly and tell all your friends about it. This situation occurs in many companies. Managers hold the employee who delivered the defective product or service accountable, even when the employee was not in a state of self-management. They then share their experience with coworkers and others, explaining how their supervisor treated them unfairly. Holding people fully accountable for errors when they are not in a state of self-management causes problems and disengagement. It also does not address the root cause of the problem, so the problem will probably recur. Ensure that the three elements of self-management are present before holding someone accountable for meeting the brand requirements.

As you implement self-management in your organization, remember: your goal is to turn every employee into a driver, empowered with the three components of self-management and accountable for their output, meeting 100% of the brand requirements.

Call to Action

1. Design self-management into every process. Start by selecting a few processes and designing in the three components of self-management.

2. Train employees how to use the three components of self-management to ensure that any output that goes to another process or customer is 100% to the brand requirements before that output is transferred to another process or customer.

3. Audit and coach to ensure that self-management is being executed 100% of the time for 100% of the operations processes. Provide positive coaching where self-management is being executed 100% of the time. Provide corrective coaching when it is not.

Key Takeaways for Chapter 18: Empower Employees to Deliver Consistent Excellence

1. To enable employees to be fully responsible and accountable for their work meeting 100% of the brand requirements, the three elements of self-management need to be built into every process.

2. The three components of self-management: Knows what the requirements are; Knows if what they are doing meets the requirements; Has the ability and authority to adjust the output until the output 100% meets the brand requirements.

The Next Chapter

We have now completed the first six elements of the People Excellence Pillar. These elements ensure that employees are adequately trained and enabled to precisely perform the process steps every time and 100% comply with the conditions of employment.

Achieving performance requires more than just enabling employees to do their jobs 100% right, 100% of the time. Just because an employee can do a job 100% right, doesn't mean they will do the job 100% right. You also need to create a work environment that encourages them to carefully follow each step of the approved processes involved in their jobs every time, even when no supervisor is present, and to fully comply with the conditions of employment. The next chapter will show how to establish such an environment for 100% execution.

CHAPTER 19

CREATE A WORK ENVIRONMENT FOR 100% EXECUTION

"Leadership is creating an environment in which people want to be part of the organization and not just work for the organization."

Horst Schulze

The Quest for Consistency: How to Ensure 100% Execution Every Time

A pressing question resonates in the world of operations management: How can a manager ensure every employee chooses to precisely perform each step of the approved process, every time, even when no supervisor is present, and 100% comply with the Conditions of Employment? Picture this: You're walking through a busy hotel. Guests arrive, are greeted, and are rapidly checked in. Guests who are leaving are thanked for their stay, checked out, and efficiently assisted with their luggage to their car and on their way. Meals are served, and all employees move with purpose. As you observe, you notice something extraordinary: every employee executes their tasks with great attention to detail and with meticulous precision. There's no supervisor nearby, yet the level of performance is impeccable. How is this possible? This scene isn't a far-fetched dream. It's the reality in organizations that have mastered creating a work environment for

100% execution. In this chapter, we'll uncover the secrets to achieving this level of operational excellence.

Setting the Stage

The People Excellence Pillar of the Path to Excellence enables each employee to precisely perform each step of the process every time, even when no supervisor is watching, and to 100% comply with the Conditions of Employment. The first six Elements of People Excellence, Hiring, Conditions of Employment, Accountability, Training to 100%, Coach to 100%, and Empower, set the employee up to precisely perform the process steps every time and to 100% comply with the Conditions of Employment. Now, we need to add an element that will ensure employees consistently choose to perform at this level.

To understand how we can influence employee behavior, let's first examine how people make decisions about their actions.

- **Assess the environment**: A person evaluates the situation they are about to enter.
- **Cultural filter**: They process this assessment through their cultural lens—their mindset, biases, and experiences. Dale Carnegie, in his book *How to Win Friends and Influence People*, provided advice that helps convey what I mean by cultural filter: "Understand that the other person has a valid view of the situation. If you were born as them with their brain and undergoing their experiences, you would, by definition, feel the same way they do." Your job is to understand what led them to believe what they believe or, in this case, what about the work environment led them to behave the way they behave.
- **Decision-making**: Based on this filtered analysis, they make a reasonable, rational, and logical decision on the actions they will take. For example, imagine you're driving on an interstate,

going about 10 miles per hour over the speed limit. You spot a police car ahead with its radar active. Your decision to slow down (and by how much) is based on your analysis of the situation, filtered through your personal risk tolerance. The key for unit operations managers is to create an environment where the reasonable, rational, and logical choice for employees is to precisely follow the steps of the approved process every time. This is achieved by adjusting the environment through legal and ethical means authorized by the company until the desired behaviors are achieved.

Debbie's Story: The Pursuit of Precision

Imagine this hypothetical scenario: A newly appointed unit operations manager, Debbie, takes charge of a high-end automotive manufacturing plant. The facility is known for producing high-quality vehicles, but inconsistencies in the assembly process lead to costly rework and occasional customer complaints. Despite having skilled workers and state-of-the-art equipment, the plant struggles to consistently achieve excellence. On her first day, Debbie observes the assembly line. She notices that while most employees follow procedures correctly, there are frequent minor deviations. A bolt not tightened to exact specifications, a component installed in a slightly different order, or a quality check performed hastily. Debbie realizes that these minor deviations, while seemingly insignificant on their own, collectively contribute to the plant's inconsistent output. She understands she needs to create an environment where following the exact process every time becomes the only logical choice for all employees. She begins by clearly communicating her expectations: every step of the approved process must be followed precisely, every time. She then implements a comprehensive coaching system where any deviation is addressed immediately, regardless of how minor. She also introduces positive reinforcement, rewarding employees who consistently follow the process with positive feedback. But Debbie doesn't stop there. She recognizes that to truly transform the environment, she needs to go deeper.

- Redesigns workstations: the new design makes following the correct process the easiest option.

- Implements visual aids and checklists: these reinforce the correct procedures at each station.

- Establishes a peer recognition program: these recognitions reward employees for consistently following the approved processes and helping others do the same.

- Creates a feedback system: Allowing this system allows employees to suggest improvements to the processes, giving them a sense of ownership.

Over time, Debbie observes a change in the company's culture. Employees begin to take pride in their accuracy, and the idea of "good enough" is replaced by a dedication to excellence. This hypothetical scenario demonstrates the challenges and initial steps managers might encounter when creating a work environment focused on 100% execution.

Data Speaks: The Case for 100% Execution

Research in behavioral psychology supports the approach outlined in our scenario. A study published in the *Harvard Business Review* found that clear expectations and immediate feedback are critical components of high-performing teams. These factors significantly impact employee performance and adherence to procedures. Moreover, data from manufacturing plants that have implemented similar strategies show remarkable results:

- A 30-50% improvement in productivity.

- A significant reduction in defects.

These statistics underscore the power of creating an environment that fosters 100% execution. Real-world examples further illustrate the impact of this approach:

- **Toyota's Production System**: Known for its "lean" manufacturing principles, Toyota has created an environment where continuous improvement and strict adherence to standardized processes are ingrained in the culture. This led Toyota to consistently rank among the top automotive manufacturers for quality and reliability.

- **Amazon's Fulfillment Centers**: Amazon designed its warehouse environments to make following the correct processes the most efficient option for employees. Through careful layout design, clear visual cues, real-time feedback systems, and AI and technology, Amazon consistently achieved remarkable accuracy in order fulfillment across its vast network.

The Key Principles: How to Achieve 100% Execution

To create a work environment for 100% execution, several key principles must be applied:

- **Employees Control Their Behavior**: Every individual decides their actions, making it critical for managers to create an environment that encourages the right choices.

- **Rational Decision-Making**: Employees make decisions based on their assessment of the environment. If shortcuts are easier or less time-consuming, they will likely choose that path unless the environment makes the correct process the logical choice.

- **Impact of Management**: Managers in most companies are authorized to use between 25 and 65 tools to manage the work environment, so operation employees will choose to precisely perform each step of the approved process every time, even when no supervisor is present and 100% comply with the conditions of employment. Some of these tools include training, coaching, checklists, audits, scheduling, the discipline process, hiring, firing, job assignments, pay, and praise. They have the tools to make following the approved process the reasonable, rational, and logical option for employees.

- **Managerial Responsibility for Quality**: Unit Operations managers must ensure products and services meet brand requirements 100% of the time, under 100% of the conditions. Consistent quality must be their primary measure of success.

- **Providing Adequate Tools**: Managers must have the resources and authority to adjust the work environment to achieve consistent execution. This includes corrective coaching, positive reinforcement, and, when necessary, progressive discipline.

- **Role-Modeling**: Employees often look to management and peers for cues on how to behave. Ensuring consistent role-modeling from leaders is one of the most powerful ways to influence employee behavior.

- **Immediate Feedback**: Immediate and consistent feedback has the most significant impact on shaping employee actions, especially when deviations from the process are identified.

The Objections: Is 100% Execution Unrealistic?

Some might argue that striving for 100% execution is unrealistic or could create an overly rigid work environment. They might say, "Isn't 95% good enough? Won't pushing for perfection stress out our employees?" While these concerns are understandable, they overlook several key points:

- **The Compounding Effect of Small Errors**: Even 95% accuracy in a complex process can lead to significant issues. For example, in a 20-step process where each step has a 95% chance of being completed 100% correctly, the probability of completing the entire process without error is only 36%.

- **Cost of "Good Enough"**: The expenses associated with rework, customer dissatisfaction, and lost market share far outweigh the investment required to achieve 100% execution. "Good enough" quality affects both revenue and costs.

- **Employee Satisfaction**: A well-designed environment for 100% execution often reduces employee stress by removing ambiguity and setting them up for success. Clear guidelines and logical processes make it easier for employees to perform at their best.

- **Continuous Improvement**: The goal of striving for 100% execution isn't to achieve perfection immediately but to establish a constant refinement and improvement culture with a standard of continually improving as close to 100% as possible.

The Manager as Architect: Shaping the Work Environment for Success

When you create the right work environment, excellence becomes the default, not the exception. By understanding that employees make reasonable, rational, and logical decisions based on their work environment, managers can strategically shape the environment so employees decide on the desired behaviors. It's not about constantly policing employees or creating a culture of fear. Instead, it's about making the right choices so intuitive and rewarding that they become second nature. This insight transforms the role of a manager from a taskmaster to an environment architect. The focus shifts from controlling employees to creating a context where the desired behavior is the only logical choice. If the employee's behavior is not what the company needs, change the work environment until it is.

Consider the analogy of a river: You can expend enormous amounts of energy trying to make water flow uphill, or you can design the riverbed so that the water naturally flows where you want it to go. Creating a work environment for 100% execution is about shaping the "riverbed" of your organization. Please don't blame the water for where it is flowing. Water will always take the path of least resistance. If you want the water to flow somewhere else, change the terrain so it flows there.

The cost of a work environment where processes are not precisely performed and conditions of employment are not 100% met is enormous and is often just accepted as an unavoidable cost of doing business. One example, based on surveys of leaders of thousands of managers in our AWCR class, reported that 25% of their day is spent on things that never should have happened in the first place—a clear waste of talent and resources.

When you shape an environment where precisely performing the steps of the process, every time, is the only logical choice, you don't just change behaviors—you transform your entire organization. The result is unlocked levels of quality, employee engagement, efficiency, and innovation you never thought possible.

Every organization is perfectly designed to achieve the results it is currently achieving. One key element that must change to achieve different results is the design of the work environment. You want to design the work environment so that the desired behaviors of the employees are the reasonable, rational, and logical choice, from their perspective, every time. You want employees to choose to precisely perform the steps of the approved process because the work environment you have designed makes that the reasonable, logical, and rational choice.

Implementation: Steps to Build an Environment for 100% Execution

To implement these insights and create a work environment for 100% execution, follow these steps:

1. **Assess Your Current Work Environment**:
    -   Measure the percentage of customer engagements where products and services meet 100% of brand requirements.
    -   Measure the percentage of steps of the approved processes that are precisely performed.
    -   Measure the percentage of time employees are standing around doing nothing.
    -   Compare your employee turnover to similar companies in your area.
2. **Ensure Unit Operations Managers Have Adequate Methods**:
    -   Review available tools, capabilities, and authority that managers are authorized to use to manage the work environment.
    -   Identify gaps in managerial tools, capabilities, or authority.
3. **Train Managers**:
    -   Equip managers with the skills to use available methods and shape the work environment so employees choose to follow the process 100% of the time, every time, even when there is no supervisor in the area.
4. **Managers Manage the Work Environment**:
    -   Managers use the tools to manage the work environment. Two key measures are the percentage of their unit's products and services that meet 100% of the brand requirements, and the percentage of process steps performed precisely by their unit's employees.

- Identify gaps between current performance and 100% for these two measures, determine the root cause, address the root cause by changing the way the work environment is being managed, and determine if the gap has been reduced. Repeat this improvement cycle until the gap is significantly reduced, and repeat with another process or unit.

5. **Modify the Set of Tools Authorized:**
   - Company-wide management should consider modifying the set of tools that managers are authorized to use if that is one of the root causes of the work environment not being managed to 100% execution.

Continue this process until all work environments are managed to 100% execution.

Call to Action

1. Start small. Select a unit or a process to improve the work environment.
2. Follow the implementation steps outlined in this chapter.
3. Gradually expand until it covers all operation areas and processes.

Creating a work environment for 100% execution is not a one-time event but an ongoing process of refinement and improvement. Stay committed to the journey, and you'll see remarkable results.

Key Takeaways for Chapter 19: Create a Work Environment for 100% Execution

1. Create a work environment that makes it reasonable, rational, and logical for employees to choose to precisely perform each step of the approved process, every time, even when no supervisor is present, and 100% comply with the conditions of employment.

2. Only the employee controls their behavior. Employees choose their behavior based on their analysis of the work environment.

3. The manager can systematically influence the employees' behavior by using tools they are authorized to use to manage the work environment, until the desired behavior, precisely following the process steps, and 100% complying with the conditions of employment, is chosen by employees every time.

4. Managers in most companies already have adequate tools and authority to manage the environment. In many cases, what is needed is teaching managers to fully use the set of tools they are already authorized to use. McClaskey Excellence Institute surveys of thousands of managers show that unit operations managers are authorized to use between 25 and 65 tools to manage the work environment, so operation employees will choose to precisely perform each step of the approved process every time, even when no supervisor is watching, and 100% comply with the conditions of employment. Some of these tools include training, coaching, checklists, audits, scheduling, the discipline process, hiring, firing, job assignments, pay, and praise. If root cause analysis reveals gaps in their toolset, company management needs to determine how to close those gaps.

The Next Chapter

Now that we've established how to create a work environment that fosters 100% execution, we'll explore another key element that significantly impacts employee respect, productivity, and self-esteem: how best to utilize your employees' full time and abilities. In the next chapter, we'll look at strategies for fully engaging the full time and abilities of each team member, further supporting your journey toward operations excellence.

CHAPTER 20

FULL USE OF TIME AND ABILITIES: SECONDARY JOBS

*"This time, like all times, is a very good one,
if we but know what to do with it."*

Ralph Waldo Emerson, essayist, lecturer, philosopher, and poet

Maximizing Potential: The Hidden Power of Full Engagement

Imagine entering a bustling workplace where every employee is fully engaged, purposeful, and productive. No one is idly standing around, checking their phone, or engaging in non-work-related chatter. Now, consider this shocking statistic: On average, only 40% of employees fully use their time and abilities toward their organization's mission. For managers, this figure rises to 60%. This begs the question: What percentage of your employees fully use their time and abilities toward your organization's mission? What could your organization achieve if you raised these numbers to nearly 100%? And the biggest surprise is, who benefits most when employees' time is fully utilized toward the mission?

The Respect Factor: Creating an Environment of Full Utilization

Maximizing employees' time and abilities isn't just about productivity—it's about respect, engagement, and unlocking human potential. It's about creating an environment where every second an employee spends on the job adds value to the organization's mission. Historically, many organizations have accepted a certain level of "downtime" as unavoidable. However, companies with extraordinary operations have learned that this doesn't have to be the case. They have put systems and policies in place that ensure full utilization of every employee's time and skills, benefiting the customer, the organization, and most of all, the employee. This approach isn't about making employees work harder but about respecting your company's most valuable resource—its people. It's about eliminating wasted time and unproductive effort, thereby increasing productivity, boosting employee self-esteem, fostering an environment where employees are proud of their work, and, most importantly, showing you respect your employees by not wasting their time.

Pal's Story: The Power of Secondary Jobs

When I worked at Pal's making french fries, not every customer ordered french fries. Pal's has a policy that states: Every second you are on the clock, you will be doing the most important thing you can do to contribute to the mission from your position. As part of my training, I was not only trained in my primary job but also in secondary jobs. I was empowered to switch to secondary jobs when there was nothing I could do related to my primary job. These secondary jobs included:

- Cleaning up my immediate work area (5-10 seconds).
- Restocking the french fry station (2-10 minutes).
- Helping teammates at other stations (2 minutes or longer, depending on how many teammates need help).

- Cleaning of the entire french fry station (20-30 minutes).

The result? I was never standing around doing nothing during my work shift. Contrary to what some might think, this didn't tire me out. It made me feel respected, valued, and an essential part of the team. Because I was 100% engaged, I was always shocked by how quickly my shift passed. I left each shift feeling great about myself and my contribution to Pal's mission.

At Pal's, we turned having your station clean and fully prepped for the next rush into a game: "Can you have your workstation in 100% shape at the end of the shift?" You won if, when the next shift worker came in, they couldn't find anything to do to set up the station because it was already perfectly set up and clean.

Numbers Don't Lie: The Case for Full Utilization

As previously mentioned, some of the surveys of thousands of managers we took during our classes at the McClaskey Excellence Institute revealed some startling statistics:

- On average, only 40% of employees fully use their time and ability toward the mission from their position.
- For managers, this figure rises to 60%, still leaving significant room for improvement.
- Perhaps most concerning, managers reported that 25% of their day is spent on things that never should have happened in the first place—a clear waste of talent and resources.

These figures highlight the significant potential for improvement in most organizations. A Gallup study revealed that only 21% of employees worldwide are engaged at work, pointing to a need for better use of employee time and abilities. Furthermore, highly engaged teams are 21% more profitable, showing the financial advantages of boosting employee engagement. Poor management practices cost the U.S. economy an estimated $7 trillion annually in lost productivity, stressing the importance of effective management. Additionally, companies with high employee engagement experience 59% less turnover, leading to substantial cost savings and greater stability. Prioritizing employee well-being is also vital, as organizations that do so see a 10% boost in productivity. Work environments optimized for 100% efficiency can significantly reduce stress, which is especially important since 44% of employees reported experiencing significant stress during the previous workday — a major factor in burnout. Lastly, only 33% of employees strongly agree that they understand their company's purpose, revealing a notable disconnect between employees and their organization's mission. Employees need a clear connection to purpose to be genuinely engaged.

Key Principles for Full Utilization of Time and Abilities

To create an environment of full-time and ability utilization, several key principles must be applied:

1. **Policy Implementation**: Establish and enforce a policy that all non-break time should be 100% productive, doing things that best contribute to the mission. Busy work that has no purpose should be avoided.

   - Example: A clear, approved written policy that all non-break time should be 100% productive, doing things that best contribute to the mission.

2. **Clear Communication**: Communicate this policy clearly during employee orientation and gain commitment.

   - Example: Clearly communicate during orientation the policy that all non-break time should be 100% productive, doing things that best contribute to the mission.

3. **Secondary Job Training**: Train all employees in secondary jobs and provide the necessary equipment and tools.
   - Example: Train employees how to restock their stations during slow times. Cross-training enables employees to assist other employees.

4. **Empowerment**: Unless managerial approval is required, authorize employees to switch to secondary jobs when primary jobs are not available and to switch back to primary jobs as soon as they need to be performed.
   - Example: Empower employees to take initiative and switch to secondary tasks without instruction.

5. **Consistent Enforcement**: Apply the policy consistently across all employees, all the time.
   - Example: Supervisors and managers monitor adherence to conditions of employment and consistently carry out the progressive discipline process.

6. **Positive and Corrective Coaching**: As noted in Chapter 17: Coaching to 100%, provide both positive reinforcement for productivity and immediate corrective coaching for non-productive behavior.
   - Example: Recognize employees who consistently follow the policy and coach those who don't.

7. **Managerial Role-Modeling**: Ensure managers exemplify this policy of full use of time and ability in their own work.
   - Example: Managers should be seen as actively engaged and following the same principles.

8. **Respect in Enforcement**: Always enforce rules and policies in a way that doesn't damage employee self-esteem.
   - Example: Deliver the positive and corrective coaching in a way that maintains self-esteem.

Addressing Concerns: Why Full Utilization is Feasible

Some might argue that pushing for 100% productivity is unrealistic or could lead to burnout. Common objections include:

- **"Employees need breaks to rest."**

  Response: Of course, scheduled breaks are essential and should be respected. This policy applies only to non-break work time. During scheduled break time, the employee should not work and may engage in any activities they choose, provided they comply with the company's break guidelines.

- **"If we force employees to work all the time, they'll quit."**

  Response: When implemented correctly, with clear communication and consistent, respectful enforcement, this policy often increases engagement and job satisfaction. Using all employees' work time to accomplish the company's mission shows you respect their time and abilities.

- **"Our business will get a reputation for not caring about employees."**

  Response: On the contrary, making full use of employees' time and abilities shows respect for their potential and contribution. It provides a work environment where employees take pride in their work.

- **"Working every second you are on the clock isn't an accepted standard for what it means to work."**

  Response: While it may not be common, full use of employees' time and abilities is a hallmark of companies with extraordinary operations. It's part of what sets them apart. If everyone else is productive the entire shift, you don't want to be the only one who is not.

A New Perspective: Time Equals Respect

The key revelation is this: When you create an environment of full-time and ability utilization for everyone, you're not just increasing productivity —you're showing profound respect for your employees. You're saying: "Your time is valuable. Your abilities are important. We want to make the most of what you have to offer." This approach transforms the workplace. It eliminates boredom and disengagement that comes from having nothing to do. It drives pride, respect, and engagement because the employee is a full contributor to the team. It creates a sense of purpose and importance in every moment of the workday. Perhaps most importantly, it significantly boosts employees' self-esteem and job satisfaction.

Steps to Implement Full Utilization in Your Workplace

To implement this approach in your organization:

1. **Establish a clear policy on the full use of time and abilities:** Create a written policy for the full use of time and abilities for all operations employees. This policy supports creating secondary jobs for all operations employees and empowers employees to switch to them when their primary job isn't needed.

2. **Communicate this policy during employee orientation:** Ensure all new hires understand this is a condition of employment and commit to complying with the policy.

3. **Train all employees in their primary and secondary roles:** Prepare employees fully by training them for both their primary and backup positions. Cross-train employees in specific tasks of other jobs so they can assist colleagues when their primary duties are not needed.

4. **Empower employees to switch to secondary tasks when primary tasks are unavailable:** Allow employees the flexibility

to take on secondary tasks without waiting for managerial approval.

5. **Implement a system of immediate positive and corrective coaching**: Provide real-time feedback to encourage adherence and address deviations.

6. **Ensure managers role-model the policy**: Managers should lead by example, demonstrating a commitment to the policy.

7. **Use progressive discipline for repeat offenders:** Create a clear, fair system for handling non-compliance. Begin with training and coaching. Disciplinary actions should only be taken after repeated violations.

8. **Consistently enforce the policy across all operations employees**: Monitor adherence and apply the policy to everyone in operations. Consistency is key to preventing HR issues.

The Bottom Line: Respecting Time for Maximum Impact

You can deliver your products and services fully aligned with your brand requirements, consistently, under all conditions. You can have highly engaged employees who are productive, always doing what they are authorized to do to best contribute to the mission, 100% of the time they are not on a scheduled break. This creates a true win-win-win for employees, the organization, and customers.

Call to Action

1. Start by assessing your current situation:
   - What percentage of your employees fully use their time and abilities?
   - What percentage of your managers fully use their time and abilities?

- How much of your managers' time is spent on unnecessary "firefighting" or other things that should not have happened in the first place?

2. Design each job and work structure so it has a reasonable break or "non-work" time built in.

3. Implement the policy of full use of time and ability.

   - This policy only addresses time that is designated as "work time" and does not include designated breaks or "non-work" time.

4. Start with one department or team as a pilot program. Carefully watch results and collect feedback from both employees and managers. Train managers to create a work environment where employees choose to use their full work time productively. Remember, this isn't just about boosting productivity. It's about creating an environment where everyone can and does contribute their best from their role to the overall mission, feels valued, and takes pride in their work.

5. Based on the pilot program being successful, systematically expand the full use of time and ability to all areas.

Key Takeaways for Chapter 20: Full Use of Time and Abilities: Secondary Jobs

1. It's about creating a work environment where every moment an employee spends on the job contributes meaningfully to the organization's mission. One, but only one of many possible tactics to achieve this, is through secondary jobs that employees switch to when work on their primary job is unavailable or not needed. A company should choose the best approach that aligns with its culture and values.

2. When you foster an environment that maximizes the use of time and ability for the mission, you're not just boosting

productivity—you're demonstrating genuine respect for your employees. You're saying: "Your time is valuable. Your abilities are important. We want to make the most of what you have to offer."

3. Maximizing time and ability prevents boredom and disengagement caused by having nothing to do. It promotes pride, respect, productivity, and engagement because you are a full contributor to the team. It creates a sense of purpose and importance in every moment of the workday, boosting pride in work and reducing turnover. Most importantly, it greatly enhances employees' self-esteem and job satisfaction. What it does not do is lead to exhaustion. It is assumed that work includes built-in, reasonable breaks or "non-work" time. The full use of time and abilities applies only during designated work hours. We assume that break time can be spent doing anything employees want within company restrictions.

The Next Chapter

We have now covered eight of the nine elements of People Excellence. All of your employees can and do choose to accurately perform each step of the approved process every time, even when no supervisor is watching. They decide to fully comply with the Conditions of Employment 100% of the time. However, there remains one other essential element for achieving and maintaining extraordinary operations: respect. In the next chapter, we will examine the final, vital element that applies to every interaction involving an employee.

CHAPTER 21

RESPECT FOR PEOPLE: THE GOLDEN RULE OF ALL TRANSACTIONS

"Our mission statement about treating people with respect and dignity is not just words but a creed we live by every day. You can't expect your employees to exceed the expectations of your customers if you don't exceed the employees' expectations of management."

Howard Schultz, former Chairman and CEO of Starbucks

The Power of Respect: A Foundation for Success

A Harvard Business Review study finds that being treated with respect is a top factor for employees.

Imagine two identical companies with the same products, processes, and market position. Company A views respect as a nice-to-have, while Company B makes respect a core value in every interaction. Which company do you think will succeed in the long run? This question highlights why the final element of the People Excellence pillar isn't just another "what" to do but a transformative "how" that influences all interactions and touches every part of your organization.

Respect: The Cornerstone of Extraordinary Operations

Respect is not just an inherent right of each person; it's the foundation of extraordinary operations. It's the secret ingredient that elevates good companies to great ones, encouraging high performance and low turnover. This final element of People Excellence is unique — it's not about what we do, but how we do it. Dr. Christine Porath, a leading researcher on workplace civility, states, "Respect is the currency of trust. When people feel respected, they are more trusting of the organization and willing to put in extra effort."

Research from the Society for Human Resource Management (SHRM) found that respectful treatment of employees is the top factor in job satisfaction, even ahead of pay.

Stories of Respect: Transforming Everyday Interactions

Let's look at three scenarios that illustrate the power of respect:

- **New Employee Experience:** Miguel, a recent hire at TechInnovate, is pleasantly surprised when the CEO remembers his name and asks about his first week during a chance encounter in the elevator. This small act of respect makes Miguel feel valued and motivates him to share his best ideas from week one.

- **Mistake Handling:** Aisha, a project manager at GlobalHealth, realizes she's made a significant error in a report. Instead of being criticized, her supervisor, Jack, calmly discusses the mistake with her, focusing on learning and prevention. This respectful approach turns a potential crisis into a growth opportunity.

- **Cross-departmental Collaboration:** The marketing and engineering teams at EcoSolutions often clashed due to differing priorities. The CEO introduces a respect-based communication workshop. As a result, both teams begin to appreciate each other's perspectives, leading to more innovative and successful product launches. After the workshop, the time to complete cross-departmental projects at EcoSolutions decreased by 20%.

I also want to share a firsthand story about how a large, established Fortune 50 company showed respect for its diverse, multilingual employees. Johnson & Johnson leadership asked me to train a group of their leaders from around the world on the Malcolm Baldrige National Quality Award. The goal was to prepare these leaders for a discussion on whether Johnson & Johnson should apply U.S.-based award criteria globally. This alone demonstrated respect. But the bigger example was still to come. I found myself teaching a class of over 50 managers from 7 different countries speaking five different languages. Many participants from non-English-speaking countries had limited English proficiency, and I only spoke English. Moreover, there was no designated interpreter. This was way before the now common translation apps.

I was worried that most of the class wouldn't understand what I was about to say over the next two days, which would be very disrespectful. The organizer reassured me: "We have groups in the same class with multiple languages all the time. We never disrespect our employees. We've set it up so everyone will learn." And that's precisely what happened. How did they do it? People who shared the same language sat together at round tables. At each table, one or two bilingual individuals fluent in both English and their native language helped facilitate understanding. My instructions from Johnson & Johnson were to teach for about 20 minutes, then pause for 10 minutes to let the bilinguals explain what was covered to the rest of the group at each of their table. They would give the go-ahead, and I'd move on with the next segment. We had intentionally built in extra time, and I now understood why. It worked perfectly. Everyone expressed confidence that they understood the material and could discuss how the Baldrige

Award criteria might be helpful in their cultures. This was a powerful example of respect.

These narratives demonstrate how respect, when woven into an organization's fabric, can transform employee experiences and drive excellence at all levels.

The Business Case for Respect: Research and Results

Recent research underscores the tangible benefits of fostering a culture of respect:

- A Deloitte Global Human Capital Trends report revealed that organizations with a strong sense of purpose, including respect as a core value, significantly outperformed the S&P 500.
- Research published in the Harvard Business Review found that employees who feel respected are:
    - 56% healthier.
    - 1.72 times more trustful and trusting.
    - 89% more likely to stay with their organization.
    - 92% more focused on their work.
    - 26% more engaged in their work.

These statistics highlight the profound impact respect has on organizational success.

Guiding Principles: Building a Culture of Respect

To create a culture of respect, organizations must embrace these key principles:

1. **Universal Application:** Treat everyone with respect in every conversation and interaction, no matter the hierarchy or situation.

Example: At Zappos, every employee, including the CEO, answers customer service calls during busy periods, demonstrating respect for customers and frontline staff.

2. **Full Utilization:** One of the best ways to show respect for an employee is to make sure their time and abilities are fully used to accomplish the mission.

    Example: Google's "20% time" policy respects employees' creative abilities by allowing them to spend one day a week on projects of their choosing.

3. **Professional Treatment**: Treat all employees as professionals at all times.

    Example: Pixar's "Braintrust" meetings, where everyone's opinion is valued equally, regardless of their position.

4. **Respectful Conflict Resolution:** Address challenging conversations with respect.

    Example: At Bridgewater Associates, employees are encouraged to provide honest, respectful feedback to anyone in the organization, including the CEO.

5. **Dignified Discipline**: Apply progressive discipline respectfully.

    Example: Starbucks' approach to performance improvement focuses on coaching and support rather than punitive measures.

6. **Setting Up for Success:** Offer the tools, training, and support necessary for every employee to succeed.

    Example: Amazon's "Career Choice" program, which pre-pays 95% of employees' tuition for training in high-demand fields.

Addressing Criticisms: The Balance of Respect and Results

Critics might argue that an emphasis on respect could lead to:

- **Lack of Candor**: "If we're always respectful, won't we avoid necessary hard conversations?"

Response: Respect doesn't mean avoiding difficult topics. It means addressing them in a way that preserves dignity and promotes understanding.

- **Decreased Productivity**: "Won't all this focus on respect slow us down?"

Response: Research shows that respectful environments are more productive. Disrespect leads to disengagement and decreased output.

- **Cultural Misunderstandings**: "In a global company, isn't it impossible to define respect that works for everyone?"

Response: While expressions of respect may vary culturally, the underlying principle of valuing each individual is universal. Training bridges cultural divide.

Example: Global organizations like IBM have successfully addressed these challenges by implementing respect training tailored to various cultures, ensuring a unified yet culturally sensitive approach to respect.

The Strategic Advantage of Respect

The key revelation is this: respect is not just a moral imperative; it's a strategic advantage. It acts as the catalyst that turns good processes into extraordinary operations and ordinary employees into high-performing teams. It's also crucial for maintaining 100% success once it is achieved. This insight shifts respect from being a "soft skill" to a core business strategy. It's not just about being kind; it's about fostering an environment where respect thrives, collaboration becomes the norm, and every individual feels motivated to give their best. As Satya Nadella, CEO of Microsoft, says, "Respect is the foundation of our culture. It's not just how we treat each other, but how we think about our products, our customers, and our impact on the world."

Implementing Respect in Your Organization

To implement a culture of respect:

1. **Assess the Current State**: Conduct a company-wide survey to gauge your organization's current level of respect.

2. **Develop a Respect Policy**: Create a clear, actionable policy that outlines expectations for respectful behavior. Consider listing respect as a company value.

3. **Leadership Alignment**: Ensure all leaders understand and commit to role modeling respectful behavior in all interactions. It starts at the top of the organization.

4. **Training Program:** Create comprehensive training on respectful communication and conflict resolution. Equip managers and all employees to recognize their own and others' disrespectful behavior, as well as tactics to address such behavior.

5. **Embed Respect into the Culture:** Respect should be a characteristic of every interaction. Begin by establishing this as a practice among top managers and gradually extend it throughout the hierarchy until all employees adopt it and it is part of the culture.

6. **Create Feedback Systems:** Set up ways for reporting disrespectful behavior and offering suggestions for improvement.

7. **Respect in Assessments:** Respectful behavior should be a key factor in annual evaluations and a primary consideration for promotions. Can you afford to promote a leader who shows disrespect?

   Example: Jack Welch, former CEO of GE, made Six Sigma training a requirement for promotion, ensuring employees adopted essential behaviors. Respect can similarly serve as a key criterion for advancement.

8. **Recognition Program:** Create a program to identify and reward respectful behavior.

9. **Evaluate and Modify:** Frequently review the effectiveness of your respect initiatives and make adjustments as necessary.

Call to Action: Creating a Respectful Workplace

- Perform respect audits within your organization.

- Make respect a core value and company policy that applies to all company-related interactions. Consider making respect a mandatory behavior for promotions and include it in annual management and employee performance evaluations.

- Begin with top management, ensuring all interactions are respectful, then gradually extend this approach through the hierarchy to include all employees.

Key Takeaways for Chapter 21: Respect for People: The Golden Rule of All Transactions

1. This final element of People Excellence is unique—it's not about what we do, but how we do it.

2. Respect is a fundamental right of everyone who works for or is connected to a company. The company must have systematic, meaningful policies on respect that are enforced. For example, high ratings on respect are required for managerial promotions. The company must not permit any disrespectful interactions.

3. Show respect in every conversation and interaction, regardless of hierarchy or circumstances. It is important to understand that respect does not mean avoiding difficult conversations. Instead, it means having those difficult conversations respectfully.

4. Employees rank "respectful treatment of all employees at all levels" as one of the top factors influencing job satisfaction.

5. Respect is not just a moral obligation; it's a strategic advantage. It is the cultural trait that turns good processes into extraordinary operations and ordinary employees into high-performing teams.

6. Respect is a key cornerstone of extraordinary operations. Respect is required to both obtain extraordinary operations and to maintain it.

7. An essential aspect of respect is designing jobs that maximize employees' time and abilities.

The Next Chapters

We have completed all four pillars and elements of the McClaskey® Triple 100® Path to Excellence. Understanding the process is the first step. Congratulations on reaching this milestone!

The next steps involve implementing the Path to Excellence to achieve and maintain extraordinary operations. The upcoming section of the book will review the McClaskey® Triple 100® Path to Excellence, share best practices for its implementation, discuss strategies for maintaining extraordinary operations, and offer resources for further assistance with both implementation and maintaining gains. It will begin with a high-level overview of the Path to Excellence, ensuring the entire Path remains clear as you design and execute your plans.

IMPLEMENTING THE PATH TO EXCELLENCE AND MAINTAINING EXTRAORDINARY OPERATIONS

"Vision without execution is hallucination."

Thomas Edison, one of America's greatest inventors and businessmen

The rest of the book offers guidance and best practices for achieving and maintaining extraordinary operations. The following four chapters are:

1. **Chapter 22:** The McClaskey® Triple 100® Path to Excellence: Bringing It All Together: This chapter provides a high-level summary of the book and an overview of the Path to Excellence. This helps keep the key concepts top of mind as you put them into practice. You will see how the four pillars and key concepts are interconnected and integrated, creating a holistic path that leads to extraordinary operations.

2. **Chapter 23:** Implementing the Path to Excellence: Based on years of helping companies implement the Path to Excellence, I will share best practices for implementation and what does and does not work. This will guide you on a proven path for implementation as you transform your company from ordinary to extraordinary operations.

3. **Chapter 24: Maintaining Extraordinary Operations:** Reaching excellence is a significant milestone worth celebrating. However, achieving extraordinary operations is only half the battle. The other half is keeping your operations at 100% to ensure your extraordinary operations and results are maintained.

4. **EPILOGUE: Where to Get More Assistance: Your journey to excellence continues with resources, training, and support to elevate your operations from ordinary to extraordinary. Here, I will show you that you don't have to achieve and maintain extraordinary operations on your own. I will list some specific help and support available.**

CHAPTER 22

THE MCCLASKEY® TRIPLE 100® PATH TO EXCELLENCE: BRINGING IT ALL TOGETHER

"Greatness is not a function of circumstance. Greatness, it turns out, is largely a matter of conscious choice and discipline."

Jim Collins

Overview

Now that you understand all four pillars of the McClaskey® Triple 100® Path to Excellence, the next step is to focus on implementing what you learned. To do this, I first want to give you a brief overview of the Path to Excellence and its four pillars. Chapter 23 will focus on implementing the Path to Excellence so you achieve extraordinary operations, and Chapter 24 will focus on maintaining extraordinary operations.

To be successful, you need to give your customers a reason to choose you over your competitors. One of the best ways to build customer loyalty is to consistently deliver on your promises—not just most of the time, but every time. This approach will give you a sustainable competitive advantage because few competitors will ever aim for 100%. Focusing on delivering your products and services 100% to your brand requirements, 100% of the time, under 100% of the conditions, will generate high revenue with lower costs and less stress. This strategy creates the Triple Win™: (a) making your customers 100% delighted, (b) empowering your employees for 100% success, and (c) growing your business to maximize revenue, repeat business, and profits.

The Foundation of Extraordinary Operations

The McClaskey® Triple 100® Path to Excellence is designed with a specific purpose: to achieve extraordinary operations. The objective of extraordinary operations is to deliver your company's products, services, and customer experiences:

- **100% to brand requirements.**
- **100% of the time.**
- **Under 100% of the conditions.**

This isn't just a lofty goal; it's a practical way to transform your operations from ordinary to extraordinary. By implementing the four pillars of the Path to Excellence, you will no longer deliver your products and services mostly right, most of the time, but instead will deliver them 100% to your brand requirements, 100% of the time.

The Four Pillars of the Path to Excellence

McClaskey® Triple 100®
Path to Excellence
Ordinary ➜ Extraordinary Operations

Pillar 1:
Think
Excellence

Pillar 2:
Process
Excellence

Pillar 3:
People Excellence

Pillar 4:
Focus
Excellence

Summary: The Four Pillars of Excellence

Our journey through the Path to Excellence is built on four fundamental pillars:

1. **Think Excellence**: Setting your mindset and the company standard to deliver the products, services, and customer experience 100% to the brand requirements every time. Anything below 100% is unacceptable.

2. **Focus Excellence**: Aligning every aspect of your operations with your mission and KCRs.

3. **Process Excellence:** Designing processes so that when the steps of the approved process are precisely followed, your employees will consistently deliver your products, services, and customer experience 100% to the brand requirements, 100% of the time.

4. **People Excellence**: Engaging, empowering, and enabling your employees to precisely perform the steps of the approved process every time, so they can deliver your products, services, and customer experience 100% to the brand requirements, 100% of the time.

These interconnected pillars create a comprehensive framework that transforms your operations from ordinary to extraordinary; from mostly meeting your brand requirements to consistently fulfilling them. This is how you encourage your customers to pass your competitors and choose your business instead. They can rely on you to deliver. They cannot rely on your competitors to do so.

Let us review the essence of the four pillars of the Path to Excellence:

Think Excellence

Think Excellence
Your Target is Every Instead of Most

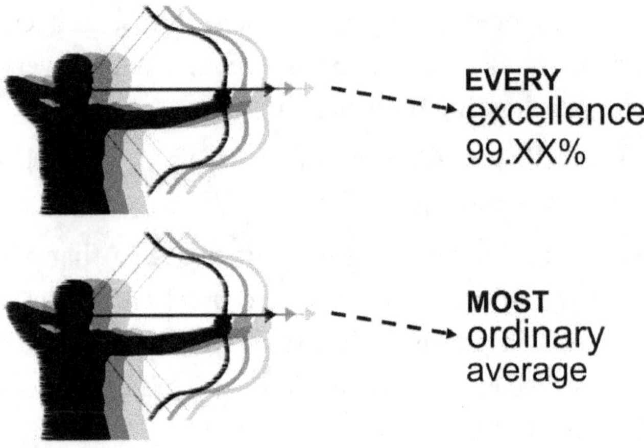

The journey to extraordinary operations begins with leaders having a 100% mindset. This is a crucial starting point because the quality level leaders deem acceptable determines the maximum outgoing quality an organization can deliver to customers. It is so important because the percentage of time the organization's products and services meet 100% of the brand requirements will not consistently exceed the leaders' acceptance threshold.

The quality standards leaders accept are mainly shaped by their mindset and beliefs. Ordinary leaders accept "most," which is the standard for nearly all leaders in service organizations. In these organizations, products, services, and customer experiences will generally meet your brand requirements most of the time and under most conditions. Why? Because they believe that is the best their organization can do. Accepting "most" as the standard creates a self-fulfilling prophecy. Leaders believe it and accept it, thereby limiting the organization's performance. Their standard of "most" is the problem. Since they accept that only "most" of the products will meet 100% of the brand requirements, they also accept that "some" of the products and services delivered to the customers will not meet the brand requirements.

Extraordinary leaders only accept "every" or 100%. The products, services, and customer experience will consistently meet 100% of your organization's brand requirements, 100% of the time, under 100% of the conditions. Even leaders who only accept "every" may still deal with a few products and services that don't meet 100% of the standards, but such instances will be much less frequent than with a mindset of "most."

Toyota's Production System (TPS) exemplifies this principle. According to a Harvard Business Review study, Toyota's relentless pursuit of excellence often results in their plants having 50% fewer defects than comparable facilities, and their vehicles lead in sales and reliability.

Focus Excellence

McClaskey® Triple 100® Path to Excellence
Focus Excellence

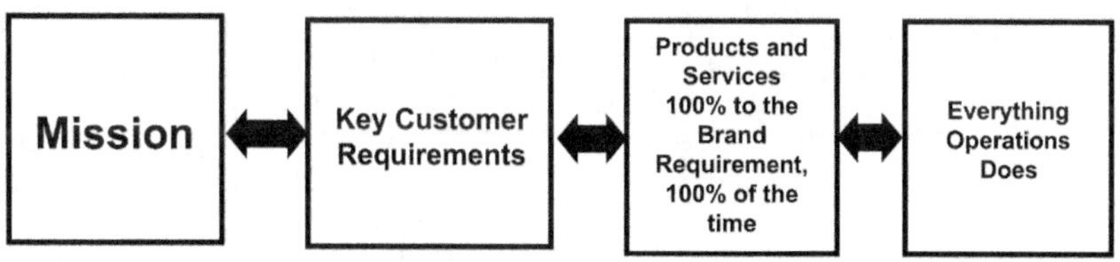

This pillar aligns everything the company does with the best-known way to achieve the organization's mission. The mission is an organization's purpose or reason for existence. The fundamental mission of every company is to delight its customers in a way that builds loyalty, encourages repeat business, and generates positive recommendations. A company fulfills its mission by meeting all its KCRs every time. The KCRs are the critical few requirements the customer has, all of which must be satisfied for the customer to be delighted with the experience with your organization. KCRs are what you promise customers when they do business with your organization. The role of operations and the operations unit manager in meeting the KCRs is to deliver products, services, and the customer experience 100% to the brand requirements, 100% of the time, under 100% of the conditions. Everything operations do is focused and aligned to delivering the products, services, and customer experience 100% to the brand requirements.

Amazon's customer-centric approach illustrates this perfectly. Jeff Bezos, in his letter to shareholders, emphasized, "Obsessive customer focus is by far the most protective of Day 1 vitality."

Process Excellence

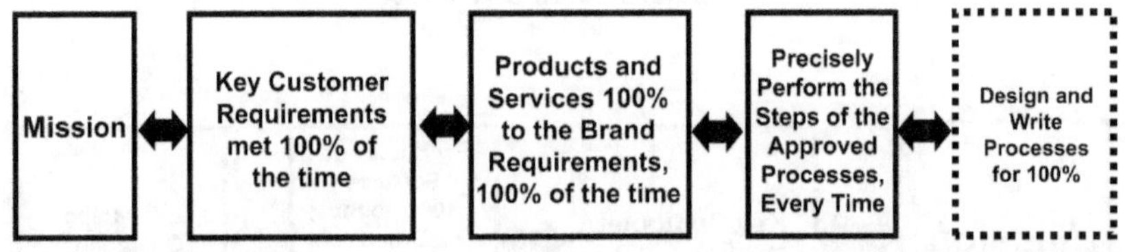

In this pillar, we design processes to 100%. This means that when a trained employee precisely performs the steps of the approved process, they will deliver the product or service 100% to the brand requirements; 100% of the time; under 100% of the conditions, and will be done in the most efficient way possible. Once the processes are designed for 100% and incorporate the best-known methods, they are standardized and mandated for use everywhere applicable. Standardized processes are systematically reviewed using the company's systematic improvement process.

General Electric's implementation of Six Sigma in the 1990s is a prime example. According to GE's 1999 annual report, the company estimated that Six Sigma, a method they used to ensure their products were delivered 100% of the time, generated $2 billion in benefits in 1999 alone.

People Excellence

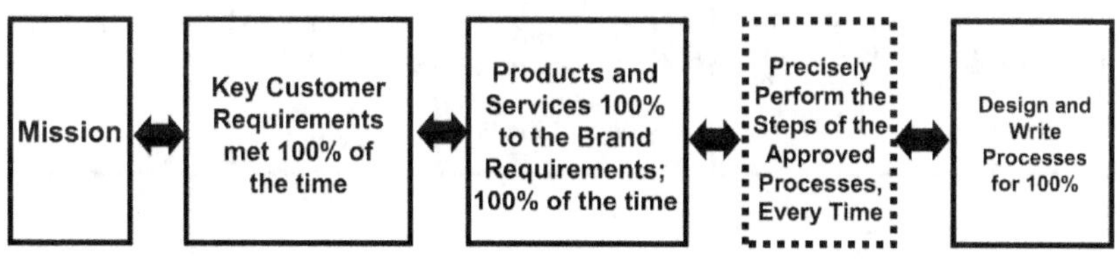

During the People Excellence Pillar, the process is executed to produce and deliver the product, service, or customer experience 100% to the brand requirements, every time. The key behavior that the People Excellence pillar aims to develop is that everyone working in operations chooses to precisely perform each step of the approved process, every time, even if no supervisor is present, and fully complies with the conditions of employment. People Excellence establishes the conditions that make this possible through the implementation of nine elements: Hiring; Conditions of Employment; Accountability; Training to 100%; Coaching to 100%; Empower; Environment for 100% Execution; Full Use of Time and Abilities; and Respect for People.

Zappos, the online shoe retailer, demonstrates this through its culture of employee empowerment. Tony Hsieh, the late CEO of Zappos, said in his book Delivering Happiness that "If you get the culture right, most of the other stuff — like great customer service, or building a great long-term brand, or passionate employees and customers — will happen naturally on its own."

Implementing the Four Pillars Causes the Mission to be Accomplished

Implementing the four pillars achieves the mission by creating a seamless flow from process design to mission.

As a result of the Process Excellence pillar, all processes are designed for 100%. Implementing the People Excellence pillar ensures that employees perform the steps of the processes accurately every time. When processes that are 100% designed are followed precisely every time, products and services consistently meet 100% of the brand requirements, leading to the operations portion of the KCRs being fulfilled 100% of the time. When the KCRs are consistently satisfied, the organization achieves its mission to delight customers in a way that creates loyalty, with every customer, every time. Satisfied customers return and recommend your organization.

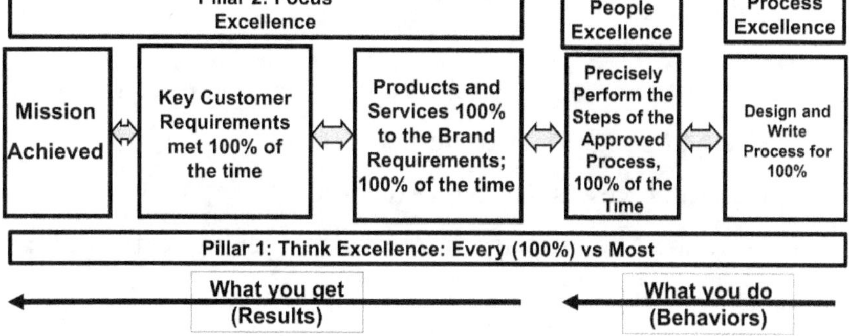

The Triple Win

The outcomes of implementing the McClaskey˚ Triple 100˚ Path to Excellence result in extraordinary operations that create a triple win for the customers, employees, and the company:

1. **Customers:** Customer delight and loyalty because the products and services consistently meet the KCRs.

2. **Employees:** Engaged workforce because they are set up for 100% success, which leads to higher productivity, greater job satisfaction, and lower turnover.

3. **Company:** Increased revenue, profits, recommendations, and a sustainable competitive advantage.

This isn't just about improving operations; it's about creating a culture that fosters sustainable success for all stakeholders. This culture is sustainable because all three major stakeholders win simultaneously, so everyone is motivated to do their part to keep it working.

Key Learnings Along the Path

Through the McClaskey® Triple 100® Path to Excellence, you've discovered how to:

- Achieve more repeat business than your competitors.

- Design for legendary customer service.

- Design processes for 100% execution.

- Describe the manager's role in achieving extraordinary operations.

- Communicate and reinforce conditions of employment that are understood and followed 100% by all.

- Develop training that gets 100% of your employees enabled to do the job 100% right under 100% of the conditions (Triple 100® Training).

- Hire the right people to reduce turnover while keeping productivity high.

- Design jobs to fully use employee time and abilities and design out employee problems.

- Implement lasting improvements that are used by all and never go away.

- Create operations that are easy to manage and operate at "best-in-class" levels.

The Three Extraordinary Principles

Underlying the entire Path to Excellence are three key principles:

1. Set everyone up for 100% success.

2. Eliminate gray.

3. Improve operations so it is a win/win/win for Customers, Employees, and the Company, all at the same time.

These principles guide every decision and action along the Path to Excellence. They are characteristic of everything done in each of the four Pillars.

The Role of Respect for People: I have emphasized that respect is not just a moral imperative and an inherent right of every person, but also a strategic advantage. It's the invisible force that turns ordinary operations into extraordinary achievements. Respect is a key ingredient that transforms good processes into extraordinary operations and ordinary employees into high-performing teams. It also plays a vital role in helping us maintain excellence over time. And it is free. It costs nothing extra to deliver a strong message respectfully. A significant benefit is that if you respectfully let someone know something that can help them improve, they are more likely to use your advice. One of the most important ways to show respect is to follow our first principle of setting everyone up for 100% success. Respect is one of the few elements that applies to every part of the Path to Excellence. It extends beyond the Path to Excellence and should be incorporated into every company interaction.

Call to Action

You are now familiar with the McClaskey® Triple 100® Path to Excellence and its advantages. The path and its benefits are straightforward, making it one of the safest and most worthwhile investments to enhance your business. You have just received an overview of the key points of the Path to Excellence. Now, let's move on to Chapter 23 to develop a clear implementation plan and then begin the implementation.

Key Takeaways: Chapter 22: Triple 100® Path to Excellence: Bringing It All Together

1. McClaskey® Triple 100® Path to Excellence is the proven path to go from ordinary to extraordinary operations.

2. The Path to Excellence consists of four Pillars: Think Excellence, Focus Excellence, Process Excellence, and People Excellence.

3. The Path to Excellence has three underlying principles that apply to all four pillars: Set everyone up for 100% success; Eliminate gray; Improve operations so they are a win/win/win for Customers, Employees, and the Company, all at the same time.

The Next Chapter

The McClaskey® Triple 100® Path to Excellence offers a complete framework for achieving and maintaining extraordinary operations. Incorporating these elements into your organization creates a seamless flow in which operations excellence becomes the norm and every part of your operations reliably delivers top results.

In the next chapter, I will share best practices for implementing the Path to Excellence that will elevate your organization from ordinary to extraordinary operations. I have learned these best practices over the past 50 years while helping various companies adopt them. Based on this experience, I will guide you in developing a successful implementation plan. I will explain what works and what doesn't, helping you avoid costly and difficult mistakes. I have found that having a partner familiar with these best practices and experienced in guiding companies through the Path to Excellence can significantly accelerate your implementation, reduce frustration, and boost your chances of success.

Are you ready to take your operations from ordinary to extraordinary? The path is clear, and the rewards are within reach. Let's continue this journey toward operational excellence together.

Mark Sanborn clearly articulated your biggest challenge in his book The Fred Factor: "The true competitor is mediocrity." We must always remain dedicated to excellence and avoid settling for mediocrity. It's so easy to accept being ordinary. And when you do, you are just like all the other ordinary companies that are competing with each other based on price rather than excellence.

CHAPTER 23

IMPLEMENTING THE PATH TO EXCELLENCE

"All good thoughts and ideas mean nothing without action."

Mahatma Gandhi, Indian lawyer, anti-colonial activist

The Path Forward to Obtaining 100% Extraordinary Operations

As we reach the summit of our journey through the McClaskey® Triple 100® Path to Excellence, I want you to pause and reflect on how much you've accomplished. You've learned about the four pillars of excellence: Think Excellence, Focus Excellence, Process Excellence, and People Excellence. We have explored the details of each element and started to see how they connect to create a tapestry of extraordinary operations.

This holistic approach to operations excellence distinguishes truly extraordinary organizations from others. It's about instilling a mindset of excellence at every level, from strategic decision-making to daily operations.

As you implement the Path to Excellence, I encourage you to think holistically. Strive to use the Path to Excellence to develop a 100% mindset where operations excellence is the norm and not the exception; to align every task with your mission and KCRs; and to design and execute processes that consistently deliver 100% to your brand requirements, every time. Maintain a clear focus on the culture of excellence you are cultivating. A work culture where:

- It is a win-win for all three stakeholders: Customers, Employees, and the Company.
- Customers, employees, and managers would all place the McClaskey® $1000 Bet on the products and services meeting 100% to the brand requirements.
- Employees are set up for 100% success.
- Employees self-manage their work so they only deliver products and services 100% to the brand requirements, 100% of the time.
- Your company isn't doing extraordinary things; it is doing ordinary things at an extraordinary level.
- You are making full use of everyone's time and abilities to accomplish the mission.
- Everything is done with respect.

The journey toward operational excellence starts with you. Set your personal and the company's standards to 100%, aiming to meet your brand requirements every time, not just most of the time. No longer accept mediocrity. With this mindset, evaluate your current practices against each of the four pillars of the Path to Excellence. Based on that evaluation, identify areas for improvement. Implement the Path to Excellence pillars to address these gaps. The Path to Excellence provides proven practices to close the gaps and build extraordinary operations.

As we move into implementation, the key is to start small and stay consistent. We recommend choosing one process and fully implementing it at 100% in one unit or store. Then, build on that success by taking the same process to 100% in all relevant areas. After that, select another process and repeat the steps until all processes are at 100% where they are applicable.

The winning formula for implementation is the two P's: Persistence and Patience. Managers guided by both successfully lead their organizations from ordinary to extraordinary operations. Track your progress, stay open to feedback, and make adjustments. Persistence involves making consistent progress each week, while Patience means understanding it will take 1-2 years to transform from ordinary to extraordinary operations.

Remember, making your organization a model of operations excellence is challenging but highly rewarding. It requires commitment, discipline, and a willingness to rethink current approaches. With each step you take, you'll move closer to a workplace where excellence is the norm, not the exception.

I encourage you to embrace this journey. It isn't a single destination but an ongoing process of growth and improvement that benefits all three main stakeholders: the customer, the employee, and the company. As you follow and implement the Path to Excellence, you will customize the approach for your company. Commit to building a culture of accountability, engagement, and excellence. The result will be an inspired, empowered, aligned, and dedicated management and workforce committed to achieving and maintaining operations excellence at every level of your organization.

In People Excellence, I highlighted the importance of hiring the right people, establishing clear conditions of employment, holding people accountable, providing training to 100%, coaching to 100%, empowering employees only to deliver products and services that fully meet the brand requirements, setting an environment conducive to flawless execution, making full use of time and abilities, and doing every interaction with respect. These principles lay the foundation for achieving extraordinary operations. People Excellence is the most challenging pillar to implement and maintain. Most of your implementation efforts will be focused on People Excellence.

The first three pillars set up People Excellence. They focus on creating an environment where excellence will thrive. This involves using these pillars to lay a foundation for an environment of excellence. Process Excellence aims to design processes that ensure 100% execution. Focus Excellence is about aligning every task with your mission and KCRs. Think Excellence encourages cultivating a mindset in which delivering the company's products and services to 100% of brand standards is the only acceptable level across your organization.

Implementing and Obtaining Extraordinary Operations

The McClaskey Excellence Institute has helped thousands of organizations on the journey from ordinary to extraordinary operations. Here is a proven implementation plan that is highly effective. This plan provides a solid foundation that you can use as is or customize to fit your specific needs and project management process.

1. Have company leadership attend our AWCR class as they begin implementation, and then continue with consulting to support the implementation.

    a. The McClaskey Excellence Institute's Achieving World-Class Results class is designed to guide your leadership team through the initial implementation. It breaks the process into manageable parts so that each week, you implement a segment of the Path to Excellence. By the end of the class, you will have completed the initial implementation. Its success comes not only from teaching the Path to Excellence outlined in this book but also from providing each leadership team with structure, accountability, timely identification of best practices, and access to McClaskey Excellence Institute implementation experts to support implementation.

2. Make implementation of extraordinary operations a 1-2 year strategic initiative.

    a. As part of your strategic plan or annual planning, make implementing extraordinary operations a company initiative.

    b. Assign an executive to lead your company's extraordinary operations initiative. Usually, it is either the head of operations, the President, or the owner.

3. Have a project plan that follows the McClaskey® Triple 100® Path to Excellence. Have all the action items in the plan resourced. The plan is actively managed by company management, with progress reviewed vs. the plan at least every other week. When action items in the action plan are not implemented by their due dates, management takes steps to get them back on track.

    a. The first priority of the extraordinary operations initiative team is to develop a project plan for implementing the McClaskey® Triple 100® Path to Excellence. This team must set goals that are Specific, Measurable, Achievable, Realistic, and Timely—commonly known as SMART goals. Once the plan is complete, the company will be operating with extraordinary operations. The project plan needs to be resourced and carried out at a pace suitable for your company. Typically, it takes between 12 and 18 months to fully implement the Path to Excellence and have all processes running at 100%.

4. Form your initial group of managers to start the Implementation of the Path to Excellence.

    • I recommend that the initial group be all the operations managers above the store or unit management level, as well as some store or unit managers from stores/units where you will initially implement the ordinary to extraordinary initiative.

5. Train your managers in the McClaskey˚ Triple 100˚ Path to Excellence

    a. Train your managers, as they will be actively involved in the implementation.

        I. Train your initial team of managers:

            - Typically, the first step in the project plan is to train the initial group of leaders on the McClaskey® Triple 100® Path to Excellence. This is included early in implementation because the Path to Excellence training provides all involved leaders and managers with a shared language, a common goal, a unified 100% mindset, a proven path to follow, and the knowledge of how to implement it in their operation. This is exactly what we have observed happening with management teams that have completed the McClaskey Excellence Institute's Achieving World-Class Results (AWCR) class.

        II. Train the remaining operations managers as they get involved in the implementation.

            - Two formats for the AWCR training are to attend a public class where multiple companies attend, and a private class where everyone in the class is from your company.

                i. We have trained thousands of companies on the Path to Excellence through our public and private McClaskey Excellence Institute's Achieving World-Class Results (AWCR) courses. Although our public AWCR classes are very effective, we have found that companies prefer to train

> their managers in our private AWCR classes. This is because, in a private class, all discussions and implementation examples are tailored to their specific company.

6. Start every other week progress reviews

    a. The leaders of the extraordinary operations initiative hold weekly or every other week progress review meetings. These 20 to 45-minute meetings assess whether the planned action items for the last week or two were completed and set new action items for the following two weeks.

    b. Celebrate reaching milestones and major action items. Assist in removing barriers when action items are not completed.

    c. Proceed at a pace that ensures all your operations processes are fully implemented and maintained at 100% within 1-2 years. Any month without progress is a problem. The management of the operations excellence initiative identifies the cause and takes immediate action to get the project back on track. When consulting with businesses affected by seasonal factors, such as being busier in the summer than at other times of the year, we recommend that they incorporate their improvement plan to focus on more process enhancements during slower months and fewer during busier months.

7. Begin collecting measures to monitor progress toward achieving and maintaining extraordinary operations. Start capturing some of this data early to establish your baseline. The initial measures can be gathered while managers are being trained. Some categories of measures, along with examples for each category, include:

a. Satisfaction measures that come directly from the customer. Examples include:

   1. Overall satisfaction.

   2. How well their KCRs were met.

   3. Level of repeat business or other measures of customer loyalty.

   4. Likelihood to recommend.

b. Measures that come from the company indicate how well the company is achieving extraordinary operations. Examples include:

   1. What percentage of your customer visits did the customer experience everything 100% to your brand requirements?

   2. What percentage of your products, services, and customer experience are 100% to your brand requirements when delivered to or experienced by the customer?

   3. What percentage of the employees are precisely performing each step of the approved process?

c. Measures that indicate how well the company is managing the extraordinary operations initiative. Examples include:

   1. How many processes did you start to implement to 100% in the last four weeks?

   2. What percentage of your operations processes are designed for 100%?

   3. What percentage of your operations processes are operated at 100%?

   4. What percentage of your operations processes are maintained at 100%?

5. In the last two months, has your leadership team met at least every other week to manage the extraordinary operations Initiative?

6. What percentage of your leaders have attended the McClaskey Excellence Institute's Achieving World-Class Results class or other training that teaches implementing the Path to Excellence?

8. Implement Pillar 1: Think Excellence

    a. Ensure all managers complete the AWCR or similar training and are committed to the only acceptable level of operations is 100% to the brand requirements every time.

9. Implement Pillar 2: Focus Excellence

    a. Get the mission and KCRs developed to meet the criteria, approved, memorized by all employees, used by everyone to make daily decisions, and provide purpose for all parts of their jobs.

    b. Plan to thoroughly execute Pillar 2 within the first three months.

10. Implement Pillars 3 and 4: Process Excellence and People Excellence: Follow the Path to Excellence to design and implement your processes to 100%.

    a. Begin by selecting and developing a straightforward process that affects a KCR to be designed and implemented at 100% in all relevant stores or units.

    b. Implement 2-5 processes each month until all operations processes are designed, implemented, and maintained at 100%.

    c. List your key operations processes. Over the next 12 months, decide which month you will design and implement each process to 100%. Make this part of your project plan and manage it according to your action items. We have found that most companies have between 20 and 50 key operations processes.

    d.   Implement as fast as you can maintain 100% execution.

    e.   Implement the nine elements of People Excellence. Over the next 12 months, decide which parts of the nine elements you will implement each month. Incorporate this into your project plan.

11. Link up Your Support for Ongoing Implementation

    a.   As part of the implementation process, identifying and engaging internal and external resources dedicated to the implementation of the Path to Excellence has a significant impact on successful execution. The McClaskey Excellence Institute's training and consulting have served this role for many companies. They have found it an effective way to accelerate their progress and ensure consistent improvement. Usually, AWCR training is given to all operations managers, and then consulting support is added as you begin your implementation.

Implementation: Can You Follow the Same Recipe?

Although the benefits of extraordinary operations are clear, some may argue that achieving such levels of excellence is too costly or unrealistic. Common objections often question whether such a transformation is even possible. But what if these objections are just misconceptions that can be easily clarified? These misconceptions are why companies often fail to transition from ordinary to extraordinary operations.

Consider the objection, "It's too expensive to implement." At first glance, the investment needed for extraordinary operations might seem too costly. As Pal's Sudden Service showed, the small initial costs are often recovered through significant increases in revenue, efficiency, and profit. By cutting waste, improving processes, and boosting customer loyalty, extraordinary operations save significantly more money than they cost, providing a strong return on your investment.

Another common critique is, "It only works in simple industries like fast food." This view underestimates the versatility of the Path to Excellence and extraordinary operations. I have found that the principles of excellence are universally applicable across nearly every type of service business. While the way they are applied may vary, the fundamentals remain consistent across industries. These principles apply across sectors, from healthcare to manufacturing. The key is to implement the Path to Excellence in a way that addresses the challenges of each industry and culture. We have had the pleasure of helping many companies do this. Whether you serve hamburgers or provide medical care, operations excellence is universally beneficial. All of them have successfully applied the McClaskey® Triple 100® Path to Excellence.

I know this is true through firsthand experience. The McClaskey Excellence Institute and I have worked with nearly every type of service business and many manufacturing companies as they have implemented the Path to Excellence and enhanced their process execution. Some of the service businesses we've partnered with include restaurants, convenience stores, hospitals, hotels, banks, professional services like accounting and legal, real estate, landscapers, as well as city, state, and federal agencies, the Veterans Administration (VA), and military bases, just to name a few.

Skeptics also say, "We can't afford to invest that much in training." When people say that, they are focusing only on the costs, not the benefits of better training. While training does require an upfront investment, consider the alternative. High turnover, customer dissatisfaction, and lost revenue are much more expensive in the long run. Well-trained employees build a cycle of service excellence, loyalty, revenue, and efficiency that leads to lasting success. Investing in your team and processes, as outlined in the Path for Excellence, is one of the best investments you can make for your future.

Finally, some claim, "Our industry is too volatile for such consistency." Extraordinary operations can help you effectively manage volatile markets. By building a strong foundation of excellence, companies can better adjust to changing conditions without sacrificing quality or customer satisfaction. Flexibility and resilience are results of a well-oiled operational system. As the market or business evolves, you can adapt quickly because of your operations excellence.

Common Challenges and Solutions to Implementing Extraordinary Operations

The journey to extraordinary operations isn't without obstacles, but each challenge presents an opportunity for growth and improvement. The challenge must be addressed, or it could hinder the implementation. Drawing on McClaskey Excellence Institute's experience with nearly every type of company, here are some common implementation challenges and how they were resolved.

Challenge #1: Don't have the time or money. We have better ways to invest our limited resources.

You might wonder whether you have enough time, money, or labor to make the necessary changes to turn your company's operations from ordinary to extraordinary operations.

Solution:

No company has unlimited resources for improvements. However, it is equally true that every company has some resources available for improvement. The key is to use these resources as effectively and efficiently as possible. The implementation process I mentioned earlier in this chapter aligns available resources with the number of processes you work on at any given time. Focusing on just a manageable few processes at once ensures you do not exceed your resource limits. Most of the operations processes you are improving are already in use: the changes you make are value-added enhancements, and a 5% to 15% improvement in an existing process will deliver immediate benefits.

At the McClaskey Excellence Institute, we suggest two key strategies to keep implementation manageable. First, do your initial implementation as part of the AWCR class, where you benefit from structure, accountability, and expert guidance to model best practices and resolve any issues that arise during implementation. The second suggestion is to start with a small, straightforward process that impacts KCRs but requires minimal effort or resources to elevate it from ordinary to extraordinary operations. Aim for an early win by targeting low-hanging fruit to achieve quick results. Achieving success in these areas builds momentum, gains support, and justifies further investments of time and effort. This approach also helps develop your skills in transforming ordinary processes into extraordinary operations.

An example of a starter process chosen by one company was placing three hot sauces in a specific mild-to-spicy order on every table, every time, not just most of the time, but always. They knew they had succeeded when all managers would place a McClaskey® $1000 bet that the next guest's table would have the sauces in the correct order.

After successfully improving, implementing, and maintaining all low-hanging-fruit processes, gradually shift focus to more impactful processes, building your skills along the way. A good practice is to prioritize operations processes that directly affect KCRs. Working on the most impactful processes ensures resources are used effectively to drive meaningful improvements. Selecting the number of processes your resources can handle each month will help you stay within your capacity limits. Following this method ensures steady and consistent progress. Your speed depends on your resources and your ability to maintain processes at 100%.

Often, a few key resources are needed for many of the processes you are upgrading. If many processes involve IT or HR changes or require specific managers' time, these resources can become bottlenecks. In such cases, you'll need to free up those resources as much as possible. Once the extraordinary operations team has identified the resource causing the bottleneck, provide support to those employees so they can dedicate more time to transforming processes from ordinary to extraordinary. This can be done cost-effectively once the bottlenecking resources are identified and addressed. If there are processes that do not depend on resources that would otherwise hinder other improvements, those processes can also be chosen for enhancement.

Challenge #2: We've attempted to improve operations before, but it didn't succeed. Why is this one different? Nearly every manager has faced improvement efforts that either weren't finished or didn't work.

Solution:

This is a proven approach based on how companies truly progress from ordinary to extraordinary. 'Proven' is a keyword. Every company that has engaged with this process through our AWCR class has implemented essential parts of the Path to Excellence, including reaching at least one process at or near 100% before the class ends. It doesn't require much in the way of resources to get started, and most companies already have them. Companies have adopted the McClaskey® Triple 100® Path to Excellence with varied resources and have transformed from ordinary to extraordinary. This proven method can work for you, but it doesn't do so automatically. You need to allocate some resources to make it happen. The key is your leader's motivation to achieve excellent company performance rather than settle for ordinary, which almost guarantees you will disappoint some customers. Suppose you believe the company's leaders are satisfied with the current ordinary level of operations or have a history of struggling to focus on long-term improvements. In that case, I recommend exploring other ways to improve.

Another advantage of this path is that you can receive help and support when needed. You don't have to figure everything out on your own. The McClaskey Excellence Institute has assisted many companies in transforming their operations from ordinary to extraordinary.

Challenge #3: Resistance to Change. Even when managers want change, you will often hear employees who work for me resist it and keep doing things the way they have in the past.

It's natural for people to resist new procedures. Change can be intimidating, especially when it disrupts the familiar. When companies are not facing a crisis, there's a strong desire to stick with the status quo. We have always done it that way; we're making money, so leave it alone.

Solution:

The solution is to foster a culture of open communication and involve all managers and employees in the change process. Additionally, start by implementing the change in one area or store and show what's in it for both employees and managers, as well as how it improves customer service and benefits the company. Initiating pilot programs allows employees and managers to see extraordinary operations and their advantages firsthand. It also demonstrates that success is achievable within their company. It's crucial to train and engage operations managers first so they can lead the implementation of Extraordinary Operations in their areas. Work through the hierarchy, not around it. Managers should clearly communicate to each employee the benefits of moving from ordinary to extraordinary operations. Include in the explanation how all three stakeholders — employees, customers, and the company — benefit from this change. The question "What is in it for me?" is key, and because advantages are available for everyone, they must be continually communicated and demonstrated. Also, inform employees about the support they will receive during the transition.

You can significantly decrease resistance to change by implementing effective change management practices. This involves engaging managers and employees early in the process, clearly communicating the benefits for employees, customers, and the company, preparing managers and employees for complete success within a culture of extraordinary operations, and providing ongoing coaching and support. When employees understand the "why" behind the changes, they are more likely to accept the "how." Creating a sense of ownership and involvement can turn resistance into enthusiasm.

Challenge #4: "The Program of the Month" Syndrome - Company Leaders Are Not Consistent. In many organizations, managers have worked for companies where leaders seem eager to implement the latest improvement idea they have just heard.

Solution:

Consistency is essential. A culture of extraordinary operations requires that company leaders be dedicated to operations excellence as a permanent trait of their organization, not just a focus for one month, one quarter, or one year. The leadership must remain committed to achieving and maintaining extraordinary operations. This involves a cultural change. Extraordinary operations need to be deeply embedded in the company's values and culture. When employees and managers see that this focus is a priority for all leaders and is demonstrated by everyone, gaining buy-in for lasting change will be easier. One way company leaders become committed to extraordinary operations is by seeing the significant benefits of a culture that fulfills their promise to customers by getting their products and services right every time.

Challenge #5: Leading the Change. Since it is essential to change employees' behavior to improve the process, the challenge arises with managers who have most of their employees directly reporting to them.

How do you engage and prepare the unit operations managers to lead the effort?

Solution:

After top-level operations management, the most important group to engage is your unit operations managers. While getting buy-in from operations managers at all levels is crucial, securing the support of your unit operations managers is especially vital. These managers lead the efforts for their unit or store, and to do so, they must change first. Effective manager enablement and engagement are key to transforming an organization from ordinary to extraordinary operations.

Many successful companies recognize this and start by having their unit operations managers and all levels of operations management above the store or unit level take classes in leading a change from ordinary to extraordinary operations. They invest in their managers' development. While there are many ways to do this, one course I highly recommend based on firsthand experience is sending all managers and leaders to the McClaskey Excellence Institute's Achieving World-Class Results (AWCR) class. This course is specifically designed to teach the what, why, and how of implementing the McClaskey® Triple100® Path to Excellence, while also equipping managers with the skills to lead their units toward extraordinary operations. As part of this course, managers transform an existing company process from ordinary to extraordinary, allowing them to practice the skills they are learning in real time.

Getting all unit operations managers involved in the Path to Excellence encourages them to work together as a team. This helps guide the entire organization toward achieving and maintaining extraordinary operations. They will support each other because they are using the same path and the same language to describe the various elements of the path.

Challenge #6: Managers Losing Commitment to Operations Excellence. If the unit operations managers don't consistently and over time lead and maintain the change, the change won't happen in their unit or store.

One common reason for failing to achieve extraordinary operations is when managers lose their commitment. When this occurs, they stop doing their part to reach exceptional results in their area. As more managers stop contributing, the resulting drag becomes too heavy to sustain the effort. How do you keep all managers engaged in and committed to the journey toward extraordinary operations?

Solution:

Secure your managers' support by engaging them in the operations excellence effort for their area, rather than bypassing them. This requires each manager at every level to be enabled, empowered, and committed to transforming their area from ordinary to exceptional operations.

Having everyone enabled and engaged in the same proven process, working as a team, will maintain engagement. Don't isolate managers so they feel they are on their own to accomplish extraordinary operations. They need to be part of a company initiative that provides clear direction and offers support to help them do their part. Part of this support is enablement. Another part is accountability. They need to be held both responsible and accountable.

Piloting processes that consistently operate at 100% in a few stores or locations demonstrates that transforming from ordinary to extraordinary operations is achievable within your company and advantageous for everyone involved. Processes running at 100% make it easier to manage an area or unit, not more difficult. This keeps managers motivated to elevate processes from ordinary to extraordinary.

As mentioned earlier, an essential component of keeping managers engaged is the company's leaders' unwavering commitment to a culture of operations excellence. Managers do not want to invest time and effort in a significant change if they feel company leaders are not committed to doing what it takes to make it permanent.

Call to Action

Implement the McClaskey® Triple 100® Path to Excellence.

It's time to take action. Review and adjust if necessary, then start using the implementation plan outlined in this chapter under the "Implementing and Obtaining Extraordinary Operations" heading to achieve the Path to Excellence today.

Now, let's implement the McClaskey® Triple 100® Path to Excellence to realize its benefits. While Chapter 23 offers helpful guidance on implementation, it often isn't enough for successful execution. The key to successful implementation is to build on the guidance in Chapter 23 and combine it with your company's leadership and external support.

I strongly recommend the McClaskey Excellence Institute's Achieving World-Class Results (AWCR) course for your company's leaders, along with coaching, to effectively put the Path to Excellence into practice. Enrolling in the AWCR class at the start of implementation is highly beneficial. This class builds on the guidance in Chapter 23 and provides a solid, supportive framework along with tailored, practical advice and accountability to help you succeed in applying the Path to Excellence. The AWCR training provides all involved leaders and managers with a shared language, a common goal, a unified 100% mindset, a proven path to follow, and the knowledge to implement it in their operations.

As you follow the Path for Excellence in your organization, remember that this is a continuous journey. Patience and persistence are essential. Excellence isn't a destination; it's a continuous process of improvement and maintaining the gains. There's no need to rush; focus on making steady progress each month toward achieving 100% extraordinary operations, maintaining the gains, and using the Path to Excellence to keep moving steadily toward that goal. Every step brings you closer to 100% excellence.

As part of the implementation, gather the necessary resources to successfully follow the Path to Excellence, which will elevate your operations from ordinary to extraordinary. As mentioned, you don't have to do this alone. Take advantage of the tools and references provided in this book, as well as those offered by the McClaskey Excellence Institute. Engaging your team is key to a successful implementation. Have your unit-level leaders and above attend classes on the McClaskey® Triple 100® Path to Excellence and read this book so they can fully understand, buy in, engage, and help lead the effort toward extraordinary operations. I recommend participating in the McClaskey Excellence Institute's AWCR class, which many companies have used as part of their successful implementation. The AWCR class was developed explicitly for implementing AWCR.

Key Takeaways for Chapter 23: Implementing the Path to Excellence

1. Make implementation of extraordinary operations a 1 to 2 year strategic initiative, which has a resourced project plan and is managed using project management with at least every other week meetings.

2. Train your entire management team in the McClaskey® Triple 100® Path to Excellence using the AWCR class.

3. As part of the AWCR class, you will start by getting your first process from ordinary to extraordinary operations. The

AWCR class will provide support in beginning to implement the key elements of all four pillars of the Path to Excellence in your company.

4. Measure to track and manage progress toward achieving 100% design and execution of all your processes, and maintain 100% once you have achieved it.

5. Use the McClaskey Triple 100 Path to Excellence to design, implement, and maintain all your operations processes to 100%.

6. Implement 2-5 processes per month until all operations processes are designed, implemented, and maintained to 100%.

7. Implement Pillars 1 and 2, Think Excellence and Focus Excellence, over the first 3 months of your implementation. You will be doing this while you are also implementing Pillars 3 and 4, Process Excellence and People Excellence, to get processes designed and implemented to 100%.

8. Only implement as fast as you can maintain 100% execution.

9. Persistence and Patience are key attributes of leaders who are successful in going from ordinary to extraordinary operations.

The Next Chapter

You're on track to implement all your processes to 100% within the next 1 to 2 years. But your journey doesn't end once your processes are fully executed to 100%. The true test of excellence isn't just achieving it once but consistently maintaining 100% execution across all processes day after day, year after year. That's what we'll explore in the next chapter: how to maintain 100% execution for all your processes.

CHAPTER 24

MAINTAINING 100% EXTRAORDINARY OPERATIONS

*"I'm here to build something for the long-term.
Anything else is a distraction."*

Mark Zuckerberg, Founder, Chairman, CEO of Facebook/Meta

Key Practices for Maintaining 100% Extraordinary Operations

As you work towards 100% extraordinary operations, remember, the goal isn't just to make changes; it's to make changes that stick. You are wasting your time if you cannot maintain the gain. It would be like trying to fill a water bucket that has huge holes. In this chapter, I will show you how to maintain your gains. To maintain 100% execution, focus on making excellence the way of life in your organization. Your goal shouldn't be about quick fixes or temporary improvements. Your goal should be to fundamentally shift your organization's culture by no longer accepting 'most' as the standard and instead setting the bar at 100%.

Many organizations struggle to maintain their gains. They achieve a level of excellence and, over time, lose the gains they'd made.

The key to maintaining excellence is to integrate it into your organizational DNA. This means continually reinforcing the principles and practices discussed throughout this book, particularly those in the People Excellence pillar, chapters 13-21. It means regularly evaluating your operations to determine whether each process is executed to your standard 100% of the time. If it's not meeting the 100% standard you set, use the processes outlined in this book to identify why and take corrective action.

Let's review what maintaining processes at 100% means. This is the key point covered in the Think Excellence pillar. Vince Lombardi captured the essence so well when he said, "Perfection is not attainable, but if we chase perfection, we can catch excellence."

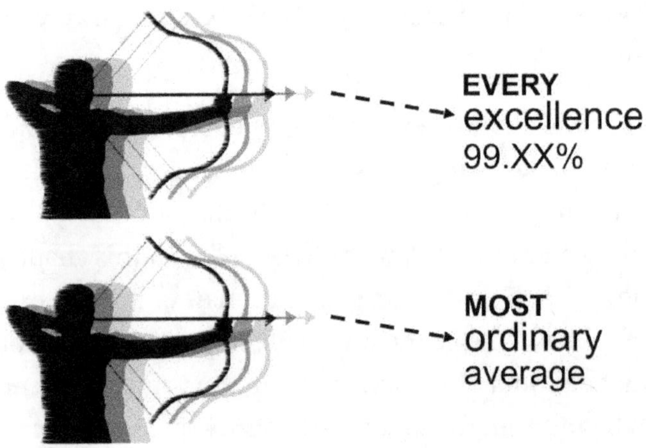

In other words, your standard is always 100%. It is never acceptable to deliver a product, service, or customer experience that does not 100% meet the brand requirements. But we also understand that, in reality, even our best employees will, on rare occasions, deliver a product or service that does not meet the brand requirements. A company operating at 100% extraordinary operations will have occasional errors. However, even one error is unacceptable. We know we will never get every product and service 100% right, but we are always targeting and taking actions to get there. Every customer deserves to get what we promise them every time they do business with us.

Companies with extraordinary operations are always finding ways to get closer to the 100% target. Because they only accept 100% to the brand requirements and are actively working toward achieving 100%, they deliver their products and services many times more accurately than their competitors.

Pal's Sudden Service delivers their products and services 10 times more accurately than their nationally known competitors while going four times faster. They accomplish this year after year.

When your company operates with extraordinary operations, you deliver your products and services 100% to your brand requirements better than 99% of the time. Customers choose you over your competitors because they know they can count on you to deliver what you promised every time. And you'll continue to improve by working the system to target errors, update processes for 100% execution, and train your employees to 100%.

Maintaining processes to consistently operate at 100% is a special management skill set. This skill set is not a strength for most managers. This is understandable, because most of the processes they have managed were focused on achieving mostly right outputs, or ordinary operations, rather than 100% right or extraordinary operations. Therefore, they have had minimal experience managing operations processes whose standard is 100%, 100% of the time.

Process for Maintaining 100% Operations Once It is Achieved

Here are several methods managers of companies with extraordinary operations use to maintain gains and keep processes executed at 100%. I saw and experienced these methods in practice during my 6 weeks working at Pal's as a crew member, as well as seeing them work with other companies. Many of these are commonly used management methods, but they are upgraded to get 100% performance rather than ordinary, mostly right performance.

1. **Set up a management system for Maintaining Extraordinary Operations**

    a. **Maintain Momentum and Progress with Regular Operations Excellence Planning and Accountability Meetings**: Have extraordinary operations progress review meetings to align, focus, and keep progress to your implementation plan. During each meeting, you will track your implementation progress on implementing extraordinary operations, maintaining processes to 100%, and planning the next action items. We recommend these progress review meetings every two weeks. The meetings are usually 30-45 minutes. As part of every meeting, the manager determines which processes that were 100% are still operating at 100%. When a process is no longer operating at 100%, the team conducts a root cause analysis to identify the cause, develops an action plan, and brings the process back to 100% operations. Also, address the root cause of why the process stopped operating at 100%.

    b. **Ensure All Leaders and Managers Stay Engaged:** When hiring leaders and managers, ensure they are fully trained in the McClaskey® Triple 100® Path to Excellence.

Doing this will ensure they are fully committed to extraordinary operations from day one.

c. **Measure and Grade managers against how well they manage the Extraordinary Operations Initiative:**

1. What percentage of your processes are designed for 100%

2. What percentage of your processes are operated at 100%

3. What percentage of your processes are maintained at 100%

4. In the last 2 months, has your leadership team met at least every other week to manage the Extraordinary Operations Initiative

5. What percentage of your leaders have attended the AWCR class

6. What percentage of your leaders have attended the Lean class

7. What percentage of your leaders are Coaching to 100%

h. Based on the measures, take the appropriate actions

2. **Set up a cultural structure that makes 100% extraordinary operations the norm within your company:** Some of the elements include integrating the above measures as part of the managers' and employees' evaluation, and consistently applying all nine elements of the People Excellence Pillar

3. **Change the Assessment Factors for Unit Operations Managers:** In ordinary operations, general managers, unit, and store operations managers are assessed based on many different factors. With extraordinary operations, the assessment is focused on three main factors: 1) Delivering the

products and services 100% to the brand requirements, 100% of the time, 2) having all employees precisely perform the steps of the approved process every time; and 3) 100% complies with the conditions of employment. Focusing on these three assessment factors to assess your managers sets a supportive work environment that promotes extraordinary operations.

4. **100% Standard:** Make delivering your products and services 100% to the brand requirements 100% of the time, the only acceptable standard. Remember from Think Excellence that your company's performance will never be higher than the standards the management accepts.

5. **Set Employees up for 100% Execution**: The key to maintaining 100% for all your processes is to create a work environment where each employee is enabled, empowered, responsible, accountable, and chooses to precisely perform each step of the approved process, every time, and the process outputs are 100% to the process requirements, 100% of the time. Employees operate the processes. Managers set up the work environment that causes the employees to choose to precisely follow each step of the approved process, every time. When process steps are not precisely followed, the manager determines what needs to change in the work environment so employees will find it reasonable, rational, and logical to precisely follow the process steps. Positive and corrective coaching is one of the most versatile and easy-to-use tools managers use to shape the work environment.

6. **Go from "Pick your Battles" to "See it, Say it" Coaching:** Do corrective coaching whenever you observe an employee not performing a process step precisely as written in the approved process. "If you see it, say it" is the corrective coaching practice, regardless of how slight the deviation from the standard is. In companies with ordinary operations, there are so many deviations that managers sometimes focus only on significant

deviations from process steps, while ignoring minor ones. "Pick your battles" is the mantra of ordinary companies. This creates a work environment where minor deviations from steps appear to be acceptable.

Once a process is performing at or near 100%, management's attention must transition to the details. No deviation is too small to do corrective coaching. The real standard is what a manager sees and ignores. "See it, say it." This is the mantra of managers who manage companies that maintain extraordinary operations. Coaching and feedback are most effective at influencing behavior when it is certain and immediate. In other words, you never walk by an employee performing a process step incorrectly without providing corrective coaching. Train, coach, and assess your managers on how consistently they practice "See it, say it" coaching. It is one of the key differences between coaching that maintains extraordinary operations and coaching that leads to ordinary operations.

7. **Frequent Positive Coaching:** The second key difference between coaching that leads to ordinary operations and coaching that supports extraordinary operations is always to give at least equal to or more positive coaching than corrective coaching. Positive coaching boosts morale and increases employee engagement. It is important to note that while you are providing equal to or more positive than corrective coaching, you are still providing corrective coaching for any deviation from the process steps.

   Practicing positive or corrective coaching doesn't mean managers shy away from having tough conversations. However, they do them respectfully. The emphasis on equal or more positive coaching is rooted in the fact that it is disrespectful to employees to ignore the fact that they do the job right most of the time. It is challenging to maintain extraordinary operations when most coaching is corrective.

8. **Train to 100%:** While all the elements within People Excellence are important, training to 100% has one of the most significant impacts. You cannot achieve 100% execution without 100% training. Training to 100% means equipping employees with the skill, knowledge, and attitude needed to perform the process at 100%, every time. This ensures employees develop the habit of precisely performing each step of the approved process consistently. Our survey of thousands of service managers showed that, on average, they were training their employees to 75%. The managers seemed satisfied with that level of training. They believe employees learn on the job, often through making mistakes, many of which could have been avoided through 100% training. Managers who train their employees to less than 100% set them to deliver products and services mostly right, and they consider that good enough.

   Now that you've raised your standards to 100%, you must train every employee to 100% every time. Designing a process to 100% also involves developing training that achieves 100%. Training to 100% initially requires more upfront resources than a company's previous 75% or "mostly" training level. However, once you've fully implemented training to 100%, your annual training costs are similar to when you were training to 75%. This happens because you find cost-effective ways to train to 100% without compromising the 100% level, and you experience lower employee turnover by setting your employees up for 100% success. This means you train fewer people each year. Additionally, training to 100% reduces costs through fewer mistakes, increased repeat business, more positive recommendations, and boosts in revenue and profits.

9. **Find the Root Cause of Non-Compliances:** When the products or services are not delivered 100% to the brand requirements or the employees are not precisely performing the steps of the approved process, determine the root cause

and take actions that address the root cause and not just the symptom. The symptom is what you observed. To get to the root cause, ask "why" of the previous cause 3 to 5 times. You have reached the root cause when you identify a management process, practice, or policy as the cause. For example, the symptom of the problem is that the product does not 100% meet the brand requirements. Why? Because some key steps of the process were not followed. Why? The shift manager rarely notices or coaches related to those steps not being performed precisely according to the approved process. Why? Because the shift managers rarely get coached by their General Manager for not doing corrective coaching when employees are not precisely following the process steps. Why? Because the store's General Manager is okay with products not meeting the brand standard, as long as it doesn't result in a complaint. Now you have found the root cause.

10. **Obey the "Triple 100® Sustainable Change Speed Limit":** As I consulted with many companies, I found that the speed limit for sustainable change is to "only go as fast as you can maintain the gain." I first learned this from Thom Crosby, the CEO of Pal's, and then confirmed it with many other companies. This is a key to sustainable excellence. If you try to improve too many processes at once, it can overwhelm a company's ability to sustain the gain, and the entire change effort may collapse. Although the speed at which a company can change varies, it's best to improve only a small number of processes each month and increase the rate if you can maintain 100% execution. For most companies, we have found that improving two to five processes a month allows adequate progress while maintaining the gains.

11. **Use both Persistence and Patience:** Successful managers who lead their companies from ordinary to extraordinary operations balance persistence with patience. A company needs

to move at a pace that has enough momentum (persistence) but not so fast that it becomes overwhelming and unsustainable (patience). One sign of moving too fast is when you cannot maintain the processes at 100%. Conversely, a sign of moving too slow is when you're not converting two to five processes from ordinary to extraordinary operations each month. Most companies that transition from ordinary to extraordinary operations take one to two years.

The Journey Continues

Your journey toward operational excellence is an ongoing process that requires dedication, resilience, and a commitment to continuous improvement. Embrace the principles outlined in this book, apply them consistently, and adapt as needed to maintain sustained excellence. Keep learning from your experience and from the best proven practices. By doing this, you will reach your organizational goals and foster a culture of high performance and continuous growth.

I want to emphasize that this isn't the end of your journey; it's a new beginning. You now have the tools and knowledge, in fact, the entire proven path to excellence, to create and sustain 100% extraordinary operations. But knowledge alone isn't enough; it's what you do with this knowledge that truly matters.

Take action today by applying what you've learned. Focus on one area of your operations and strive to make it 100% excellent. Then, move on to another. Before long, extraordinary operations will become your new standard.

Remember, the pursuit of excellence is not a destination but a journey. It's a journey that will challenge, inspire, and ultimately transform your organization. As you continue on this path, know you're not just improving your operations; you're changing lives. You're creating an environment where employees thrive, customers are consistently delighted, and your business reaches its full potential while gaining a sustainable competitive advantage.

With a culture of extraordinary operations, you can grow your business and expand to new locations while maintaining operations excellence. You can be the leader who breaks the cycle of the bigger your business is, the worse it operates. I knew the founder and owner of several dealerships. He said the only time he felt proud of his operation was when he owned and ran a single dealership. Now that he owns many dealerships and doesn't run any of them, he's embarrassed by their level of operation. Don't let this happen to you.

The path is clear, the tools are in your hands, and the potential is limitless. Your journey to 100% operations excellence continues now. Embrace it, enjoy it, and never stop striving for excellence. The extraordinary awaits you.

Call to Action

1. Use the "Process for Maintaining 100% Operations Once It is Achieved" section of this chapter to establish your company's systems for sustaining 100% operations after they are achieved.

2. Establish a management system for Maintaining Extraordinary Operations

3. Establish a cultural framework that makes 100% extraordinary operations the norm within your company. Some key aspects include integrating the above measures into managers' and employees' evaluations and consistently applying all nine elements of the People Excellence Pillar.

Key Takeaways for Chapter 24: Maintaining 100% Operations Excellence

1. Develop a company culture where consistently delivering your products and services 100% to the brand requirements 100% of the time is the only acceptable standard. This involves structuring and shaping your company's culture to reliably implement all elements within the four pillars of the Path to Excellence, with a strong focus on the nine elements of the People Excellence pillar.

2. Set Employees up for 100% execution.

3. The key to maintaining 100% for all your processes is to create a work environment where each employee is enabled, empowered, responsible, accountable, and consistently chooses to perform each step of their processes precisely. This ensures process outputs meet 100% of the brand requirements, 100% of the time, and fully comply with the conditions of employment.

4. Regularly monitor that all your processes are maintained at 100%. When processes fall below 100% execution, take action to restore them to 100% operation. Also, identify and address the root causes of why the process stopped executing at 100% and resolve them.

5. As new processes are created or changed, make sure they are designed and executed at 100%.

6. Follow the "Triple 100® Speed Limit for Sustainable Change" of "only go as fast as you can maintain the change."

7. Use both persistence and patience to guide the journey from ordinary to extraordinary.

8. Assess managers based on their ability to ensure that everyone they oversee does the following three things: 1) consistently perform the steps in the approved process every time; 2) produce products and services that meet 100% of the brand

requirements, 100% of the time; and 3) fully comply with the conditions of employment.

9. Require all managers to be trained in the McClaskey® Triple 100® Path to Excellence so they are enabled to engage and lead extraordinary operations in their area.

The Epilogue

Where to Go to Get More Assistance

Build your knowledge and skills by learning from your own experiences and from those of others. In the next chapter, I will list where you can learn from the experiences of others who have built extraordinary operations. Their journeys will help you develop your skills as you learn proven role-model practices.

If what you just read feels insightful and valuable, do me three favors: implement extraordinary operations in your company, share this book and the McClaskey® Triple 100® Path to Excellence with all your friends and colleagues, and email me at info@mcclaskeyexcellence.com to tell me how you have used the Path to Excellence to create extraordinary operations. I would sincerely appreciate it. The McClaskey Excellence Institute (McClaskeyExcellence.com) is here to support you on your journey from ordinary to extraordinary operations. It would be our privilege to work with you to achieve extraordinary operations for your company.

WHERE TO GO TO GET MORE ASSISTANCE: YOUR EXCELLENCE JOURNEY CONTINUES

"Success is not a goal to reach or a finish line to cross. It is a system to improve, an endless process to refine."

James Clear

An Element of Successful Leadership is Gathering the Right Team for Success

You're not alone in your pursuit of 100% operations excellence. The McClaskey Excellence Institute provides a variety of resources and support systems to guide and assist you along the way. We have partnered with thousands of companies and can help you with implementation and resolving any issues you encounter. It would be a great privilege to work with you and your company on your journey from ordinary to extraordinary operations.

Classes and Consulting:

1. **Public and Private Classes:** From the book, you see the potential. Now, let us activate that potential and make it

happen. What if I told you there is a course that will guide you through every aspect of implementing the McClaskey® Triple 100® Path to Excellence? A course that provides active coaching and practice as you lead your organization on a journey from ordinary to extraordinary operations. The course, which I personally developed and others have enhanced, is the McClaskey Excellence Institute's Achieving World-Class Results (AWCR) class. 100% of the companies that take this class implement the path to excellence. Another great feature of the AWCR class is that during the class, you get guided practice on every aspect of the Path to Excellence, including designing and fully implementing one of your processes to 100%, as well as developing your company's mission and key customer requirements.

The AWCR class has two formats. Both are great options, and you can choose whichever suits you best to get started.

a. **Private AWCR classes:** These are the most popular and recommended format. They are customized for your company, focusing discussions on implementation specific to your organization. Your company's implementation challenges are identified and addressed in detail. The sessions are more engaging and in-depth. Private classes enable you to train a large management group at once, ensuring everyone listens and contributes during and after the class. Since they are all working on implementing the path during the class, they collaborate more effectively. The classes foster lively discussions that reveal implementation issues and promote the sharing of best practices.

b. **Public AWCR classes:** This is an excellent option for companies with small management teams or those wanting to review the class before enrolling their management team in a private session. Public AWCR classes include multiple leaders from various companies and industries attending the same session. This allows you to learn how others are applying the Path to Excellence within their organizations. Public classes are held regularly.

2. **Consulting Services:** This complements our training classes well. Consulting allows us to provide personalized guidance and support. Work with certified McClaskey Excellence Institute operations experts to receive timely, tailored implementation advice. Our decades of combined experience will help you and your leadership team overcome and prevent real-world challenges, keeping you on track toward exceptional operations. We have seen that companies that engage us for both training and consulting achieve faster, more assured progress.

3. **Management Development Programs:** Enhance your management team's skills to achieve and maintain higher levels of operations excellence. We can customize this training to meet the specific needs of your management team.

Contact us to answer any questions about the right training for your management team, or view our public class schedule.

McClaskey Excellence Institute:

- **Website:** www.McClaskeyExcellence.com
- **Contact:** info@McClaskeyExcellence.com

More In-depth Training and Certification:

1. **Broaden Your Knowledge:** While the AWCR class is the one almost everyone starts with, there are some excellent classes at the McClaskey Excellence Institute to add more depth, capabilities, and breadth to your expertise. Three of these classes are: Lean, which delves into efficiency and waste

elimination; Spectacular Customer Service; and Training to 100%.

Lean for Service and Healthcare: Remove waste, unnecessary complexity, and costs to make your processes more efficient by identifying and eliminating non-value-adding activities. The AWCR class helps you design effective processes. But you also want your processes to be efficient. That's where lean comes in. Managers who have taken both AWCR and Lean describe AWCR as one side of a coin of excellence, with Lean being the other side. They complement each other. First, make your processes effective—they meet the brand requirements every time. Then, make your processes efficient.

Spectacular Customer Service: Learn how to design and implement customer service that "wows" your customers.

Embed outstanding hospitality into your service processes so every customer feels appreciated and valued. One of the main benefits of providing exceptional customer service is that it doesn't cost more than standard service yet significantly impacts customer satisfaction, repeat business, and positive word of mouth. You can deliver average or extraordinary customer service in roughly the same amount of time and at similar costs. So why not choose to provide exceptional service to your customers?

Training to 100%: An in-depth workshop focused on designing Training for 100%. One of the key elements of the Path to Excellence is mastering Training to 100%. While we cover the basics in the AWCR class, there is much more to teach about Training to 100%. Usually, the participants are the leaders responsible for designing the training. Companies want their primary training leaders to gain more in-depth knowledge of how to deliver Training to 100% so they can apply it within their companies. This class enables participants to take an actual company process and design training for that process to reach 100%. Once the training is designed, they pilot it within the company to verify that it will achieve 100% and that the organization can effectively carry out the Training to 100%. Attendance in this class requires prior participation in the AWCR class, so attendees understand the other components necessary for Training to 100% to succeed in a company.

2. **McClaskey° Triple 100° Leadership Certification Program:**

   i.   Certification for leaders who spearhead efforts within their company to transform ordinary operations into extraordinary ones. This program encourages leaders to develop the deep expertise necessary to achieve outstanding operational results in their organization. This is accomplished through personalized mentoring as they apply these extraordinary practices across multiple units or departments.

   Two Leadership Track Certifications are available:

   McClaskey° Triple 100° Certified Leader.

   McClaskey° Triple 100° Certified Leader with Sustainable Results.

Ongoing Support and Resources from McClaskey Excellence Institute:

1. **Monthly Consulting:** Engage for 1-2 hours per month for us to keep sharing proven practices that solve problems and overcome obstacles during implementation. Keeps progress steady and maintains momentum. Provide accountability and structure.

2. **Regular Mentoring Meetings:** Set up meetings between the McClaskey Excellence Institute experts and your key leaders to mentor them in role-model leadership practices that transform ordinary operations into extraordinary ones.

3. **Regular Planning and Accountability Meetings:** Monitor progress, resolve issues, and plan and document next steps and action items.

4. **Leadership Development:** Make sure your leadership team keeps growing and improving. Think about enrolling in a certification program for leaders aimed at achieving extraordinary operations and maintaining results.

5. **Checklists and Templates:** Utilize the provided checklists and templates within the book to support your implementation efforts.

6. **Online Resources:** Visit the McClaskey Excellence Institute website for additional reading and resources. Follow us on LinkedIn and other social media platforms. Listen to our Operations Experts podcast.

Recommended Reading: Additional Books to Support Your Journey

Visit the McClaskey Excellence Institute website under resources for a recommended list of books. Some of these recommended books include:

1. *Change: How Organizations Achieve Hard-to-Imagine Results in Uncertain and Volatile Times* by John P. Kotter,

2. *Crucial Accountability: Tools for Resolving Violated Expectations, Broken Commitments, and Bad Behavior* by Kerry Patterson

3. *Customer Service Experience: It's All in the Details* by David McClaskey

4. *Developing Human Service Leaders* by Deborah Harley-McClaskey

5. *Excellence Wins: A No-Nonsense Guide to Becoming the Best in a World of Compromise* by Horst Schulze

6. *Good to Great: Why Some Companies Make the Leap and Others Don't* by Jim Collins

7. *Influence: The Psychology of Persuasion* by Robert Cialdini

8. *Juran on Quality by Design: The New Steps for Planning Quality into Goods and Services* by J. M. Juran

9. *Multi-Unit Leadership: The 7 Stages of Building Profitable Stores Across Multiple Markets* by Jim Sullivan

10. *Root Cause Analysis: The Core of Problem Solving and Corrective Action* by Duke Okes

11. *Setting the Table: The Transforming Power of Hospitality in Business* by Danny Meyer

12. *Simple Numbers, Straight Talk, Big Profits!* by Greg Crabtree

13. *Simply Brilliant: How Great Organizations Do Ordinary Things in Extraordinary Ways* by William C. Taylor

14. *Start with Why: How Great Leaders Inspire Everyone to Take Action* by Simon Sinek

15. *The 21 Irrefutable Laws of Leadership: Follow Them and People Will Follow You* by John C. Maxwell

16. *The 7 Habits of Highly Effective People: Powerful Lessons in Personal Change* by Stephen R. Covey

17. *The Advantage: Why Organizational Health Trumps Everything Else in Business* by Patrick Lencioni

18. *The Baldrige Excellence Framework (Business/Nonprofit)* by NIST

19. *The New Gold Standard* by Joseph A. Michelli

20. *What Great Brands Do: The Seven Brand-Building Principles that Separate the Best from the Rest* by Denise Lee Yohn

Call to Action

Be that company with extraordinary operations whose customers will place the McClaskey® $1000 Bet: the next time they do business with your company, they will bet their money that you will fulfill your promise of delivering your products and services 100% to your brand requirements. Why? Because you have extraordinary operations.

You don't have to face this alone. If I or the McClaskey Excellence Institute can assist, reach out to us. The book offers insights on the Path to Excellence, and our training and consulting help you make extraordinary operations a reality for your company. It would be a privilege to support you.

The second thing I would like you to do is contact us and let us know how it's going. We would love to hear about your progress, questions, and issues you're facing. We might know how others solved the same problem you're having and would be happy to share it.

You have our contact information.

McClaskey Excellence Institute:
- **Website**: www.McClaskeyExcellence.com
- **Contact**: info@McClaskeyExcellence.com

ACKNOWLEDGMENTS

I feel incredibly privileged to have learned from and worked alongside leaders whose profound knowledge and abilities led them to create companies so excellent that the United States recognized them as national role models. They truly are the best of the best. This book, and the proven Path to Excellence it teaches, is only possible because they shared their insights on how they achieved role-model excellence so others could improve their companies and make the world a better place. Thank you.

These leaders include Thom Crosby and Pal Barger of Pal's Sudden Service, who developed systems that ensure their customers' orders are correct every time; Horst Schulze of The Ritz-Carlton Hotel Company, who built exceptional guest service systems that prioritize guest care and comfort, delighting every guest with the philosophy of "Ladies and Gentlemen serving Ladies and Gentlemen"; Ken Schiller and Brian Nolan of K&N Management, whose "love of excellence" inspired initiatives that became ingrained in their culture forever; Rulon Stacey and Priscilla Nuwash of Poudre Valley Health System, who fostered a culture where everyone wants to jump out of bed and get to work so they could serve their patients; Joe Alexander of the Monfort College of Business at Northern Colorado University, who was part of a 20-year process involved 5 Deans of the college that created role-model results; Don Evans and Roger Quayle of OMI, who established a system enabling managers of city water and wastewater treatment plants nationwide to collaborate and solve each other's problems; Earnie

Davenport of Eastman Chemical Company, where a comprehensive quality management system was implemented across all plants, ensuring superior operational levels; and Jerry King, whom I learned about how Owner-Operators manage Pal's stores and had the privilege of working for him to experience first-hand the role model operation.

I would especially like to thank Thom Crosby, who, over hundreds of conversations over 20 years, shared his profound knowledge and wisdom on how to create holistic, integrated systems that consistently deliver excellence. And to Horst Schulze, who allowed me into his inner circle for two years so I could see firsthand and understand what systems created Ritz-Carlton's excellence.

I would also like to thank the many thousands of company leaders who have attended our training classes. You trusted us to provide you and your leadership teams with the proven Path to Excellence, and then to implement it in your companies. The true heroes are those who lead their companies to excellence. To mention a few of these many outstanding leaders with whom we have had a long-standing relationship would include: Raji Sankar, Joe Douglas, Jeff Offutt, Dan Rowe, Greg Crabtree, Billy Schaefer, Tom Holliday, Chuck Gault, John Kemp, Kevin Malhame, Tony Lofrezo, Glenn Mueller, Alan Lovelace, Kevin Santiago, John Puckett, Casey Norris, John Kemp, Neil Farmer, Blair Christianson, Brooke Christianson, Jim Overman, David Marzich, and Jaffar Wahdat.

I want to thank the leaders who reviewed the book and provided valuable feedback. They include Thom Crosby, Joe Douglas, Raji Sankar, Jeff Offutt, Joe Alexander, Russell Justice, Kate Craig, Billy Schaefer, Kate McClaskey, Betty McClaskey, Teresa Keller, Deborah Harley-McClaskey, and Tom Holliday.

I want to thank my excellent writing team, Chip Hopper and Levi McPherson, who played an indispensable role in helping me write a book that conveys this very game-changing message. I also want to thank my editor, Kate Craig, who did a superb job editing the book to improve its clarity and consistency and eliminate textual errors.

GLOSSARY OF KEY TERMS

5S: A 5-step workplace organization method that focuses on improving the organization of the work area. The five steps are: Sort, Set in order, Shine, Standardize, and Sustain.

Benchmarking: The practice of comparing business processes and performance metrics to industry bests and best practices from their own and other companies.

Brand Requirements: The specific standards and specifications that define the quality and characteristics of a company's products or services.

Change Management: The collective term for all approaches to prepare, support, and help individuals, teams, and organizations in making a successful change.

Coaching to 100%: A management technique focused on providing both positive and corrective feedback that is sincere, specific, immediate, and personal to help employees consistently meet 100% of brand requirements.

Conditions of Employment: The specific requirements and expectations that an employee must meet to maintain their position within an organization.

Continuous Improvement: A systematic and ongoing effort to enhance processes, products, or services over time.

Customer Satisfaction: how well pleased the customer is with the experience they had with the company. One way to determine the level of customer satisfaction is through a customer-based measure of how well the company's products, services, and overall experience met their key customer requirements and expectations.

Employee Engagement: The extent to which employees feel passionate about their jobs, are committed to the organization, and put discretionary effort into their work.

Extraordinary Operations: A state where an organization consistently delivers its products, services, and customer experiences to 100% of brand requirements, 100% of the time, under 100% of conditions.

Focus Excellence: The second pillar of the McClaskey® Triple 100® Path to Excellence, emphasizing the alignment of all aspects of operations with the organization's mission and KCRs, and that the role of the unit operations manager is to deliver the products and services 100% to the brand requirements, 100% of the time, under 100% of the conditions.

Gemba Walk: The practice of walking around a workplace to identify first-hand the current practices. This can identify both what is going right and wasteful activities.

Gray Areas: Aspects of operations or communication that are ambiguous or open to reasonable interpretation, potentially leading to inconsistencies in performance.

Just-In-Time (JIT): An inventory strategy companies employ to increase efficiency and decrease waste by receiving goods only as they are needed.

Kaizen: A Japanese term meaning "change for the better" or "continuous improvement."

Key Customer Requirements (KCRs): The essential expectations that customers have for a product, service, or customer experience, all of which must be met to ensure customer satisfaction and loyalty.

Key Performance Indicators (KPIs): Measurable values that demonstrate how effectively a company is achieving key business objectives.

Lean: A systematic method for identifying and reducing/eliminating non-value adding activities.

McClaskey' Triple 100' Path to Excellence: A comprehensive methodology for achieving extraordinary operations that delivers the products, services, and customer experience 100% to brand requirements, 100% of the time, under 100% of conditions.

Operational Excellence: Operations that deliver the products, services, and customer experience 100% to the brand requirements, 100% of the time, under 100% of the conditions.

PDCA Cycle: Plan-Do-Check-Act, a four-step model for carrying out change. Plan what you are going to do; Do carry out your plan; Check to see if your got what you planned to get; If you got the desired results, then standardized the plan as the way to get the results; If you did not get the desired results, determine the root cause, modify the plan and repeat the cycle until you develop a plan that successfully and reliably gets the desired results.

People Excellence: The fourth pillar of the McClaskey' Triple 100' Path to Excellence, which is a comprehensive approach to empowering, enabling, and setting a work environment that ensures every employee is enabled and will choose to precisely perform their processes to 100% of the brand requirements. For operations employees, they are enabled and will choose to precisely follow each step of the process, every time, under any conditions they would encounter on the job, and will 100% comply with the Conditions of Employment.

Poka-Yoke: A Japanese term that means "mistake-proofing" or "inadvertent error prevention."

Process Excellence: The third pillar of the McClaskey' Triple 100' Path to Excellence, centered on designing and documenting processes that when the steps of the process are precisely followed, it will deliver the product, service or customer experience 100% to the brand requirements; 100% of the time; under 100% of the conditions and this is done in the most efficient manner possible.

Process Mapping: A workflow diagram or flowchart to bring forth a clearer understanding of a process or series of related processes.

Progressive Discipline: A structured approach to addressing employee performance issues, typically involving a series of increasingly severe steps.

Respect for People: A fundamental principle emphasizing the importance of treating all individuals with dignity and consideration in all interactions. Treat and communicate with all individuals in ways that enhance their self-esteem rather than diminish it, while still having the difficult conversations.

Root Cause Analysis: A method of problem-solving used for identifying the underlying causes of faults or problems.

SDCA Cycle: Standard-Do-Check-Act, a systematic approach to operating standardized processes so they are delivered exactly according to the standard process. Standard is the standardized process for whatever you are going to do; Do perform the standardized process exactly as it is written; Check to see if your got the desired results as stated in the standard; If you got the desired results as stated in the standard, then continue; If you did not get the desired results as stated in the standard, take the action that the that been authorized to take when the desired results were not obtained. Self-Management is a process by which the Check and Act steps can be operationalized.

Secondary Jobs: Additional tasks or responsibilities that employees can perform when their primary job duties are not immediately required.

Self-Management: The ability and authorization of employees to monitor and adjust their own performance to consistently meet brand requirements.

Six Sigma: A set of techniques and tools for process improvement.

Standard Operating Procedure (SOP): A set of step-by-step instructions approved by an organization that specifies the way that employees are to carry out their work.

Standardization: The process of using the approved process or standard operating procedure (SOP) everywhere it is applicable.

Think Excellence: The first pillar of the McClaskey® Triple 100® Path to Excellence, focusing on cultivating a mindset of extraordinary operations where the only acceptable standard is to deliver the products, services, and customer experience 100% to the brand requirements, every time. This is contrasted to ordinary operations, where achieving 100% to the brand requirements most of the time is the accepted standard.

Total Quality Management (TQM): is an organization-wide management approach to systematically and consistently improve all aspects of the company and its products and services so that the organization's mission and key customer requirements are consistently met at the highest possible level, consistent with the brand requirements. This leads to long-term success through improved customer satisfaction. It has four main components: quality planning, quality assurance, quality control, and quality improvement.

Training to 100%: A comprehensive approach to employee training that ensures every employee can perform their processes to 100% of brand requirements. For operations processes, the employee is Trained to 100% when they can precisely follow each step of the process, every time, under any conditions they would encounter on the job.

Triple Win: Extraordinary operations are implemented in such a way that all three major stakeholders win. Customers consistently receive products, services, and a customer experience that meet their key customer requirements and are thus consistently delighted.

Employees are set up for 100% success on the job, which leads to employee engagement, pride, discretionary effort, and job satisfaction. The business or company gets increased revenue, profitability, and customer recommendations.

Value Stream Mapping: A lean technique used to analyze and design the flow of materials and information required to bring a product or service to a consumer. This technique helps identify where and to what extent non-value-adding activities (waste) occur so that the process can be improved.

Visual Management: The practice of displaying critical information in a highly visible manner in the workplace.

BIBLIOGRAPHY, CHAPTER NOTES, AND RESOURCES

Preface: The Journey to Extraordinary Operations

Collins, Jim. *Good to Great: Why Some Companies Make the Leap... and Others Don't.* New York: Harper Business, 2001.

Chapter 1: Extraordinary Operations: A Great Investment

Gartner, Inc. "Customer Experience Survey Research." Stamford, CT: Gartner, Inc., various years.

American Express. "American Express Customer Service Barometer." New York: American Express, various years.

National Institute of Standards and Technology. "Malcolm Baldrige National Quality Award Recipients." Gaithersburg, MD: U.S. Department of Commerce, NIST, various years. https://www.nist.gov/baldrige.

American Express. (2011). *American Express Global Customer Service Barometer.* American Express. Retrieved from American Express Newsroom.

Aristotle. (2004). *Nicomachean Ethics.* Cambridge University Press. ("We are what we repeatedly do. Excellence, then, is not an act, but a habit.").

Baldrige Performance Excellence Program. (2010). *K&N Management: Baldrige Award Recipient Profile.* National Institute of Standards and Technology. Retrieved from the Baldrige Program.

Bureau of Labor Statistics. (2020). *Job Openings and Labor Turnover.* U.S. Bureau of Labor.

Forrester. (2016). *The Business Impact of Customer Experience.* Forrester Research, Inc. Retrieved from Forrester Research.

Gartner. (2012). *Customer Experience Is the New Competitive Battleground.* Gartner Press Release. Retrieved from Gartner Press Release.

Gartner. (2018). *Market Share Analysis: Customer Experience and Engagement Software.* Gartner Research. Retrieved from Gartner Research.

McClaskey Excellence Institute. (n.d.). *Achieving World-Class Results: Case Studies and Best Practices.* McClaskey Excellence Institute. Retrieved from McClaskey Excellence Institute

National Institute of Standards and Technology (NIST). (2021). *Baldrige Performance Excellence Program.* Retrieved from NIST Baldrige Program

Pal's Sudden Service. (n.d.). *Pal's Sudden Service: History and Achievements.* Company Website. Retrieved from Pal's Sudden Service

Chapter 2: Overview and Origin of the McClaskey® Triple 100® Path to Excellence

Maxwell, John C. *The 21 Irrefutable Laws of Leadership: Follow Them and People Will Follow You.* Nashville: Thomas Nelson, 1998.

Deloitte. "The Deloitte Global Millennial Survey." New York: Deloitte, various years.

Chapter 3: Think Excellence: How Extraordinary Leaders Think Differently

Maraniss, David. *When Pride Still Mattered: A Life of Vince Lombardi.* New York: Simon & Schuster, 1999.

Schulze, Horst, and Dean Merrill. *Excellence Wins: A No-Nonsense Guide to Becoming the Best in a World of Compromise.* Grand Rapids, MI: Zondervan, 2019.

O'Neill, Paul H., and Charles Duhigg. *The Power of Habit: Why We Do What We Do in Life and Business.* New York: Random House, 2012.

National Safety Council. "Injury Facts: Deaths by Transportation Mode." Itasca, IL: National Safety Council, various years. https://injuryfacts.nsc.org.

USAFacts. "Is Flying Safer Than Driving?" USAFacts, accessed January 2025. https://usafacts.org/articles/is-flying-safer-than-driving/.

Arnold Barnett, *The Risk of Flying: Airline Safety in Perspective* (Cambridge, MA: MIT Press, 2000).

Bain & Company, *Commitment to Excellence and Sustained Value Creation* (Bain & Company, 2019).

Horst Schulze, *Excellence Wins: A No-Nonsense Guide to Becoming the Best in a World of Compromise* (Grand Rapids: Zondervan, 2019).

Jeffrey Liker, *The Toyota Way: 14 Management Principles from the World's Greatest Manufacturer* (New York: McGraw-Hill, 2004).

Jim Collins, *Good to Great: Why Some Companies Make the Leap and Others Don't* (New York: HarperBusiness, 2001).

Malcolm Gladwell, *Outliers: The Story of Success* (New York: Little, Brown and Company, 2008).

"Pal's Sudden Service: Performance Excellence," Baldrige Performance Excellence Program, accessed August 12, 2024, https://www.nist.gov/baldrige/pals-sudden-service.

Pat Williams, *Vince Lombardi on Leadership: Life Lessons from a Five-Time NFL Championship Coach* (Gainesville, FL: Health Communications Inc., 2012).

Paul O'Neill and Alcoa, *Case Study: Paul O'Neill's Transformational Leadership at Alcoa,* Harvard Business Review, accessed August 12, 2024, https://hbr.org.

Tom Peters, *The Excellence Dividend: Meeting the Tech Tide with Work That Wows and Jobs That Last* (New York: Vintage, 2018).

Tony Hsieh, *Delivering Happiness: A Path to Profits, Passion, and Purpose* (New York: Business Plus, 2010).

Chapter 4: Mission: The Purpose of Everything an Organization Does

Drucker, Peter F. *The Practice of Management.* New York: Harper & Brothers, 1954.

Deloitte. "Culture of Purpose: 2014 Core Beliefs and Culture Survey." New York: Deloitte University Press, 2014.

Fortune Magazine. "Troy Bader on Warren Buffett's Advice." Fortune, various issues.

Bain & Company study on the impact of clearly articulated and widely understood missions on employee engagement and customer advocacy. Source: Rogers, P., & Blenko, M. (2006). Who has the D? How clear decision roles enhance organizational performance. Harvard Business Review, 84(1), 52-61.

Deloitte study on the impact of mission-driven companies on innovation and retention. Source: Deloitte. (2014). Culture of purpose - Building business confidence; driving growth. Deloitte Core Beliefs & Culture Survey.

Harvard Business Review survey on the impact of strong, mission-driven cultures on net income and shareholder value. Source: Kotter, J. P., & Heskett, J. L. (1992). Corporate culture and performance. New York: The Free Press.

Peter Drucker quote: "The most important thing in communication is to hear what isn't being said." Source: Drucker, P. F. (2008). Management. Harper Collins.

The concept of the "100% mindset" is drawn from the author's previous work and is referenced throughout the chapter.

The examples of Company A and Company B in the compelling narrative section are hypothetical and used for illustrative purposes.

The implementation steps and call to action sections are based on the author's insights and recommendations, drawing from the principles and evidence presented throughout the chapter.

Chapter 5: Identify Key Customer Requirements

Godin, Seth. *Purple Cow: Transform Your Business by Being Remarkable.* New York: Portfolio, 2003.

Bezos, Jeffrey P. "Amazon.com Annual Shareholder Letters." Seattle: Amazon.com, Inc., various years. https://www.aboutamazon.com/news/company-news/shareholder-letters.

Gartner, Inc. "Customer Experience Management Research." Stamford, CT: Gartner, Inc., various years.

Deloitte. "Global Customer Experience Benchmarking Report." New York: Deloitte, various years.

Forbes Insights. "The Power of Customer Experience." New York: Forbes Media, various years.

Walker Information. "Customers 2020: A Progress Report." Indianapolis: Walker Information, various years.

Bain & Company. "Customer Experience Economics." Boston: Bain & Company, various years.

Bain & Company, *Customer Experience: Why It Matters and How to Get It Right* (Bain & Company, 2019).

"Chick-fil-A: The Obsession with Speed and Service," *Fast Company*, accessed August 12, 2024, https://www.fastcompany.com/chickfila-speed-service.

Deloitte, *Customer-Centric Companies Are More Profitable* (Deloitte, 2019), accessed August 12, 2024, https://www2.deloitte.com.

Forbes, *Customer Experience Statistics: Why It's Important and How to Improve It*, Forbes, accessed August 12, 2024, https://www.forbes.com/sites/forbescoachescouncil/2018/11/27/customer-experience-statistics

Gartner, *Customer Experience Trends: Competing on the Customer Experience*, Gartner, accessed August 12, 2024, https://www.gartner.com/en/newsroom/press-releases/2020-05-07-gartner-survey-reveals-customer-experience-trends

Jack Dorsey, *Business Leadership Lessons from Twitter's CEO* (New York: Wiley, 2020).

Jeff Bezos, *Amazon Annual Shareholder Letter, 2018*, accessed August 12, 2024, https://www.amazon.com/ir/shareholder-letter

Kate Zabriskie, *Business Quotes: Wisdom for the Workplace* (CreateSpace Independent Publishing Platform, 2012).

"Mercedes-Benz: Customer Experience Driven by Anthropology," Mercedes-Benz USA, accessed August 12, 2024, https://www.mbusa.com/mercedes/benz/anthropology.

Seth Godin, *Purple Cow: Transform Your Business by Being Remarkable* (New York: Portfolio, 2003).

Steve Jobs, *Steve Jobs: The Exclusive Biography* by Walter Isaacson (New York: Simon & Schuster, 2011).

"The Value of Customer Experience, Quantified," *Harvard Business Review*, accessed August 12, 2024, https://hbr.org/2014/08/the-value-of-customer-experience-quantified

Tony Hsieh, *Delivering Happiness: A Path to Profits, Passion, and Purpose* (New York: Business Plus, 2010).

Walker, *Customers 2020: A Progress Report* (Walker Information, 2017), accessed August 12, 2024, https://www.walkerinfo.com/knowledge-center/reports/customers-2020

Chapter 6: Align Every Task to the Mission Through Key Customer Requirements

Drucker, Peter F. *The Essential Drucker: The Best of Sixty Years of Peter Drucker's Essential Writings on Management.* New York: HarperBusiness, 2001.

Malcolm Baldrige National Quality Award. "Award Recipients and Their Journeys." National Institute of Standards and Technology. https://www.nist.gov/baldrige.

Harvard Business Review. "Organizational Alignment and Performance." Cambridge, MA: Harvard Business Publishing, 2020.

Journal of Business Strategy. "Strategic Alignment and Organizational Agility." Bingley, UK: Emerald Publishing, 2019.

Baldrige Performance Excellence Program, *Baldrige Excellence Framework: A Systems Approach to Improving Your Organization's Performance* (Gaithersburg, MD: National Institute of Standards and Technology, 2019).

David McClaskey, *The McClaskey˚ Triple 100˚ Path to Excellence* (Kingsport, TN: McClaskey Excellence Institute, 2021).

"Donor Alliance: Commitment to Saving Lives Through Organ Donation," Donor Alliance, accessed August 12, 2024, https://www.donoralliance.org/about-us.

Gallup, *The State of the American Workplace Report* (Gallup, 2017), accessed August 12, 2024, https://www.gallup.com/workplace

Harvard Business Review, *Strategic Alignment: Understanding Line-of-Sight and Its Impact on Performance* (Harvard Business Review, 2020).

Journal of Business Strategy, *Strategic Alignment and Its Role in Achieving Business Agility* (Journal of Business Strategy, 2019).

Larry Potterfield, *MidwayUSA's Commitment to Excellence and Continuous Improvement* (Columbia, MO: MidwayUSA, 2015).

"MidwayUSA: A Journey to Performance Excellence," Baldrige Performance Excellence Program, accessed August 12, 2024, https://www.nist.gov/baldrige/midwayusa

Peter Drucker, *The Practice of Management* (New York: Harper & Row, 1954).

Peter F. Drucker, *Managing for Results* (New York: Harper Business, 2006).

"Strategic Planning and Alignment Best Practices," *McKinsey & Company*, accessed August 12, 2024, https://www.mckinsey.com/business-functions/strategy-and-corporate-finance/our-insights

"Tri County Tech: A Model for Student-Centered Education," Baldrige Performance Excellence Program, accessed August 12, 2024, https://www.nist.gov/baldrige/tri-county-tech.

U.S. Department of Commerce, *Baldrige Performance Excellence Program: Case Study of Eastman Chemical Company*, accessed August 12, 2024, https://www.nist.gov/baldrige/eastman-chemical-company

Walter Isaacson, *Steve Jobs* (New York: Simon & Schuster, 2011).

Chapter 7: How to Use Your Mission and KCRs to Make Decisions

Schultz, Howard, and Joanne Gordon. *Onward: How Starbucks Fought for Its Life without Losing Its Soul.* New York: Rodale, 2011.

Hsieh, Tony. *Delivering Happiness: A Path to Profits, Passion, and Purpose.* New York: Grand Central Publishing, 2010.

Deloitte. "Business Trends: Purpose-Driven Companies." New York: Deloitte Insights, various years.

Strategic Management Journal. "Mission Statements and Organizational Performance." Hoboken, NJ: Wiley, various years.

Harvard Business Review. "The Power of Mission-Driven Organizations." Cambridge, MA: Harvard Business Publishing, various years.

3M Company, *Innovation at 3M: A Mission-Driven Culture* (3M, 2020). https://www.3m.com/3M/en_US/company-us/about-3m/innovation/

A.G. Lafley, *Playing to Win: How Strategy Really Works* (Cambridge, MA: Harvard Business Review Press, 2013).

David McClaskey, *The McClaskey° Triple 100° Path to Excellence* (Kingsport, TN: McClaskey Excellence Institute, 2021).

Deloitte, *Purpose-Driven Companies Outperform Their Peers: The 2019 Deloitte Global Millennial Survey* (Deloitte, 2019)., accessed August 12, 2024, https://www2.deloitte.com.

Harvard Business Review, *Leading Change: Creating a Culture of Strategic Alignment* (Harvard Business Review, 2018).

Harvard Business Review, The Value of a Well-Crafted Mission Statement: Fostering Innovation and Employee Retention (Harvard Business Review, 2020).

Howard Schultz, *Onward: How Starbucks Fought for Its Life without Losing Its Soul* (New York: Rodale Books, 2011).

Jim Collins, *Good to Great: Why Some Companies Make the Leap and Others Don't* (New York: HarperBusiness, 2001).

Johnson & Johnson, *Our Credo* (Johnson & Johnson, 1943), accessed August 12, 2024, https://www.jnj.com/credo.

McKinsey & Company, Mission-Driven Leadership: The Role of Purpose in Transforming Organizations (McKinsey & Company, 2021), accessed August 12, 2024.*McKinsey & Company, Mission-Driven Leadership: The Role of Purpose in Transforming Organizations* (McKinsey & Company, 2021). https://www.mckinsey.com/business-functions/strategy-and-corporate-finance/our-insights

Paul Polman, *Net Positive: How Courageous Companies Thrive by Giving More Than They Take* (Cambridge, MA: Harvard Business Review Press, 2021).

Peter Drucker, *The Practice of Management* (New York: Harper & Row, 1954).

Strategic Management Journal, The Impact of High-Quality Mission Statements on Firm Performance (Strategic Management Journal, 2017).

Walter Isaacson, *Steve Jobs* (New York: Simon & Schuster, 2011).

Chapter 8: The Manager's Role in Embedding Mission and KCRs into Organization Culture

Deloitte. 2020. "The Global Marketing Trends 2020: Purpose-Driven Companies." Deloitte Insights. https://www2.deloitte.com/us/en/insights/topics/marketing-and-sales-operations/global-marketing-trends/2020/purpose-driven-companies.html.

Cone Communications and Porter Novelli. 2018. "2018 Cone/Porter Novelli Purpose Study." Boston: Cone Communications, May 30, 2018. https://www.prnewswire.com/news-releases/americans-more-loyal-and-willing-to-defend-purpose-driven-brands-according-to-new-research-by-cone-300656014.html.

Schulze, Horst, and Dean Merrill. *Excellence Wins: A No-Nonsense Guide to Becoming the Best in a World of Compromise.* Grand Rapids, MI: Zondervan, 2019.

Zabriskie, Kate. *Customer Service Training 101: Quick and Easy Techniques That Get Great Results.* New York: AMACOM, 2012.

Deloitte. "2019 Deloitte Global Millennial Survey." New York: Deloitte, 2019.

Gartner, Inc. "Organizations Executing CX Strategies." Stamford, CT: Gartner, Inc., 2018.

Spotify. "Company Mission and Values." Stockholm: Spotify AB, various years. https://www.spotify.com.

Chapter 9: The Unit Operations Manager's Role

National Institute of Standards and Technology. "Baldrige Excellence Framework." Gaithersburg, MD: U.S. Department of Commerce, NIST, various years. https://www.nist.gov/baldrige.

Chapter 10: Design and Document Processes for 100%

Clear, James. *Atomic Habits: An Easy & Proven Way to Build Good Habits & Break Bad Ones.* New York: Avery, 2018.

Pronovost, Peter, Dale Needham, Sean Berenholtz, David Sinopoli, Haitao Chu, Sara Cosgrove, Bryan Sexton, Robert Hyzy, Robert Welsh, Gary Roth, Joseph Bander, John Kepros, and Christine Goeschel. "An Intervention to Decrease Catheter-Related Bloodstream Infections in the ICU." *New England Journal of Medicine* 355, no. 26 (December 2006): 2725-32. https://doi.org/10.1056/NEJMoa061115.

Clear, James. *Atomic Habits: An Easy & Proven Way to Build Good Habits & Break Bad Ones.* New York: Avery, 2018.

Gawande, Atul. *The Checklist Manifesto: How to Get Things Right.* New York: Metropolitan Books, 2009.

Pronovost, Peter, Dale Needham, Sean Berenholtz, David Sinopoli, Haitao Chu, Sara Cosgrove, Bryan Sexton, et al. "An Intervention to Decrease Catheter-Related Bloodstream Infections in the ICU." *New England Journal of Medicine* 355, no. 26 (December 2006): 2725–32. https://doi.org/10.1056/NEJMoa061115.

Bosco, Joseph A., III, Roshan P. Khanuja, Nicholas M. Demris, Kester Ramsay Ashworth, Nicolas S. Piuzzi, and Javad Parvizi. "The Contralateral Hip: At-Risk or Not for Infection After Hip Arthroplasty?" *Journal of Arthroplasty* 32, no. 9S (September 2017): S252–S255. https://doi.org/10.1016/j.arth.2017.03.034.

Kurtz, Steven M., Edmund C. Lau, Heather Watson, Jasvinder K. Schmier, and Javad Parvizi. "Economic Burden of Periprosthetic Joint Infection in the United States." *Journal of Arthroplasty* 27, no. 8 (September 2012): 61–65. https://doi.org/10.1016/j.arth.2012.02.022.

Liker, Jeffrey K. *The Toyota Way: 14 Management Principles from the World's Greatest Manufacturer.* New York: McGraw-Hill, 2004.

Chapter 11: Standardizing Processes

Gawande, Atul. *The Checklist Manifesto: How to Get Things Right.* New York: Metropolitan Books, 2009.

Haynes, Alex B., Thomas G. Weiser, William R. Berry, Stuart R. Lipsitz, Abdel-Hadi S. Breizat, E. Patchen Dellinger, Teodoro Herbosa, Sudhir Joseph, Pascience L. Kibatala, M. C. Mishra Lapitan, Alan F. Merry,

Krishna Moorthy, Richard K. Reznick, Bryce Taylor, Atul A. Gawande, and Safe Surgery Saves Lives Study Group. "A Surgical Safety Checklist to Reduce Morbidity and Mortality in a Global Population." *New England Journal of Medicine* 360, no. 5 (January 2009): 491-99. https://doi.org/10.1056/NEJMsa0810119.

Chick-fil-A. "About Chick-fil-A." Chick-fil-A Corporate Website. Accessed January 2025. https://www.chick-fil-a.com/about.

Chapter 12: Improve Processes

How 1% Performance Improvements Led to Olympic Gold: https://hbr.org/2015/10/how-1-performance-improvements-led-to-olympic-gold

How 1% Performance Improvements Led to Olympic Gold; Harvard Business Review, October 30, 2015, by Eben Harrell

Tracy, Brian. *Eat That Frog!: 21 Great Ways to Stop Procrastinating and Get More Done in Less Time*. San Francisco: Berrett-Koehler Publishers, 2001.

Juran, Joseph M., and A. Blanton Godfrey, eds. *Juran's Quality Handbook*. 5th ed. New York: McGraw-Hill, 1999.

Chapter 13: Selecting the Right Employees for Operations

Collins, Jim. *Good to Great: Why Some Companies Make the Leap... and Others Don't*. New York: HarperBusiness, 2001.

Gallup. "The Benefits of Employee Engagement." Gallup Workplace. Accessed October 1, 2025. https://www.gallup.com/workplace/236927/employee-engagement-drives-growth.aspx.

Society for Human Resource Management (SHRM). SHRM website. Accessed January 2025. https://www.shrm.org.

Chapter 14: The Power of Crystal-Clear Conditions of Employment

Carnegie, Dale. *How to Win Friends and Influence People.* New York: Simon and Schuster, 1936.

Cialdini, Robert B. *Influence: The Psychology of Persuasion.* Rev. ed. New York: Harper Business, 2006.

Chapter 15: Accountability: Progressive Discipline

Welch, Jack, and Suzy Welch. *Winning.* New York: Harper Business, 2005.

Schmidt, Eric, and Jonathan Rosenberg. *How Google Works.* New York: Grand Central Publishing, 2014.

Daniels, Aubrey C. *Performance Management: Changing Behavior That Drives Organizational Effectiveness.* 4th ed. Atlanta: Performance Management Publications, 2000.

Rockwell, Theodore. *The Rickover Effect: How One Man Made a Difference.* Annapolis, MD: Naval Institute Press, 1992.

Chapter 16: Training to 100%

Barger, Thomas E. *The Pal's Sudden Service Story: How One Company Built the Best Drive-Thru Restaurant Business in America.* Self-published, 2015.

Chapter 17: Coaching to 100%: The Cornerstone of Sustained Excellence

Porath, Christine, and Christine Pearson. "The Price of Incivility." *Harvard Business Review* 91, no. 1-2 (January-February 2013): 114-121.

Gallup, Inc. "State of the American Workplace." Gallup Report. Washington, DC: Gallup, Inc., 2017.

Deloitte. *Global Human Capital Trends*. Annual report series. New York: Deloitte University Press, various years.

Nadella, Satya. *Hit Refresh: The Quest to Rediscover Microsoft's Soul and Imagine a Better Future for Everyone*. New York: Harper Business, 2017.

Chapter 18: Empower Employees to Deliver Consistent Excellence

Drucker, Peter F. *Management Challenges for the 21st Century*. New York: HarperBusiness, 1999.

Carnegie, Dale. *How to Win Friends and Influence People*. Rev. ed. New York: Simon and Schuster, 1981. Initially published in 1936.

Covey, Stephen R. *The 7 Habits of Highly Effective People: Powerful Lessons in Personal Change*. New York: Free Press, 1989.

Hsieh, Tony. *Delivering Happiness: A Path to Profits, Passion, and Purpose*. New York: Grand Central Publishing, 2010.

Chapter 19: Create a Work Environment for 100% Execution

Carnegie, Dale. *How to Win Friends and Influence People*. New York: Simon and Schuster, 1936.

Gallup. "Employee Engagement Drives Growth." 2013. https://www.gallup.com/workplace/236927/employee-engagement-drives-growth.aspx

Harvard Business Review. "The Neuroscience of Trust." January 2017.

McKinsey & Company. "Unlocking Industrial Productivity: How Digital Manufacturing Can Escape Pilot Purgatory." October 2018.

Gallup. "Employee Engagement Drives Growth." 2013. https://www.gallup.com/workplace/236927/employee-engagement-drives-growth.aspx

Harvard Business Review. "The Neuroscience of Trust." January 2017.

McKinsey & Company. "Unlocking Industrial Productivity: How Digital Manufacturing Can Escape Pilot Purgatory." October 2018.

Chapter 20: Full Use of Time and Abilities: Secondary Jobs

Gallup, Inc. "State of the Global Workplace." Annual report. Washington, DC: Gallup, Inc., various years.

Society for Human Resource Management (SHRM). "Employee Job Satisfaction and Engagement" reports. Alexandria, VA: SHRM, various years.

American Psychological Association (APA). "The Impact of Employee Well-being on Productivity."

Atlassian. "The State of Meetings Report."

Gallup (2017). "Employee Engagement and Turnover."

Gallup (2019). "The Cost of Poor Management."

Gallup (2020). "State of the American Workplace Report."

Gallup's Re-Engineering Performance Management Paper.

Gallup's State of the Global Workplace: 2022 Report.

Chapter 21: Respect for People: The Golden Rule of All Transactions

Hsieh, Tony. *Delivering Happiness: A Path to Profits, Passion, and Purpose.* New York: Grand Central Publishing, 2010.

Porath, Christine L., and Christine Pearson. "The Price of Incivility." *Harvard Business Review* 91, no. 1-2 (January–February 2013): 114–21.

Porath, Christine. *Mastering Civility: A Manifesto for the Workplace.* New York: Grand Central Publishing, 2016.

Society for Human Resource Management (SHRM). "2017 Employee Job Satisfaction and Engagement Survey." Alexandria, VA: SHRM, 2017. https://www.shrm.org.

Nadella, Satya. *Hit Refresh: The Quest to Rediscover Microsoft's Soul and Imagine a Better Future for Everyone.* New York: Harper Business, 2017.

Deloitte. *2020 Deloitte Global Human Capital Trends.* New York: Deloitte Insights, 2020. https://www2.deloitte.com/us/en/insights/focus/human-capital-trends.html.

Welch, Jack. "Developing Leaders: Jack Welch on How to Find and Cultivate Talent." Interviewed by Adi Ignatius. *Harvard Business Review,* November 2013.

Porath, Christine L., and Christine Pearson. "The Price of Incivility." *Harvard Business Review* 91, no. 1-2 (January–February 2013): 114–21.

Porath, Christine. *Mastering Civility: A Manifesto for the Workplace.* New York: Grand Central Publishing, 2016.

Note: Dr. Porath's research on workplace civility and respect is well-documented. Her statement that "respect is the currency of trust" aligns with themes in her published work.

Society for Human Resource Management (SHRM). "2017 Employee Job Satisfaction and Engagement Survey." Alexandria, VA: SHRM, 2017. https://www.shrm.org.

Note: SHRM's research consistently identifies respectful treatment as a top factor in job satisfaction, though specific report titles and years vary.

Nadella, Satya. *Hit Refresh: The Quest to Rediscover Microsoft's Soul and Imagine a Better Future for Everyone.* New York: Harper Business, 2017.

Note: Nadella's perspectives on respect as foundational to Microsoft's culture are documented in his book and public statements.

Deloitte. *2020 Deloitte Global Human Capital Trends.* New York: Deloitte Insights, 2020. https://www2.deloitte.com/us/en/insights/focus/human-capital-trends.html.

Note: Deloitte's annual Human Capital Trends reports examine organizational culture, purpose, and values, including respect-based cultures.

Welch, Jack. "Developing Leaders: Jack Welch on How to Find and Cultivate Talent." Interviewed by Adi Ignatius. *Harvard Business Review,* November 2013.

Note: Welch's quote about Six Sigma training as a requirement for promotion at GE is documented in various sources about GE's management practices during his tenure.

Chapter 22: The McClaskey® Triple 100® Path to Excellence

Sanborn, Mark. *The Fred Factor: How Passion in Your Work and Life Can Turn the Ordinary into the Extraordinary.* New York: Currency, 2004.

Collins, Jim. *Good to Great: Why Some Companies Make the Leap... and Others Don't.* New York: HarperBusiness, 2001.

Hsieh, Tony. *Delivering Happiness: A Path to Profits, Passion, and Purpose.* New York: Grand Central Publishing, 2010.

Amazon.com, Inc. "2016 Letter to Shareholders" by Jeffrey P. Bezos. Seattle: Amazon.com, Inc., April 2017. https://www.aboutamazon.com/news/company-news/2016-letter-to-shareholders.

General Electric Company. *1999 Annual Report*. Fairfield, CT: General Electric Company, 2000.

Toyota Motor Corporation. *The Toyota Way 2001*. Internal document. Toyota City, Japan: Toyota Motor Corporation, 2001.

Liker, Jeffrey K. *The Toyota Way: 14 Management Principles from the World's Greatest Manufacturer*. New York: McGraw-Hill, 2004.

MacDuffie, John Paul, and John F. Krafcik. "Integrating Technology and Human Resources for High-Performance Manufacturing: Evidence from the International Auto Industry." In *Transforming Organizations*, edited by Thomas A. Kochan and Michael Useem, 209–26. New York: Oxford University Press, 1992.

Chapter 23: Implementing the Path to Excellence

Sanborn, Mark. *The Fred Factor: How Passion in Your Work and Life Can Turn the Ordinary into the Extraordinary*. New York: Currency/ Doubleday, 2004.

Chapter 24: Maintaining 100% Extraordinary Operations

Lombardi, Vince. Multiple sources attribute various versions of Lombardi's quote about perfection and excellence. See:

Maraniss, David. *When Pride Still Mattered: A Life of Vince Lombardi*. New York: Simon & Schuster, 1999.

AUTHOR BIOGRAPHY

David J. McClaskey

President, McClaskey Excellence Institute

David McClaskey has trained and coached over 15,000 leaders during his 50-year career, helping organizations of all types achieve extraordinary levels of operational excellence. As co-founder and President of the McClaskey Excellence Institute, he developed the McClaskey® Triple 100® Path to Excellence. This proven framework enables companies to get their products and services 100% right, every time.

Recognized by the U.S. Department of Commerce for his expertise, David was selected to develop and deliver training for the first Malcolm Baldrige National Quality Award examiners and judges. Baldrige is the nation's highest honor for performance excellence. He also contributed to shaping the Baldrige assessment and scoring systems still in use today.

Few can match David's legacy. He has guided **seven organizations to win eight Baldrige Awards,** including **The Ritz-Carlton Hotel Company** (twice) and the first two restaurants ever to win. He also helped **Florida Power & Light** become the first U.S. company to earn Japan's prestigious **Deming Prize.**

A **Master Six Sigma Black Belt, American Society for Quality Fellow (ASQ),** and **Institute of Industrial Engineering Fellow,** David has received numerous honors, including ASQ's **Distinguished Service Medal**, Tennessee's **Ned R. McWherter Leadership Award,** and the U.S. Department of Commerce recognition for **"outstanding service to the nation".**

David has a Bachelor's in Industrial Engineering from the **University of Florida** and a Master's degree in Industrial Engineering from the **University of Tennessee.**

His lifelong passion is to make the world a better place by **helping companies become extraordinary in their operations**—so they delight customers, empower and set up employees for 100% success and pride in work, and achieve sustainable success.

David McClaskey and the McClaskey Excellence Institute are available for training, consulting, webinars, keynotes, and other conference presentations.

Learn more at **<u>McClaskeyExcellence.com</u>**

www.ingramcontent.com/pod-product-compliance
Lightning Source LLC
Chambersburg PA
CBHW051458150726
47997CB00001B/23